EDMO
THE HAZAI

THE EUROPEAN HUMANITIES RESEARCH CENTRE

UNIVERSITY OF OXFORD

Director: Martin McLaughlin
Fiat-Serena Professor of Italian Studies

The European Humanities Research Centre of the University of Oxford organizes a range of academic activities, including conferences and workshops, and publishes scholarly works under its own imprint, LEGENDA. Within Oxford, the EHRC bridges, at the research level, the main humanities faculties: Modern Languages, English, Modern History, Classics and Philosophy, Music and Theology. The Centre stimulates interdisciplinary research collaboration throughout these subject areas and provides an Oxford base for advanced researchers in the humanities.

The Centre's publications programme focuses on making available the results of advanced research in medieval and modern languages and related interdisciplinary areas. An Editorial Board, whose members are drawn from across the British university system, covers the principal European languages. Titles currently include works on Arabic, Catalan, Chinese, English, French, German, Italian, Portuguese, Russian, Spanish, Greek and Yiddish literature. In addition, the EHRC co-publishes with the Society for French Studies, the Modern Humanities Research Association and the British Comparative Literature Association. The Centre also publishes a Special Lecture Series under the LEGENDA imprint, and a journal, *Oxford German Studies*.

Further information:
Kareni Bannister, Senior Publications Officer
European Humanities Research Centre
University of Oxford
76 Woodstock Road, Oxford OX2 6LE
enquiries@ehrc.ox.ac.uk
www.ehrc.ox.ac.uk

LEGENDA

EUROPEAN HUMANITIES RESEARCH CENTRE

University of Oxford

Edmond Jabès in his Paris apartment, 1973
Photo: Edith Herrenschmidt (Archives Edmond Jabès)

Edmond Jabès

The Hazard of Exile

❖

STEVEN JARON

LEGENDA

European Humanities Research Centre
University of Oxford
2003

Published by the
European Humanities Research Centre
of the University of Oxford
47 Wellington Square
Oxford OX1 2JF

LEGENDA is the publications imprint of the
European Humanities Research Centre

ISBN 1 900755 71 8

First published 2003

British Library Cataloguing in Publication Data
A CIP catalogue record for this book is available from the British Library

LEGENDA series designed by Cox Design Partnership, Witney, Oxon
Printed in Great Britain by
Information Press
Eynsham
Oxford OX8 1JJ

Chief Copy-Editor: Genevieve Hawkins

IN MEMORY OF MY GRANDFATHERS

Marque d'un signet rouge la première page du livre, car la blessure est invisible à son commencement.

Reb Alcé in *Le Livre des Questions* (1963)

La langue a, pour lieu, la langue.
L'exil de la langue est la condition de l'exilé.

Un Etranger avec, sous le bras, un livre de petit format (1989)

CONTENTS

Abbreviations		xii
Acknowledgements		xiv
Introduction		1
1	Judaism in the Margin	15
2	A Still-Born Poet	48
3	'La Patrie de l'humain'	87
4	Exile Confirmed	114
5	On Not Belonging	155
	Bibliography	169
	Index	185

ABBREVIATIONS

Footnotes have been kept to the necessary minimum by the use of abbreviations, followed by page number, for works frequently cited. I have nevertheless allowed myself a handful of digressions in order to clarify or develop a point. In the first instance full citation details are given in footnotes for periodicals and other references, while the short title is subsequently used (e.g. *Marelles sur le parvis* for *Marelles sur le parvis: essais de critique poétique*). Italics in quotations from Jabès's writings are his own, unless otherwise indicated.

Alo	Edmond Jabès, *Avec l'ombre*
A	Maurice Blanchot, *L'Amitié*
Ap	Edmond Jabès, *Arrhes poétiques*
Au	*L'Alliance universelle*
Bé	*La Bourse égyptienne*
Dl	Edmond Jabès, *Du désert au livre: entretiens avec Marcel Cohen, suivi de L'Etranger* (2nd edn.)
Ed	Jacques Derrida, *L'Ecriture et la différence*
Ei	Maurice Blanchot, *L'Entretien infini*
Et	Edmond Jabès, *Un Etranger avec, sous le bras, un livre de petit format*
FEJ	Fonds Edmond Jabès, Département des Manuscrits, Bibliothèque nationale de France
I	*Israël*
Is	Edmond Jabès, *Illusions sentimentales*
Jbmd	Edmond Jabès, *Je bâtis ma demeure, poèmes 1943–1957* (2nd edn.)
Jta	Edmond Jabès, *Je t'attends!*
LEJ	Max Jacob, *Lettres à Edmond Jabès* (2nd edn.)
LH	Edmond Jabès, *Le Livre de l'Hospitalité*
LM	Edmond Jabès, *Le Livre des Marges*
LQ I	Edmond Jabès, *Le Livre des Questions* I (*Le Livre des Questions, Le Livre de Yukel, Le Retour au Livre*)
LQ II	Edmond Jabès, *Le Livre des Questions* II (*Yaël, Elya, Aely, · (El ou le dernier livre)*)

LR	Edmond Jabès, *Le Livre des Ressemblances* (*Le Livre des Ressemblances, Le Soupçon Le Désert, L'Ineffaçable L'Inaperçu*)
NRF	*Nouvelle Revue française*
'Op'	Edmond Jabès, 'L'Obscurité potable'
Pa	Edmond Jabès, *Les Pieds en l'air*
Pé	*Le Progrès égyptien*
Sé	*La Semaine égyptienne*

ACKNOWLEDGEMENTS

My task was greatly aided by the support I received in the initial stages of my project. Fellowships from Columbia University, French Cultural Services in New York and the American Research Center in Egypt provided funding for me to carry out my research. Antoine Compagnon, Henri Mitterand and Mark Anderson of Columbia University read an early, considerably longer version of this work, and its present shape owes much to their criticism. I was also able to read sections of it to seminars at Royal Holloway, in Montreal, Jerusalem, Recanati and Cerisy-la-Salle, and I am grateful to the organizers for their invitations. Gabriel Josipovici of the University of Sussex stands out for his support and Robert Horn for his friendship. The incisive comments of Ritchie Robertson of the University of Oxford and two anonymous readers were particularly helpful in improving my manuscript. Their authors deserve my thanks. The remaining errors, it goes without saying, are my own doing.

I have recorded in footnotes my obligations to criticism. The friends and colleagues who provided me with sources of information, printed or oral, and with whom I have enjoyed many hours of stimulating conversation, are too numerous to list; they will recognize how deep their imprint in these pages goes. Nonetheless, I must express my gratitude to Viviane Jabès-Crasson and Nimet Frascaria for permission to quote from the exchange of letters between Edmond Jabès and Gabriel Bounoure. My wish is that in reading this study they and newer readers will come to understand how Jabès's writings, from the earliest to the last, though remarkably diverse in their use of language, form, despite the frequent stylistic departures, a coherent and meaningful whole.

Paris, November 2003   S. J.

INTRODUCTION

The Problem

In 1963 a stirring book entitled *Le Livre des Questions* appeared in France by an author then unknown to the country's reading public. Edmond Jabès, aged 51, was a French-speaking, Egyptian-born writer who had emigrated from Egypt in 1957 after the Suez war and in the wake of extensive economic and cultural reforms instituted by Gamel Abdel Nasser and his corps of Free Officers. Jabès had published a previous book following his arrival in Paris. In 1959, his collected Cairene poetry appeared under the title *Je bâtis ma demeure, poèmes 1943–1957* and with a preface by a close friend from Egypt, the critic Gabriel Bounoure. While that book captured the attention of many of France's prominent writers and critics (it was reviewed no less than ten times, a large number for a poet with such obscure origins) its readership remained limited. The lyrical Surrealism of its poetry seemed outdated or, worse, *manqué*, as Existentialism, the *nouveau roman*, semiology and structuralism gained influence among the post-war French intelligentsia.

The point of departure for the new book was a moral awakening brought about by an existential crisis that effected a shift from lyricism to a fragmentary narrative, or *récit éclaté*. *Le Livre des Questions* was the beginning of a thirty-year-long project to trace the textual relations between the act of writing and Jewish identity, all of which have biographical and historic roots in Egypt.

The early cultural ambiguities Edmond Jabès experienced are at the origin of his complexity as a mature writer. With hindsight Jabès came to attribute the cause of his departure from Egypt to his Jewish origins. Proponents of Egyptian nationalism, fired by the founding of the State of Israel in 1948, viewed the Jews of Egypt as Zionist brokers of European imperialism in the Middle East. But at the time the sense of political threat was perceived as insignificant by many Egyptian Jews. In fact, the fall of the widely acknowledged corrupt monarchy in 1952 and its replacement by the Free Officers was initially greeted with enthusiasm (*Dl*, 44). Soon, however, the European enclaves broke up among the rumbling gunfire of the Suez war of 1956. Nasser did not discriminate; non-Muslim minorities, with the notable exception of the indigenous Copt population (whose residential status nevertheless remains problematical to the present day) and non-Egyptian nationals (Jabès held Italian citizenship), were advised to leave, although many elderly people, Jabès's parents included, remained, his father dying there in 1962 after which his mother came to Paris. English, French, Jews, 'sujets ennemis' all—regardless of their having been born in the country, regardless of their belonging to a family which had lived there for generations—were economically strangled, often publicly humiliated, and finally forced from Egypt.

Exile did not end when Jabès left Egypt in the summer of 1957. Added to the political expulsion was the fact that once in France, he learned first-hand of that country's xenophobic anti-Semitism. One evening shortly after his arrival, he saw this graffiti on a wall in the Odéon quarter of Paris: 'Mort aux Juifs, Jews go home.' It unleashed a psychical fury—perhaps due in part to the curious mix of French and English, probably more because he had undergone a mental shock— and resulted in the birth of his new work. 'Il a suffi de quelques graffiti sur un mur', he wrote in *Le Livre des Questions*, 'pour que les souvenirs qui sommeillaient dans mes mains s'emparent de ma plume. Et pour que les doigts commandent la vue' (*LQ* I, 30).[1] The newly arrived emigrant believed that, as a native French speaker, he would at last belong to the linguistic promised land. He was wrong. His idealized confidence in republican France as the 'patrie de l'humain'[2] vanished. As he explained to the journalist Madeleine Chapsal shortly after the book's publication, the destabilizing experience of the graffiti led him to see himself in a radically different light: 'J'avais pris conscience de ma condition juive. Il fallait maintenant que je l'assume'[3]—a distinctly *Jewish* condition, then; and the daunting, seemingly absurd necessity that he should take responsibility for that condition and that it should become integrated into his consciousness. Thus both the political expulsion from Egypt and the existential rejection from France (where he would nonetheless spend the rest of his life) triggered the composition of the new book. At home neither in Egypt nor in France, Edmond Jabès shared the experience of the dispossessed exile, a position perhaps best summarized by Adorno's terse observation: 'For a man who no longer has a homeland, writing becomes a place to live'.[4]

Le Livre des Questions combines dense aphorisms attributed to an enigmatic group of rabbis juxtaposed with the lachrymose love story of two adolescent Jews caught in the war-time maelstrom, which shuttles between Paris, Eastern Europe, Egypt and an unrecognizable 'non-lieu' situated within no identifiable time frame. Critically, it appealed to a relatively wide readership, a French public of Jews and non-Jews still quivering intellectually and emotionally from the trauma of the Vichy catastrophe and pondering further the fate of European Jewry in the post-war world. Thus did the book respond to Adorno's provocative dictum that the writing of poetry after Auschwitz was barbaric (*Dl*, 93). And it thus happened that it was representative of the cultural moment of Western Europe, and in particular of France. Representative is the operative word here, for inasmuch as it was the product of a cultural moment, Jabès's fiction portrayed not the savagery of the death camps, but the story of two ardent lovers' intimacy in contrast to death-camp inhumanity. Layered into this depiction was a narrative of the seemingly endless wandering and persecution of the Jews in history, and the principal mechanism by which they coped with their historical vulnerability, commentary:

Le *roman* de Sarah et de Yukel, à travers divers *dialogues et méditations* attribués à des rabbins imaginaires, est le *récit* d'un amour détruit par les hommes et par les mots. Il a la dimension du livre et l'amère obstination d'une question errante. (*LQ* I, 30; my emphasis)

In short, to recount (by means of a 'récit') and to comment (through the intermediary of the imaginary rabbis, who are not unlike the members of a chorus in Greek tragedy) are the two most functional discursive registers in *Le Livre des Questions*. Commentary in Jabès is explanation; explanation offered not as clarification but as a deepening of the narrative's mystery. Set apart from the main text by typographic markers such as parentheses and italics, commentary reflects the story of Sarah and Yukel while suggesting insights into their disorientation by the events of the war and post-war years:

Qui es-tu, Sarah, dans l'hiver de Yukel?
   (*Biche traquée dans les dédales d'asphalte et de plomb que j'emprunte, ce soir; biche capturée vivante pour être brûlée — Tu as échappé au feu des hommes mais pas au tien* [...]) (*LQ* I, 40–1)

Jabès's poetic reflections proclaimed that Jewish suffering was no different from any human suffering. This universalism was widely perceived. One early critic wrote: 'On a dit que c'était un livre sur "le problème juif".' But from a larger perspective, she added: 'Je crois, pour ma part, que c'est un livre sur les problèmes communs à tous les hommes, vus par un juif.'[5] The sense of Jabès's universalism remained upon his death in January 1991. The Jewish theologian David Banon reiterated that 'l'œuvre jabésienne est à la fois juive et universelle. [...O]n ne saurait occulter ou privilégier l'une des deux dimensions sans la défigurer'.[6] It is sadly ironic that, although he had abandoned the dream of Enlightenment universalism following his encounter, in long-cherished France, with the graffiti, Jabès's subsequent work nonetheless incarnated universalist ideals. But more importantly, *Le Livre des Questions*, rendered in the interrogative and composed in a minor key, confirmed in the mind of his French readers their feeling that the possible destruction of European Jewry was unthinkable, but nonetheless real. The social and psychological significance of any serious work of art or literature is never merely academic.

Jabès once said: 'Comme de l'abîme de la nuit ont surgi les astres, l'homme de la seconde moitié du XXe siècle est né des cendres d'Auschwitz.'[7] Born from the still-warm ashes of Auschwitz, he thus infused his writings with a Jewish consciousness and with collective Jewish memory, especially as they were transformed in the dread period of the death-camp revelations. As such, he could no longer be associated exclusively with that collegium of writers given up to Surrealist reverie and dream life, nor could he be identified, exclusively, as a neo-Mallarméan poet. History had made such associations impossible. Rather, from 1963 onwards, he began to share the company, uneasy though it sometimes was, of writers such as Maurice Blanchot, Emmanuel Levinas and Jacques Derrida, whose positions in the life of contemporary French and Jewish letters remain influential, having helped define the aesthetic and philosophical preoccupations of the day.

The principal aim of this monograph is to place the texts composed in the first half of Jabès's career (roughly between 1929 and 1957) in the cultural milieux (francophone-Egyptian and French-Jewish) in which he grew up, and then to show the radical change in his post-immigration writings once he assumed the consciousness of a Jew in the age of Auschwitz, a historical period which, psychically if not morally, torments this consciousness, but which is assuaged by the very act of writing. A lesser but related concern of this study is to situate Jabès in the nascent literary and philosophical environment of

Paris in the early sixties, in particular the cultural moment that sees a movement away from Existentialist preoccupations towards newer insights into problems of textuality and ontological a-theology.

One often reads in Jabès's mature work of the existence of books that somehow stand before the book in question. Jabès leads the reader across thresholds that open onto other passages, spaces, still other thresholds and, of course, other books. *Elya* (1969), for instance, opens with this very idea: 'Derrière le livre, il y a l'arrière-livre; derrière l'arrière-livre, il y a l'espace immense et, enfoui dans cet espace, il y a le livre que nous allons écrire dans son énigmatique enchaînement' (*LQ* II, 171). I understand this quotation as a plea to return to the origins of the book (here, *Elya*) and to unearth its past or, in the words of the psychoanalyst Murielle Gagnebin, to engage in a study of what she calls the 'negative presentation' or 'le lieu de l'émergence, dans l'acte même de la négation, de l'infigurabilité'. Gagnebin sees negation as, on the one hand, the artist's 'consciousness of privation' or 'absence' and, on the other, something that goes beyond the 'destruction', 'concealment' or 'elimination' of a model. For her, negative presentation 'postule une réflexion centrée sur le manque conçu en tant que *position*: l'acte est ici visé, et non l'objet de l'acte'.[8] What has been negated by the artist's or writer's mind remains present—by virtue of the psychical processes of repression or violent rejection—in his or her work. As such, Gagnebin argues cogently for a 'poïétique de la négation'.[9] I would add, a 'poetics of the stranger', by which I mean the attempt to analyse what Jabès himself called the 'absence originaire' (*Et*, 98) of his creative work dating from his Egyptian years and, more generally, the 'non-lieu' of his writing. In political terms, Jabès's violent rejection by Egypt—which followed the 'soft' repression of the country's Jews—would give him the status of a 'negatively present' subject who embodied this problem in his writings after 1957. Understood in this light, in the quotation from *Elya* Jabès would be referring not only to the books preceding that book (*Yaël*, *Le Retour au Livre*, *Le Livre de Yukel* and *Le Livre des Questions*), but also to the book that preceded his departure from Egypt, his collected poetry from the period, and, further, to his production before the Second World War. But there would be yet another book—a hypothetical, perhaps improbable book 'enfoui dans l'immense espace'. This book, Jabès notes, is 'le livre que nous allons écrire'; in other words, a book that will be collectively written in the time to come. And yet this book is the one that is supposed to be behind them all. For this reason, Jabès adds that it is going to be written 'dans son énigmatique enchaînement', that is, in a paradoxical continuity. If my analysis of this paradoxical continuity is at all successful, then it will have brought to light Jabès's earliest known writings and, more importantly, will have tried to interpret them in relation to those which have been studied in greater detail, the later texts dating from his Parisian years.

At first view, the writings dating from the Cairene period differ strikingly from those of the Parisian period. The first were strongly influenced by modernist literary trends emanating from France, whereas the texts composed in Paris stand out by their startling allusions to aspects of ancient and contemporary Jewish history and to the Jewish condition in modern Europe. A more careful reading of the post-war Cairene poetry shows that it was undeniably strong in its diverse and innovative use of Surrealist aesthetics, but was nevertheless estranged from the Surrealist movement. Its stylistic hesitancy was its most salient weakness, although Jabès demonstrated a willingness, indeed an uncomfortable need, to forge an idiom distinct from his Egyptian contemporaries, such as Georges Henein, who was enthusiastic about Surrealism. On the other hand, *Le Livre des Questions* did not dam Jabès's literary originality and moral vision. It swept broadly, and left few untouched: at its best, the reader is engaged in an empathetic relation with the tragic story of two Parisian lovers, Sarah Schwall and Yukel Serafi. At its worst, Sarah's and Yukel's tale of desperate love among the ruinous mental and physical landscapes of post-war Jewry leaves the reader confused, although 'struck' by the terrible events recounted therein. It is true that Derrida's 1964 essay 'Edmond Jabès et la question du livre' summarized with lucidity the complex relation of the Cairene texts to the Parisian ones:

On relira mieux désormais *Je bâtis ma demeure*. [...] Dans *Le Livre des Questions*, la voix ne s'altère pas, ni l'intention ne se rompt, mais l'accent s'aggrave. Une puissante et antique racine est exhumée et sur elle une blessure sans âge dénudée (car ce que Jabès nous apprend, c'est que les racines parlent, que les paroles veulent pousser et que le discours poétique est *entamé* dans une blessure). (*Ed*, 99; Derrida's emphasis)

Here, Derrida was developing key themes in deconstruction; his essay is invaluable as a document in the early history of his thought.[10] It is also important to my argument because it considered the relationship, as few have since, between the poetry of the Egyptian years and that which came after. It should be added, however, that Derrida, narrowly in my view, considered Jabès's earliest poetry to be the first poems of *Je bâtis ma demeure*, those dating from the early 1940s.

In contrast, my study examines Jabès's earliest poetry, which he began to publish in the late 1920s at the age of 17 or 18, and integrates it into the whole of his corpus. Fundamentally and not without some paradox, these juvenilia, rejected by their author, are themselves illustrative of my theme, the hazard of Jabès's poetics of exile: to my surprise and disappointment, I found that they did not belong in his bibliography as he himself set it down and which others, such as Derrida, have accepted without argument.[11] In order to bring these writings home, as it were, and to demonstrate the meaningfulness of their authorship, I have sought to reconstruct the historical and cultural contexts for Jabès's career in francophone Egypt. While the following draws heavily on many biographical sources such as unpublished correspondence, and on manuscript variants such as those scholars can now consult in the Fonds Edmond Jabès in the Bibliothèque nationale de France, it relies mainly on published editions of his books. Perhaps, then, Jabès would have to admit that a possible translation of 'Cela a eu lieu', the title of one of his very last works, inspired by a childhood memory of a visit to the Louvre with his sister, could be: 'This occurred despite my rejection of it, despite my unwillingness to re-visit it, despite my wish to place it behind me. Here, then, is the evidence; here is a plausible reconstruction of it.'

Dimensions of Exile

The position I shall argue is that Jabès was a writer-in-exile—blatantly in the period following his expulsion, implicitly while still in Egypt— by which I mean that his texts exhibit a far-reaching *étrangeté*, a foreignness or estrangement, perceptible initially when he worked as a French-speaking writer in Egypt and next as a Jewish writer in Paris, where residency was always thought of as provisional. Three aspects of the hazard of exile I consider are: (1) Jabès's self-alienation in the early years, (2) his political expulsion from Egypt and difficult settling as a refugee in France, and (3) his conscious ambivalence with regard to classical Jewish sources and religious prescriptions.

A first resonance of *étrangeté* is reflexive. The poet seeks to know himself, to examine his life from afar, as in this strophe from a poem written in Jerusalem in 1942:

> Je suis à la recherche
> d'un homme que je ne connais pas,
> qui jamais ne fut tant moi-même
> que depuis que je le cherche[.]
>   ('Chanson de l'étranger'; *Jbmd*, 46)

These lines read like a soliloquy in which the actor on stage speaks at once inwardly and outwardly, and as such the allocution is divided against itself. Despite his search, the poet remains a stranger unto himself. But self-alienation becomes meaningful because the poet-actor is, uncannily, in his element: the acknowledgement that he is a stranger unto himself is itself an authentic form of self-knowledge. I suggest (in Chapter 1) that the exilic dimension to the Cairene poetry and aphorisms begins with Jabès's teenage interest in theatre, both as an actor *and* as a playwright; it continues as he attempts to learn the idioms of French modernist poetry; and it radiates outward in the period following the Second World War when the form and content of several poems becomes theatrical or, simply, polyphonic, such as 'Le Rocher de la solitude' (1949), or when investigations into language use and dramatic performance blend, as in 'Soirées de concert ou les mots étrangers' (from the early 1950s) or 'Spectacle' (from the late 1940s):

Parfois, aidé d'un complice, le mot change de sexe et d'âme. Il rit, alors, de notre stupeur et de notre terreur. Une foule d'admirateurs se précipite pour l'applaudir. Qui jamais dira la cruauté de ces applaudissements? J'ai mis longtemps à m'apercevoir que, pour mieux jouir de ses tours, il nous entraînait à notre insu sur la scène d'un théâtre choisi. Au programme, la page de prose ou de vers que nous revendiquerons, une fois le spectacle terminé. (Jbmd, 173)

Readers of the Parisian texts know well that the theatrical dimension of the Cairene texts was never lost; on the contrary, it was modified to adapt to a new condition, the Jewish exilic condition—whence the dialogues of the stone and sand, that of the desperate Jewish lovers outside time, that of myriad voices of imaginary Talmudic sages. But it is vital to recognize that from the beginning of his career Jabès both acted and composed in theatre circles in Egypt. Later, as a refugee, he practised a kind of writing from a Jewish perspective, by which I mean his frequent allusions to Jewish thought, history, ritual, language and other aspects of culture associated with Judaism. He wrote, for example:

('Nous vivons en pays étranger, disait Reb Dambah, où le Sabbat se fête en nos cœurs. Ah! Quand les battements de notre cœur se confondront-ils avec ceux de la cité?'

Et Reb Mendel: 'Nous vivons dans l'éventail ouvert de nos voix dans le vide').
(*LQ* I, 123)

His success (or failure) in Parisian circles, no less than in Cairo, depended on his ability to interpret—in other words, to represent in his writings—the hazard of his exilic condition, which was for him unequivocally Jewish.

If texts such as 'Spectacle', dating from Jabès's Egyptian years, show signs of cultural alienation, those texts composed after his expulsion justify the designation even further. *Etrangeté*, understood as nostalgia for a lost country and as an insurmountable separation from a beloved homeland, intensified: as a French-speaking poet writing in the minority language of his native country, Jabès looked longingly to the French capital to animate his spirit; however, after his departure, now part of the linguistic majority, his gaze was cast over his shoulder to the south, to the Mediterranean, to the cities of the Near East and to the Egyptian desert:

Je garde, du pays que j'ai quitté, le souvenir d'un lit où j'ai couché, rêvé, aimé.

Je mourrai, sans doute, au pays du conquérant; mais si, par chance, je revenais dans ma patrie, pourrais-je y dormir encore, y rêver, y aimer? (*LQ* I, 391)

Jabès refused to return to Egypt in person, so he sought to recapture the memory and image of his lost homeland in his writings. He developed this second dimension of *étrangeté* in the course of his 1981 interview with the journalist Maurice Partouche. Jabès explained: 'Mon attachement à la France date de mon enfance. Je ne pouvais m'imaginer habitant ailleurs. J'aurais choisi de m'installer en Israël si je pensais que je pouvais vivre là-bas en harmonie avec moi-même. Cela n'est pas le cas. Peut-être parce que je ne me reconnais aucune appartenance. Peut-être parce que toute parole du livre n'est que parole écartelée d'une impossible appartenance.'[12] France, the 'pays du conquérant', had become, in spite of himself, home. If life in France offered no existential comfort, it did nevertheless offer him a place where he could write.

The third dimension of *étrangeté* is not without controversy. Having no formal religious education, Jabès became familiar with ancient and medieval rabbinic literature from secondary, sometimes non-Jewish sources. He had no living experience of traditional Judaism, which was for him an anachronism. While there are frequent allusions in his Parisian writings to the Kabbalah, the first known book for Jabès's reflections on God and creation is not specifically Jewish. In the early

1960s, while first exploring the possibility of integrating Kabbalistic thought into *Le Livre des Questions*, he drew his inspiration from Pierre Klossowski's translation of selected meditations on the Bible by the Christian mystical philosopher Johann Georg Hamann (Königsberg, 1730–Münster, 1788), as his correspondence with Gabriel Bounoure reveals.[13] Similarly, many contemporary orthodox Jews did not think of him as Jewish in the way they knew themselves to be. Nor was Jabès a practising or believing Jew. This theological, or, to put it differently, genealogical breach produced an extreme strain in his Parisian writing. The assimilation of Jewish themes in the Jabésian text is thus fraught with difficulty and even danger, as it proved hazardous for his reception among critics who were and remain divided between those who, according to Gary D. Mole, 'see Jabès's books as intimately related to Judaism and the history of the persecution of the Jewish people, and [...] those who see Jabès articulating a distorted view of Judaism coupled with an objectionable use of the Shoah'.[14] Jabès would have endorsed the terms of the debate: although his texts appear to have drawn on classical Jewish sources, as early as 1962–3 he was keenly aware of his distance from them, a fact evidenced in this dialogue between Yukel and some of the more severe of the imaginary rabbis.

> S'adressant à moi, mes frères de race ont dit:
> 'Tu n'es pas Juif. Tu ne fréquentes pas la synagogue.'
>
> M'adressant à mes frères de race, j'ai répondu:
> 'Je porte la synagogue dans mon sein.'
> ....
> S'adressant à moi, mes frères de race ont dit:
> 'Les rabbins dont tu cites les paroles sont des charlatans.

Ont-ils jamais existé? Et tu t'es nourri de leurs paroles impies.'
    M'adressant à mes frères de race, j'ai répondu:
    'Les rabbins dont je cite les paroles sont les phares de ma mémoire.—On ne se souvient que de soi.—Et vous savez que l'âme a, pour pétale, une parole.' (*LQ* I, 67–8)

As this exchange shows, Jabès sensed himself outside the Jewish tradition yet, in a strange and undefined way, profoundly attached to it. Again, Derrida was among the first to write about the problem: 'Pour Jabès, qui reconnaît avoir découvert très tard une certaine appartenance au judaïsme, le Juif n'est que l'allégorie souffrante. [...] Il doit alors s'expliquer avec ses frères de race et des rabbins qui ne sont plus imaginaires. Tous lui reprocheront cet universalisme, cet essentialisme, cet allégorisme décharnés [...]' (*Ed*, 112). Thus Edmond Jabès became the paradigmatic nomad, at once admired and deprecated for maintaining the position of literary outsider, not seeking answers but rather asking questions about language and identity.

The thesis that Jabès exhibited the various shades of *étrangeté* throughout his career is illustrated, seedlike, in an aphorism from the late 1940s. Although neither theatrical nor dialogic in itself, it is nonetheless representative of Jabès's theatrical preoccupation and poetoexegetical role. 'Spectacle', quoted above, concludes: 'Constamment en pays étranger, le poète se sert de la poésie comme interprète' (*Jbmd*, 176). The semantic polyvalency of the French word *interprète* captures precisely the point I wish to highlight and the topic I would like to amplify in these pages: that Jabès viewed the practice of writing in a twofold manner, as a kind of performance and as an act of exchange (*inter-pretium*). This twin purpose is implied in the various meanings of the French word *interprétation*, which refers to both the explanation of a text and the enactment of its script. It demands an interrogative engagement with language and the ability to put it to good use. It is from this meaning that our understanding of *interprète* as exegete or commentator is derived. Interpretation involves improvisation, modification and adaptation; in other words, a certain craft. Above all, interpretation requires fidelity. The moment the *interprète* strays from the text, the interpretation is rendered false. Meaning is banished from, or deformed in, inaccurate interpretation. It misleads, it becomes delusional (itself an archaic meaning of the word), it disfigures—it then requires re-examination and re-enactment—while the successful interpretation is intelligible, coherent and convincing: as a commentary, as a linguistic gloss, as a correctly executed musical composition. For Jabès, interpretation was conceived of as a means of understanding his condition as a stranger. The varieties of French modernism he drew on, as represented by Baudelaire, Rimbaud and Mallarmé, were, in a sense, a hazard, though accidental in this sense: his consciousness as a Jew emerged from the condition of being a Jew in exile, a Jew in the Diaspora[15]—a condition not unknown to other Jews since the destruction of the second Temple nearly 2000 years before Jabès left Egypt; on the other hand, French modernism was the specific stylistic expression, or garment, of Jabès's internalized historical and linguistic condition.

Organization

Following this introduction, I seek to place Jabès in the francophone Cairene milieu from the late 1920s, that is, the period dating from his first published poems and cultural activities through his immigration in 1957. Chapter 1, 'Judaism in the Margin', outlines the principal consideration under scrutiny during the Egyptian period, namely, the ambiguities associated with coming of age in the city which an Egyptian professor of English, Magdi Wahba, memorably described as 'that kingdom of illusion'.[16] What did it mean for a youth to mature in a foreign environment that was, paradoxically, home? What effect did Jabès's francophone background have on his perception of himself as a French poet and of his fellow Franco-Egyptian writers? Chapter 1 examines the origins of Jabès's Frenchness and further looks at the problem of his Jewishness. The word 'problem' is crucial. I have already alluded to Jabès's uneasiness, while in Paris, with being known as a Jewish writer, or, more precisely, to his intention of preserving his hedged 'double vocation', as Maurice Blanchot called it in an essay from 1964 (*A*, 256), as 'écrivain et juif' (*LM*, 181). I ask if the equivocation was justified by focusing on Jabès's Jewish background in Egypt, in particular his participation in Jewish youth groups against emerging Nazi anti-Semitism. It is pertinent to ask why his Cairene writings, with little exception, did not take as their reference, explicit or implicit, Jewish history and contemporary Jewish affairs in particular during and following the advent of Nazi anti-Semitism in Egypt after 1933, or again after 1945.

The next two chapters detail his professional relations with French and Egyptian literary personalities. Chapter 2, 'A Still-Born Poet', focuses on Jabès's early evolution as a writer, his first enthusiasms and subsequent difficulties in establishing his presence on the Franco-Egyptian literary scene where he was known as an 'écrivain égyptien d'expression française'.[17] Chapter 3, '"La Patrie de l'humain"', explores Jabès's relationships with the two writers who most fundamentally influenced how he wrote in his mature years. His mentor, Max Jacob, and his *éminence grise*, the critic Gabriel Bounoure, both worked with him on composition and editing, and in each case encouraged him to take a moral position *vis-à-vis* his poetry, which would be of capital importance in the years following his immigration.

Chapter 4, 'Exile Confirmed', is a discussion of *Je bâtis ma demeure*, and especially of those poems that manifest a desire to create a dwelling made of words impervious to the precariousness, the cruel caprice, of history. Furthermore, I explore the thesis that for Jabès, lyric poetry was no longer a viable medium to contain the new Jewish dimension of exile he experienced at this time. It is at this stage that the influence of Maurice Blanchot becomes visible in his evolution; similarly, in the early 1960s there begins a reciprocal relationship between Jabès's new writings and those of Jacques Derrida. The concluding discussion, 'On Not Belonging', seeks to understand the entirety of Jabès's writings through the principle of *non-appartenance*. Based on the evidence presented in the preceding chapters, I take a sceptical view of the appropriateness of calling Jabès a francophone Mediterranean, a Surrealist practitioner, a French or a Jewish writer. Upon careful examination, the inner weave of his texts suggests that all of these designations are accurate, but none is entirely so. Each is true, yet each is a falsification. Underlying this chapter, then, and ultimately the entire study, is the question: Where does Jabès belong in the annals of modern Egyptian-francophone literature, post-World War Two French literature and theory, and Jewish literature after Auschwitz?

Notes to Introduction

1. This incident is discussed in my presentation of the manuscript pages in which Jabès first described how he came across the graffiti. See 'La "matrice cachée" du *Livre des Questions*' in *Portrait(s) d'Edmond Jabès*, ed. Steven Jaron (Paris: Bibliothèque nationale de France, 1999), 88–9.
2. Emile Simon's expression from his essay by that name, published in the *Revue du Caire* 31 (1941), 109–15.
3. Interview with Madelaine Chapsal, *Express* 618 (18 Apr. 1963), 33.
4. Theodor Adorno, *Minima Moralia: Reflections from Damaged Life*, trans. E. F. N. Jephcott (London: Verso, 1974), 87. Cf. 33–4.
5. A.-M. Gentilly, *Terre retrouvée* 15 (1963), 5.
6. David Banon, 'Le livre et les livres: une écriture de l'exil', *Nouveaux Cahiers* 104 (1991), 7.
7. Edmond Jabès, 'Pages nouvelles II', *Instants* 1 (1989), ed. Lucie Ducel, 248.
8. Murielle Gagnebin, 'La présentation négative', *L'Irreprésentable ou les silences de l'œuvre* (Paris: Presses Universitaires de France/Ecriture, 1984), 13–27 (16) (Gagnebin's emphasis). Gagnebin persuasively combines German phenomenology (Husserl and Eugen Fink) and post-Freudian French psychoanalysis (Lacan, André Green and Christian David) in her intriguing study of literary and iconographic work.
9. Ibid. 22.
10. Some critics believe Jabès should be dissociated from Derrida. See, e.g., Joseph G. Kronick, 'Edmond Jabès and the Poetry of the Jewish Unhappy Consciousness', *Modern Language Notes* 106/5 (1991), 967–96. For an opposing

view, see ch. 8, 'On the Meaning of Jacques Derrida', in particular the section 'Jabès and Writing', in Allan Megill, *Prophets of Extremity: Nietzsche, Heidegger, Foucault, Derrida* (Berkeley: University of California Press, 1985), 316–20.

11. Roger E. Stoddard's *Edmond Jabès in Bibliography, 'Du blanc des mots et du noir des signes': A Record of the Printed Books*, 2nd edn., rev. and enlarged (Paris and Caen: Les Lettres modernes–Minard, 2001), has definitively done away with the notion that Jabès's writings date only from the early 1940s. Daniel Lançon, in his *Jabès l'Egyptien* (Paris: Jean-Michel Place, 1998), provides an informative *tour d'horizon* of Jabès's pre-expulsion cultural milieu. He does not, however, examine at any length his poetry from this period, nor does he investigate the relationship between it and the Parisian writings.

12. Maurice Partouche, 'Edmond Jabès, poète de l'exil et du désert', *Le Monde* suppl. to no. 11355 (2 Aug. 1981), 9–10.

13. Pierre Klossowski, *Les Méditations bibliques de Hamann* (Paris: Minuit, 1948). Jabès's and Bounoure's exchange of letters on Hamann dates from Aug. 1961.

14. Gary D. Mole, 'Edmond Jabès and the Wound of Writing: The Traces of Auschwitz', *Orbis Litterarum* 49 (1994), 295; see also his *Lévinas, Blanchot, Jabès: Figures of Estrangement* (Gainesville, FL: University Press of Florida, 1997). See further Henri Raczymow, 'Qui est Edmond Jabès?', *Cahiers obsidiane* 5 (1982), 164–6, and 'Edmond Jabès, juif contesté' in *Nouveaux Cahiers* 104 (1991), 8–9, for his objections to critics, such as Henri Meschonnic and Shmuel Trigano, of Jabès's non-rabbinic Judaism.

15. See, in this regard, Richard Stamelman's excellent essay 'The Nomadic Writing of Exile: Edmond Jabès', in his *Lost Beyond Telling: Representations of Death and Absence in Modern French Poetry* (Ithaca, NY: Cornell University Press, 1990), 223–48.

16. Magdi Wahba, 'Cairo Memories', *Encounter* 62/5 (1984), 79.

17. See Marguerite Lichtenberger, 'Les écrivains d'expression française en Egypte', ch. 11 of her doctoral dissertation, *Ecrivains français en Egypte contemporaine (de 1870 à nos jours)* (Paris: Ernest Leroux, 1934), 166–79, and Jean Desthieux, 'Poètes égyptiens de langue française', in *Revue des conférences françaises en Egypte* 15 (1938), 389–97.

CHAPTER 1

Judaism in the Margin

> ... Ah! Je voudrais,
> Je voudrais n'être pas Français, pour pouvoir dire
> Que je te choisis, France, et que dans ton martyre,
> Je te proclame, toi que ronge le vautour,
> Mon unique patrie et mon unique amour.
>
> VICTOR HUGO

Becoming French, for Georges Cattaui, was a matter of choice. When he began his *Dévotion à l'image* (1919) with an epigraph from Hugo, he did not indicate that the quotation was taken from 'A la France', from *L'Année terrible* (December 1870). The education of his Egyptian readers had trained them to recognize the poem from which the lines were excerpted. He and his readers (the book was published in Cairo by the Institut français d'archéologie orientale) shared a knowledge and affection for France that made such annotations unnecessary and even undesirable; an annotation would have fixed its meaning in a particular time and place, and would have denied its hoped-for, transcendent message. As thoughtful heirs to the Enlightenment, these out-of-place Third Republic Egyptians believed that to be French was a privilege which carried with it the duty to advance social equality. The dead whom Cattaui lamented, those of the Great War, were set on a par with the patriotic *Communards* who fell defending Paris in the Franco-Prussian war.

Born in Paris in 1896 but raised in Cairo by his family, which had been well-established in the Egyptian-Jewish community for generations, Georges Cattaui belonged at once to two countries that shared a single language, French, and furthermore, he embodied two cultures, French and Egyptian, in his writing. In temperament, however, he veered, as his quotation from Hugo and the poetry that follows it attest, towards a Third-Republican France, and he espoused the alleged universalistic values claimed by the culture which grew there. Once established in France in the early 1920s, he wrote several studies of Proust, while befriending Jewish writers such as André Spire and Catholic humanists such as Jacques and Raïssa Maritain. In 1926, he himself quietly became a Catholic.[1]

Georges Cattaui's Egyptian francophilia reflects the diffusion of French Enlightenment values into the Middle East. Love of France was not at all rare during and after the turn of the nineteenth century among subjects of the Ottoman empire, many of whom had ancestry in points bordering the Mediterranean littoral and the Levant including Greece, Italy, North Africa, Syria and Lebanon, Malta and Turkey.[2] Its origins can be traced to Napoleon's grand Expédition en Egypte begun in 1798, although the Ottoman influence, whose twilight in Egypt coincided with the outbreak of the Great War and its conflict with Britain, cannot be ignored. In the mid-nineteenth century the internal push to modernize Egypt, felt most strongly during the reigns of Mohammed Ali (1805–48) and the Khedive Ismail (1863–79)—who observed, perhaps ironically, that after the completion of the Suez Canal in 1869 'l'Egypte n'est pas en Afrique; elle fait partie de l'Europe'[3]—was followed and reinforced by the colonization of the country by the British (1882–1936). The enormous financial debt incurred during the construction of the Canal and from the Khedive's extravagant inauguration ceremonies enabled Britain to buy the majority of the shares of the Suez Canal Company, thus helping to ensure the colonization of Egypt. That the subject of the 'section scolaire' of the *Jeux floraux d'Egypte* in 1933 was a discussion of the Khedive's saying, 'Mon pays n'est plus en Afrique; nous faisons partie de l'Europe', further attests to the currency of Eurocentrism in inter-war Egypt among the French-speaking population. And while the effort to modernize produced a sometimes ignominiously destitute and volatile social backdrop to the cultural and political achievements of the late nineteenth and early twentieth centuries, Georges Cattaui knew only its opulence.

Raised in an environment which mixed French and Egyptian culture, individuals such as Georges Cattaui experienced what I call an internal uprooting, by which I mean an existential sense of exile and displacement that is not necessarily related to political expulsion. Cattaui himself was not banished from Egypt; in fact, he found himself a comfortable position in the political and economic life of the country and later, as a diplomat, in Europe. His artistic vision, predicated on an internal uprooting, was the result of a tension between his native language and culture, on the one hand, and his homeland, on the other. It may be viewed as a not so subtly constituted amalgam of the Oriental and the Occidental, both of which he absorbed at one remove from the source, as in translation.

To begin a study of Edmond Jabès's literary development with a discussion of a member of the Cattaui family is not fortuitous, first because the Cattauis were the most prominent Jewish family in Egypt for the century that runs from the end of the reign of Mohammad Ali to the dissolution of the francophone community beginning in the middle of the twentieth century, and secondly, because Edmond Jabès eventually married into it. The Cattauis counted themselves among the most wealthy and influential Jews in modern Egypt, and they contributed widely to the economic development of the country from the late nineteenth century through the mid-1950s. The first railways were laid and the first modern factories built by their companies (such as Delta Land Development) or by those of their business partners, the Mosseris, Suareses, Curiels and Rossis. Notables from the family who were active in culture and the arts, in addition to Georges, were Maurice Cattaui, an architect who helped construct the central Jewish synagogue of Cairo (*Shari Sha'ma'im*) in 1905, and the composer Hector de Cattaui (a brother of Jabès's mother-in-law), whose obituary was written by Jabès.[4] Edmond Jabès became a member of the Cattaui family upon his marriage to Arlette Cohen in 1935,[5] in the synagogue designed by Maurice Cattaui. Arlette Cohen's mother, Edith Cohen *née* Cattaui, was the daughter of one of the family patriarchs, Moïse de Cattaui pasha, who was the president of the Cairo Jewish community until his death in 1924.[6]

Our subject is the origins of Edmond Jabès's artistic vision. Whence did it come? If we are to seek a reasonable response to this question, then we must examine the Egypt of the inter-war period where he was schooled and came of age and, in particular, the combination of cultural and historical forces that shaped his thinking and writing as an adult. At that time the country numbered some 180,000 minority or non-Egyptian residents—Greeks, Italians, British, Maltese—of whom some 51,500 were Jews and among whom French was used in family, educational and social situations;[7] a minority among minorities. The total number of Jews rose through 1947 when the population reached 65,600, about 42,000 of whom lived in Cairo, although by 1956–7 the number fell to some 5,000 to 10,000 souls, who were subject to Egyptian nationalization laws.[8] 'A l'époque, le quartier à majorité européenne où j'évoluais—celui du commerce et des affaires—avait à peine les dimensions du quartier de l'Opéra à Paris', Jabès explained to the writer Marcel Cohen (*Dl*, 33). Jabès's Cairo was a fraction of the size that one might expect from such a complex cultural and linguistic crucible. Arabic was of course the most widely spoken language there, although Italian, English, Armenian and Greek could also be heard among its inhabitants.[9] Jabès himself grew up within the Egyptian linguistic diversity in a French-speaking home in the affluent Garden City section of Cairo, which was part of the city's recent plan for urban renewal and expansion. After the turn of the century, the Jabès family, with other newly wealthy Jews who had acquired capital through banking and in the cotton trade, moved to Garden City from the *haret el yahud*, Cairo's medieval Jewish quarter. 'Jusqu'au lendemain de la révolte d'Arabi Pacha, en 1882,' wrote Fernand Leprette, an inspector of French schools in Cairo until 1956, 'à peu près toute la communauté israélite du Caire a vécu au *haret el yahud*. [...] Puis, quelques Juifs s'enhardirent à s'installer à Coubrah, à l'Abassieh et au Daher et, de là les plus chanceux, les plus aisés, gagnèrent Kasr el-Doubra et Garden City où ils occupent de somptueuses demeures.'[10] Since the 1880s and the revolt of Orabi pasha against the British colonialists, at which time Edmond Jabès's paternal grandfather chose Italian nationality, the Jabès family had been exempt from laws of Egyptian taxation by the Capitulations.[11] Like many of Egypt's cosmopolitan Jewish population, they took annual holidays in France. In fact, it was on a return journey from Marseille to Alexandria in October 1929 that Edmond, 17 years of age, first met Arlette Cohen, two years younger. Immediately after his marriage, Edmond Jabès moved to the home of Arlette's affluent parents on the island of Zamalek. Jabès described it, perhaps echoing Leprette, as 'une demeure somptueuse, les oiseaux pour fenêtres' (*Jbmd*, 281). By the late 1930s, Edmond and Arlette had moved to their own apartment, also in Zamalek, where they remained until their departure from Egypt.[12] With regard to religion, nationality, legal status and language, the Jabès family was set apart from but not excluded from the Muslim, Arabic-speaking Egyptian majority.

It would be inaccurate, then, to claim that visits to France broadened the cultural horizons of francophone Egyptian youths like Georges Cattaui or Edmond Jabès since their cultural view was already oriented, by family and schooling, in the direction of the Hexagon. Moreover, the enchantment that ancient Arabic culture exerted on the imagination of the young Jabès was similarly determinative. Here, at the age of 20 and dreaming of poetry, he confesses:

Très jeune encore, les scrutant dans mon livre d'histoire où ils étaient reproduits en photographie, je rêvais à des poèmes sur papyrus que les poètes anciens d'Arabie, au mur de la Kaaba, exposaient, afin que les chefs des tribus et les savants de toutes les contrées venus en pèlerinage les emportent avec eux et les chantent et les propagent sous leur tente. Le poème offert ainsi aux yeux de l'étranger, celui-ci, s'il ne le transformait pas chez lui après l'avoir lu, ou le plus souvent, seulement écouté, du moins le situait-il dans une atmosphère propre à son tempérament. Le long cri du poète s'amplifiait de bouches en bouches, chacun retenant de lui, un seul ou deux vers qui le caractérisait en général, et vrai miracle de poésie, se construisait d'une strophe choisie et arrangée, un poème suggéré.[13]

Though born and raised in Egypt, as a boy Jabès imagined himself a foreign child, a child of the 'savants de toutes les contrées venus en pèlerinage' (perhaps not dissimilar to Champollion reading the Rosetta Stone) who had come to hear the desert poetry of ancient Arabian poets. A comparison of this quotation from Jabès's youth with another from a book written in France some thirty-five years later, demonstrates the tenacity ancient Egypt exerted on him:

Je me souviendrai toujours d'un bas-relief du temple d'Abydos où l'on voyait le dieu Horus et le dieu-soleil Rê, unis dans un même corps sous le nom de Réharakhti, Horus de l'Horizon, donnant à respirer à Ramsès II, pharaon considéré comme une incarnation du dieu Horus, le 'Ankh', symbole de vie. Ce signe qui représente, dans l'ancienne Egypte, la vie éternelle, je rêvais de l'introduire par la plume dans le vocable et de manière à ce que le sang de chaque lettre en soit chargé, enrichi. (LQ I, 40–1)

When in Paris Jabès writes of the archaeological ruins that form the history of ancient Egypt, the verb he uses is in the future tense, 'Je me souviendrai', followed by 'toujours'. Through the medium of memory, his own past is thereby placed in an eternal present. Still more, when one reads the early and later passages side by side, one discerns an intriguing parallel between them. Eerily similar expressions, such as 'je rêvais à des poèmes sur papyrus' (1932) and 'la vie éternelle, je rêvais de l'introduire par la plume' (1967), and 'les poètes anciens d'Arabie' (1932) and 'dans l'ancienne Egypte' (1967), attest to a sustained fascination and self-identification with Egyptian antiquity and, more generally, with the Orient. Studied carefully, then, the writings of Jabès's Paris period form a continuity with those of the Cairene years—not simply with those dating from after the Second World War, but even those estranged writings from his earliest years.

Like Georges Cattaui, Edmond Jabès grew up as if the cultural histories of France and Egypt had been transposed onto each other. While his cultural orientation leaned forcefully towards the former, he perceived himself to be a native of neither country ('le poème offert ainsi aux yeux de l'étranger'). It is as if he viewed Egypt with the eyes of a French schoolboy while he thought of France as a Europeanized Egyptian would. In such a way Jabès 'a grandi entre deux mondes traduits' (*LQ* I, 326), the strange amalgam of which produced an internal uprooting because neither country belonged, as to a native, to him. Yet, we see, he was and remained drawn to Egypt's ancient past. It is not odd for a boy raised in Cairo to feel the lure of the country's antiquities. What are the roots of his francophile disposition?

The passage in which Jabès scrutinized his history book for photographs where he could read poems written on papyrus was written shortly after he gained his *baccalauréat* from the Lycée français of Cairo. His first school years were spent at the Collège Saint-Jean-Baptiste-de-la-Salle (1917–24),[14] but he most likely began to see himself as non-French while he was a student at the Lycée français. It was there that he sensed himself to be an outsider to the culture with which he had been inculcated since birth. The school's administration was overseen by the Mission laïque française, a French organization established in Cairo in 1907 whose duty it was to protect French pedagogical interests in the city and in its new suburbs such as Maadi and Heliopolis. The sense of mission the Lycée français took upon itself is demonstrated in an article succinctly entitled 'L'influence de la culture française en Egypte', written by a teacher of French and Latin at the school, Jean Rapnouil. Rapnouil states confidently that French journalists and actors assuredly know that Cairene and Alexandrian French speakers can grasp the full range of meaning as well as any educated native of France. Neither plays on words nor the most diverse allusions to politics, history and culture will be lost on Egypt's French speakers. Many of the school's students work for higher degrees in the French capital, where their performance equals that of native Frenchmen, but they do not always remain there. French is their language, but Egypt is home. They remain faithful to the country and often come back, working for the betterment of its society in a 'union spirituelle entre les éléments divers qui constituent la population éclairée'.[15] From this union would flow forth 'un avenir brillant et fécond'. Rapnouil's statement may be viewed as a commentary not only on all of the graduates of this institution but equally on the young Jabès, who, after graduating from the Lycée français in 1929, did go to Paris where he enrolled in the Sorbonne's literature programme. He did not, however, attend any classes; other more pressing temptations drew him into the world of Parisian literary circles, a world which we will glimpse below, before he returned to Cairo. In any case, Rapnouil's pedagogical zeal should not be lost on us, for he was Edmond Jabès's own teacher of literature at the Lycée[16] and as such initiated him into the traditions of French poetry and its potential for adaptation to an Egyptian setting.[17] Jabès did not lose touch with his teacher after graduation. During the war years, their relationship took on a political dimension as they protested together against the onslaught of local and world Fascism and racism. In June 1945, for instance, the two attended a banquet organized jointly by the Ligue française pour la défense des droits de l'homme et du citoyen (of which Rapnouil was president), the Comité international antifasciste et antiraciste d'Egypte, the Comité démocratique espagnol and the Union rationaliste d'Egypte.[18]

The effect of Jabès's education on his writing was the object of a reflection on the correct use of language—or, rather, how language could be deformed, but for a special purpose. For Jabès, spelling errors were a springboard for creating a private language, a uniquely subjective space. The sense of questioning that accompanied the birth of poetic language may be traced to his student days and, in particular, to his relationship with his schoolmaster, perhaps Jean Rapnouil in particular. 'D'aussi loin que je m'en souvienne et autant que je puisse l'assurer,' he wrote in the second volume (1978) of *Le Livre des Ressemblances* trilogy,

je crois que ce sont les fautes d'orthographe que je faisais, enfant, adolescent, qui ont été à l'origine d'un questionnement qui s'est developpé par la suite. Je ne comprenais pas qu'un mot reproduit un peu différemment, avec une lettre en moins ou de trop, ne représentait, brusquement, plus rien; que mon maître pouvait se permettre de le biffer rageusement à l'encre rouge sur mon cahier et s'arroger arbitrairement le droit de me punir de l'avoir, pour ainsi dire, inventé. (*LR*, 201)

Humiliation at the hand of his teacher, for the young Jabès, was a source of inspiration. The corrections made on his papers were viewed as an attempt to extinguish the defiant pupil's will to create, to find new meanings. Jabès viewed his educators as violent authoritarians imposing themselves on a poor schoolboy. This feeling comes across very clearly in a poem written after the war, 'Les Condamnés':

> On dresse l'échafaud sur l'impatience Le maître avec sa pierre ponce
> frotte *les maigres doigts tachés d'encre des écoliers humiliés*
> Tu lis je lis des mots d'innocence
> que le couperet interrompt [...]
>
> (*Jbmd*, 148–9; my emphasis)

Justice, the young Jabès believed, had been disgraced. Despite the disgrace, the spelling errors he committed, and the corrections his teacher made, induced in his imagination a sense of lexical and graphic awe. How was it that using a word in one way was more correct than using it in another? Where was the fault in creating rather than simply reproducing the linguistic signs? At bottom, language was supposed to be *creative*. Here, Jabès had experienced perhaps his earliest peril regarding language and exile: when a letter was altered in a given word, its standard form and meaning were, in a sense, banished, and the boy was subsequently punished for his transgression. But it was in running the risk of banishing form and meaning that he began to question language itself. In identifying these moments at school, we have put our finger on the birth of the poet.

Indubitably, then, the Mission laïque reinforced French linguistic and cultural influences in Egypt by fixing them in the minds of its students. Active in youth theatre groups sponsored by his Lycée and by local Jewish youth groups, both of which mounted repertory pieces of the French Romantic tradition of Musset as well as of the late nineteenth-century comic school of Pierre Veber, Jabès, in his teens, regularly and literally acted French. These performances are the first known public appearances of Jabès as both actor and playwright. At one theatrical evening of the annual celebration of the Lycée français, he performed 'un amusant monologue marseillais' before an audience of more than 2000 spectators including Ismail Teymour Bey, representing King Fouad I, and Henry Gaillard, the Minister of France to Egypt. Fellow students enacted several Arabic fables during the same evening.[19] The mixture of French and Arabic culture and language seemed perfectly natural to the players and their audience. At another early performance put on by students of the Lycée, this one of *Eux* by Maurice Donnay and with the Grand Rabbi of Cairo in attendance, the press proclaimed that the 17-year-old Jabès 'fut un partenaire charmant qui s'assura la sympathie du public'.[20]

A performance of Veber's *L'Aménagement apprivoisé* in May 1930 'déchaîna le fou rire durant une demie heure et fut interprété con brio'.[21] And in January 1931 Jabès played the part of André in the local writer Robert Blum's *Beaux masques* during an evening sponsored by the Groupement littéraire et artistique of the Union universelle de la jeunesse juive (UUJJ).[22] By that time, Jabès was already a budding playwright. In November 1930 his now lost one-act, *Le 4 Septembre*, in which he 'incarna à la perfection le rôle d'un timide amoureux', was performed together with an adaptation of Alfred de Musset's poem *Durant et Dupont*, with Jabès taking one of the lead roles, and a piece of modern dance at a theatrical evening of the Cairo section of the UUJJ.[23]

Jabès's first book of poems appeared in Paris at the same time as his one-act play was performed in Cairo. *Illusions sentimentales* (1930), a selection of verse composed on the diverse models of Lamartine, Vigny and Musset, received notices in the French capital, but does not appear to have been reviewed in Parisian papers.[24] In an exceedingly rare reference to his juvenile compositions, Jabès told an interviewer in 1986 that some of these first poems had even been read at the Comédie-Française, where they enjoyed acclaim: he was accepted into the literary salon of Rachilde where 'senators, deputies, academicians' sent him letters of congratulation.[25] On the other hand, Adolf Shual, another French-Egyptian Jew, reviewed the book in November 1930 in the Egyptian cultural journal, the *Semaine égyptienne*, where he cautiously praised Jabès's 'phrase concise, frêle, d'une forme assez libre'.[26]

The most important early indicator attesting to Jabès's implantation into French cultural circles is the *Anthologie mensuelle* (renamed, after the January 1930 issue, the *Alliance universelle*). Jabès founded the journal with his older brother, Henri, in November 1929 in Paris as the house organ of the Alliance franco-égyptienne.[27] Henri Jabès acted as the magazine's director, Edmond Jabès as its Egyptian correspondent, M. C. Poinsot as its secretary general and Eugène Figuière as its administrator. Figuière, who brought out Jabès's first two books of poetry, *Illusions sentimentales* and *Je t'attends!* (1931), in Paris, was also the publisher of the journal. The first editorial co-authored by the Jabès brothers defined the humanist, cross-cultural goals of the Alliance as the 'élargissement de notre sympathie, au-delà même des frontières, à tous ceux qu'anime l'amour de la France, et cela non par nationalisme ridicule et néfaste, mais au contraire dans le but d'étendre notre amitié *humaine* aussi loin que possible'.[28] Further-more, the brothers wished to promote French writers in Cairo and Alexandria by encouraging them to visit Egypt, and to send Egyptian writers to France.[29] In an astonishing declarative *tour de force*, one of the journal's editors, Alexandre Mercereau, proclaimed: 'Si le but de l'Alliance franco-égyptienne est de nouer un lien entre la France et l'Egypte, c'est un lien purement spirituel.' The spirit of the France of 1789, its defence of human rights, liberty and justice, had inspired the Jabès brothers to wage a cultural and political combat.[30] The Egyptian press briefly described their ambitious intentions for those unfamiliar with the Alliance: 'Ses buts qui sont surtout intellectuels sont destinés à assurer une liaison amicale et ferme entre ceux qui désirent mieux que des vagues relations: une réelle fraternité entre deux pays, offrant de nombreux points de contact.'[31]

Commentaries on French-Egyptian politics and cultural relations jointly written by Henri and Edmond Jabès demonstrate a concerted effort to do away with the political obstacles that separated the two countries. In one instance they proposed having a street in Paris named after Egypt's King Fouad I;[32] in another they lamented that Egypt did not have a Fondation égyptienne at the newly established Cité universitaire in Paris's fourteenth *arrondissement* and encouraged the Egyptian authorities to build one, similar to the Fondation des Etats-Unis, as quickly as possible.[33] On the cultural side, Henri contributed to the column on the Parisian theatre scene while Edmond published his first poems and book reviews on Egyptian writers such as Jean Moscatelli and François Moutran.[34] Perhaps the Alliance's greatest success was in organizing a 'grand débat sur l'Egypte' at the Club du Faubourg Léo Poldès in May 1930. Ad-vertisements for the debate list the participants as Princess Bibesco, Jehan d'Ivray, Han Ryner, Léo Poldès, Henri Jabès and Raymond Offner, but the younger Edmond does not appear on the list! Except for Princess Bibesco and Léo Poldès, each participant had contributed to the pages of the *Alliance universelle*. Jehan d'Ivray, herself a prolific Franco-Egyptian writer, published a long excerpt from her novel *L'Appel de l'ombre* earlier in 1930.[35] In addition to founding and maintaining the Faubourg Poldès, Léo Poldès was a playwright and an outspoken Zionist. His *L'Eternel Ghetto, pièce d'actualité, en trois actes sur la question juive* (1928) reflected these interests. Bibesco had been chosen as a participant for her recently published travelogue, *Jour d'Egypte* (1929). When the debate took place, however, the participants included Henri Jabès, Alexandre Mercereau, Offner, d'Ivray, Mahmoud Bey and Baron Surcouf. The absence of Princess Bibesco, the most socially illustrious speaker, did not deter over 2000 people from attending the debate.[36]

It is clear that within a few months of the organization's inception, Henri Jabès's role had superseded his brother's. While the two continued to co-sign the editorials, Henri contributed a greater number of articles to the journal than Edmond, who only occasionally published his poems in its pages. The reason for the imbalance seems to have been primarily geographical: the former edited the journal from Paris, where the Alliance's activities were focused, while the latter remained in Cairo. Thus the 'jeune et charmant poète Edmond Jabès pour cause d'éloignement' did not attend the first luncheon of the Alliance in January 1930, which his brother sponsored with his wife (described as one of France's 'plus charmantes parisiennes') at the Carlton Hotel on the Champs-Elysées. His excuse—'Il s'occupe activement de la diffusion de la revue et des amitiés franco-égyptiennes'[37]—might refer to the intention of the Alliance to form a Société des gens de lettres en Egypte. Sadly, the roster of members did not include a single Egyptian. Rather, a diverse group of French dignitaries numbering among others Paul Brulat, Léon Riotor (municipal adviser at City Hall), Léon Frapié (author of *La Maternelle*), the attorney Maurice Prévost, the painters Maurice Dubois and Louis Plumont, the publisher Eugène Figuière, René Petit of the *Petit Journal* and his wife, the film star Suzanne Bianchetti, enjoyed one another's company.[38] An inventory of the membership also confirms the absence of Egyptians, save the Jabès brothers. In addition to the expected central committee members (Figuière, Henri and Edmond Jabès, Mercereau, etc.), the general committee included André Tardieu (President of the Council of Ministers, Minister of the Interior), Pierre Marreau (Minister of Public Education and of the Beaux-Arts) and other French high functionaries. The Alliance's very impressive list of members included the novelists, poets, critics, dramatists and politicians Juliette Adam, Henry Bordeaux, Henri Barbusse, Gustave Charpentier, Maurice Donnay, Charles Diehl, Paul Geraldy, Edouard Herriot, André Honnorat, Maurice Maeterlinck, Victor Margueritte, the Comtesse de Noailles, Charles Richet, Hélène Vacaresco, Paul Valéry and Pierre Wolff[39]—none of them Egyptian. In short, Edmond Jabès's role as the organization's repre-

sentative in Egypt was largely symbolic. Henri concluded his toast at
the luncheon with a cordial, deferential nod to his absent brother: 'Je
voudrais sceller cette amitié [between France and Egypt], d'une façon
nouvelle peut-être à Paris, mais qui est une coutume dans mon pays',
at which point he displayed a bottle of water from the Nile, which
Edmond Jabès had sent. Henri asked those present to fill their glasses
with it and wet their lips: 'je vous souhaiterai le plus de bonheur
possible en vous priant de vous souvenir de notre vieil adage: "Qui a
bu de l'eau du Nil en reboira"'.[40]

The Alliance franco-égyptienne was active for less than a single year
(the final issue of the journal dates from 31 July 1930) and Edmond
Jabès's participation was limited; but it is an unequivocal sign that he
thought of himself as a repository of cosmopolitan Egyptian and
Republican French ideals, and, moreover, as somehow responsible to
both of them. If his youthful idealism failed visibly to expand the
French cultural presence in Egypt in the late twenties and the
beginning of the next decade, it must be recalled that the house organ
of the Alliance nevertheless provided a place for the publication of his
first poems, many of which were included in *Illusions sentimentales* and
Je t'attends! Cemented by his schooling in the Mission laïque française,
the strong tendency to bridge French and Egyptian culture was
manifestly set in motion by the time he was 17 or 18.

Jabès's self-perception of himself as a Jew, in particular how he
understood himself as a Jew in contemporary history, left a further
indelible mark on his writings, even though he possessed no formal
knowledge of Jewish classical sources and had little experience with
ritual practice. Osip Mandelstam once said of himself: 'As a little bit
of musk fills an entire house, so the least influence of Judaism
overflows all of one's life. Oh, what a strong smell that is!'[41] This was,
to a large degree, also true for Jabès. Reflections on Judaism are
central to his writings, be it Jewish tradition patterned, albeit not
without imaginative modification, on the model of Talmudic sages, or
contemporary Jewish history shaped by the Holocaust. Nevertheless,
in the course of this study I advance the argument that only midway
through life, as an émigré writer in Paris, did Edmond Jabès closely
investigate his Jewish roots in Egypt and more generally his Jewish
heritage, and only then did he infuse his writing with the fruit of that
examination. Despite the virtual absence of Jewish themes in his
writings dating from the Egyptian period, Judaism was important for
him during these years. How much so, requires detailing. The second

half of this chapter thus examines the origins of the Jabès family in Egypt, and their involvement in communal Jewish affairs. Perhaps more to the point, I hope to demonstrate that although Jabès was aware of the threat to world Jewry in the early days of Hitler's rise to power, that knowledge did not greatly alter his persona as the French-Egyptian poet of the Alliance franco-égyptienne days.

The probable origins of the Jabès family are linked with the Spanish Inquisition. Their remote ancestors were Sephardic Jews (originating from North Africa and Spain following the destruction of the Second Temple in Jerusalem in 70 CE), exiles from the Iberian peninsula who made their way to Turkey in the sixteenth century. It also seems likely that at least some of Edmond's distant relatives were writers and printers. The historian of Ottoman Jewry, Stanford J. Shaw, notes: 'Between 1551 and 1553, a Hebrew language press was operated in Istanbul [...] by the Spanish exiles Solomon and Joseph Jabès, who after a short stay in Erdine operated presses in both Salonica and Istanbul, printing a series of philosophical, rabbinical and Karaite works, including editions of the Talmud'.[42] In the following centuries, other members of the Jabès family had their books printed in Izmir, Turkey. In 1757, Baruch Yabetz (here, an English transcription of the Hebrew name) published his *Sefer Lashon Arame'en*, a linguistic treatise on the Aramaic language; and in 1866 the *Sefer Tzur Ya'akov*, a commentary on the Torah and *halachot* (legal dimensions) of the twelfth-century scholar Moses Maimonides, appeared under the authorship of Ya'akov Yabetz.[43]

It is not clear how or when Jabès's family emigrated from Turkey to Egypt. That they arrived via Italy is possible. Such was the case with other Sephardic families, such as the Suareses and Mosseris, who arrived in Egypt before the mid-nineteenth century, that is, at approximately the same time as Jabès's paternal great-grandfather did. The Cattaui family was different, for, unlike other great Jewish families of Egypt, it was native to the country.[44] In any case it was Jabès's great-grandfather who initiated the move during the early to mid-nineteenth century.[45] He probably worked as a money changer, and in successive generations the family's financial activities gained increasing importance. Jabès's paternal grandfather, Haim (or, as he was also known, Vita, Italian for the Hebrew *hayim* or 'life'), worked as a financier. With his son Isaac Haim Jabès, born in 1874 in Cairo, he founded the Banque Haim Jabès et Figlio. Upon Haim Jabès's death in 1909, the banking house became the Banque Isaac Léon et les fils d'Elie A. Jabès.[46] It was under

his father's guidance that Edmond Jabès began his career in banking, which continued in stockbroking with his father-in-law René Cohen after his marriage in 1935. One book from the period, *Arrhes poétiques* (1935), reflects the relation of banking to poetry: its title plays phonetically on 'art' and 'arrhes', or 'monetary deposit'; the book itself begins with the statement: 'Un métier semblable à mon métier d'agent de Bourse' (*Ap*, 17). Jabès's image of himself as a poet does not, in this book at least, conflict with his responsibilities in finance. Later, having a profession would conflict with his wish to write. Nevertheless, working in finance occupied Jabès during the entirety of his professional life in Egypt, and his importance to the financial institutions of the country grew steadily. In fact, in the final months of his residency there, he worked as vice-president of the stock exchange and watched the work of generations of Egyptian economists crumble. As he related in an interview in the early 1980s, the Egyptian Ministry of Finances protected him as a member of the Stock Exchange Commission, which meant that the entire Stock Exchange was in his hands. Stock values tumbled in 1956–7, and he worked to stabilize them. The government was not necessarily cooperative. One day officials would restrict him from leaving his home to go to work, and the next day they would allow him to do so. The following day he would again be confined to his apartment: 'ce fut comme ça, jusqu'à la fin,' Jabès related. 'J'ai essayé de sauver quelque chose. ... Enfin, n'importe quoi, je n'ai rien pu sauver.'[47]

While Jabès's upbringing could be characterized as assimilated, the lack of a formal Jewish education was, in many ways, countered by the social affairs and philanthropy of members of his immediate and extended family. In 1933, for instance, Joseph Elie Jabès donated Hebrew Bibles and language manuals to the boys' and girls' free schools of the community. The chief rabbi of Cairo, Haim Nahoum Effendi, expressed his hope that the books would help students 'à étudier et connaître cette belle langue hébraïque qui nous a été léguée par nos ancêtres'.[48] The benefactor, with Edmond's father Isaac Jabès and his uncle Umberto Jabès and their wives, then distributed the books to the students. The Jabès family's involvement in the Cairo Jewish community went back well into the previous century. Isaac Jabès's grandfather assumed management of the fifteenth-century Reb Zimra synagogue in the *haret el yahud*; and he constructed housing around it, which was set aside for poor families. In time, the management of the small synagogue came into the hands of Jabès's

immediate family.[49] To Marcel Cohen, Jabès described the synagogue's peculiar timelessness:

J'étais, surtout, sensible à sa sobriété, à la patine des vieux murs, à la sérénité du lieu. A la mort de ma sœur, et afin de perpétuer son souvenir, mon père y avait fait suspendre un rideau de soie brodée, commandé expressément, devant la porte de l'Arche, comme il est de tradition dans toutes les synagogues. L'Arche contenait trois Torah du XVIIe siècle d'une sobre beauté. (Dl, 41)

Jabès's principal responsibility in the synagogue was to look after its administration, in particular the drive to continue the teaching of French language in a Jewish free school, named after his wife's grandfather, Moïse de Cattaui. His duties had little to do with the religious aspects of the centre. In other words, foremost in Jabès's mind at the time was not the musty odour of the cabinet of Torah scrolls, but the propagation of French among Cairo's Jewish community—a cosmopolitan view consistent with his other cultural activities in which questions of Jewish identity were not openly asked, such as the founding of the Alliance franco-égyptienne in the late 1920s or the Groupement des amitiés françaises in the immediate post-war period.

Jabès knew the medieval Reb Zimra synagogue from his boyhood, but it was to the larger, cosmopolitan Ismailia synagogue (also known as Shari Sha'ma'im) on Adly Street (formerly Maghrabi Street) in the European centre of Cairo that he went for the principal Jewish holidays,[50] and, as mentioned earlier, it was in this synagogue that he and Arlette Cohen were married. Despite his unwillingness to participate in the religious aspects of Jewish life, he was nonetheless touched by certain aspects of it, notably the liturgical music. He recalled 'dans leurs répétitions insistantes, les longs accords monotones des chants traditionnels, comme autant de sanglots et qui, en s'éployant, réveillaient, peu à peu, un obscur passé de souffrance auquel je me sentais lié malgré moi' (Dl, 41). Jabès's feelings concur with those of the Chief Rabbi of Egypt, David Prato, who wrote, in one of a series of articles devoted to the subject, that traditional Jewish music 'est parfois si puissante dans ses phrases déclamatoires vraiment majestueuses, qu'elle provoque une profonde émotion et elle fait vibrer les cordes même des moins sensibles'.[51] The weight of his experience in the family synagogue on Jabès's early feelings as a Jew cannot be underestimated, but it should not be overlooked that in the main it manifested itself in his writings in Paris, not in Cairo.

Despite the emotional distance evinced at the time, it is still essential to point out that Jabès was by no means entirely removed from important world historical events then transforming Egyptian and world Jewry. Who, in his young adulthood, first inspired him to examine his Jewish identity and to participate in Jewish communal affairs? It is true that his older brother, Henri, was active from the late twenties in Zionist youth groups, and that the influence he wielded (which we have seen in the sphere of Franco-Egyptian cultural activities) was consequential.[52] But it was Jabès's uncle, Umberto Jabès, who was most potent in forming the young man's consciousness of his Jewishness. Umberto Jabès saw to the administration of the family synagogue in the years before his nephew took responsibility for it. He was its *gabbai*,[53] or the individual who called men to recite the benediction over the Torah; traditionally, this important religious and social function fell to the president of the synagogue. Moreover, he was active in the spreading of Jewish values in Egypt, having been known to donate money and ritual objects to area synagogues,[54] and was involved in local Jewish politics. For instance, in April 1933, as anti-Semitism became an ever more pressing global issue, the Egyptian Jewish community organized an international committee with other groups in Great Britain, supported by Lionel de Rothschild, and in the United States, organized by the American Jewish Congress in New York, to show its solidarity with world Jewry. The Egyptian executive committee was headed by the Zionist lawyer Léon Castro and the president of the Jewish community, Joseph Aslan de Cattaui pasha, and it numbered among its ranks Joseph Elie Jabès and Umberto Jabès.[55]

More important still, Umberto Jabès was also at the centre of a legal battle concerning the advent of German anti-Semitism in Egypt. The case involved a German publisher based in Cairo, Wilhelm van Meeteren, and Umberto Jabès, represented by Léon Castro before the Mixed Tribunals of Alexandria from January 1934 to May 1935.[56] In the end, the legal battle generated only the most philosophical discussions, which impressed the young poet even if the cumulative effects of the incident were not to show themselves until after his departure some twenty years later when he began to draft the core of *Le Livre des Questions.*

The problem began in May 1933 when the Ligue internationale contre l'antisémitisme (LICA) distributed an unsigned pamphlet called *L'Antisémitisme en Allemagne.* The editors stated that their purpose was to provide an objective history of Hitler's anti-Semitic movement based on his own speeches.[57] The Jewish pamphlet met shortly afterwards with a response from Van Meeteren, who circulated an anti-Semitic pamphlet called *Zur Judenfrage in Deutschland* (in German as well as in French translation). The Jewish community's reaction was immediate, if restrained. On 9 June 1933, a letter from the attorney Emmanuel Mizrahi to the editor of the Egyptian-Jewish weekly *Israël* appeared. Mizrahi wanted to call attention to the pamphlet's distorted descriptions of German Jews, which included falsehoods on the Jew's base mentality, the Jewish doctor, the Jewish criminal and so on. Pitifully, moreover, the pamphlet had been published in Cairo, and the author had not even had the temerity to sign it.[58] The following week, another article appeared in the same newspaper, which further described Van Meeteren's pamphlet: 'sous une apparence scientifique', wrote the journalist, the pamphlet 's'efforce de démontrer que les sauvageries hitlériennes sont une réaction logique contre la pénétration juive en Allemagne depuis 1918'.[59] The article was printed not on the front page of the newspaper, as might be expected for something so disturbing to the Jewish community, but on page 3, which indicates that the newspaper did not want its readership to overreact to it or be alarmed by it. By late June, by which time the case had gone to court, *Israël* had covered the proceedings in greater detail while still withholding editorial outbursts of protest; an article entitled 'L'Hitlérisme, dangereuse propagande du désordre social, est traîné devant les Tribunaux', and a related one which included the complete text of the summons, appeared only on page 6, the page that covered local community news as opposed to the world news covered on the first few pages of the newspaper.[60] Despite being first marginalized in the French-Jewish press in Egypt, the affair was covered in Paris by the press organ of LICA, *Le Droit de vivre*, from the summer of 1933 until the end of the trial.[61]

As the trial neared its conclusion in May 1935, the Egyptian-Jewish community (or at least the editors of *Israël*) sensed their defeat owing to a legal technicality: since Umberto Jabès had not been named outright in the Van Meeteren pamphlet, he could not sue the publisher for libel. An *ad hominem* attack was missing from its pages, so the Mixed Tribunals could not accept the complaint. The court's dismissal of the case on legal grounds did not inhibit the local press from indulging in grand metaphysical speculation: 'Juifs et nazis devant le tribunal de l'Histoire', proclaimed one headline. The

Attorney General of the Mixed Tribunals, Hugh Holmes, announced: 'Ce n'est que devant le tribunal de l'Histoire que ces procès sont jugés et ce n'est que l'Histoire qui pourra se prononcer sur la race juive ou la race allemande, comme sur toutes les autres races du monde.'[62] Dismissing the power of the earthly court to render justice to the Jews in any immediate fashion, Holmes continued, the Jewish people 'a obtenu du seul tribunal compétent, celui de l'Histoire, un jugement favorable, qui ne peut être affecté ni par la brochure incriminée dans ce procès, ni par une décision rendue par un tribunal de trois ou de cinq magistrats même de la plus grande autorité'. In the same article the journalist Jean Lugol conferred with Holmes and called his discourse 'mémorable' and 'historique', which 'Israël fera bien d'inscrire en lettres d'or dans les annales, déjà plusieurs fois millénaires de son extraordinaire destin'. Lugol rationalized the legal defeat by reflecting that over the past twenty centuries Jews had overcome Jew-hatred, History having judged in their favour. Even in contemporary Europe instances of rehabilitation of Jews forsaken by Christian Europe occurred periodically: Lugol pointed out that during a festival celebrating the great Sephardic philosopher and legal scholar, Maimonides, the mayor of Cordova had proclaimed Spain's regret for expelling the Jews five centuries earlier; more recently the Dreyfus affair in France had demonstrated that all racism 'n'est que l'expression plus ou moins fidèle d'un complexe national d'instincts combatifs trop violemment refoulés'.

Argument did not cease with the end of the trial. In the following weeks the LICA organized a conference, with Umberto Jabès in attendance, at which Léon Castro compared the Jabès–Van Meteeren affair to a trial in Berne only a week before, which had determined that the *Protocols of the Elders of Zion* contained erroneous information about the Jews and that the author or authors of the document were themselves falsifiers.[63] Although the Tribunals in Alexandria were powerless to halt the distribution of the Van Meeteren pamphlet, Castro could still appeal, by analogy, to the legal authority of Berne to discredit the Nazi document and its distributors.

Ink and paper proliferated in the course of the Jabès–Van Meteeren affair as the story occupied the francophone and Jewish presses and as depositions were published in legal circles. Perhaps the most interesting of these documents, for our purposes, is the German club's counter-complaint and summary of the trial in Cairo.[64] The document described the Kairoer Judenprozeß from the German perspective. Thus, readers were provided with the legal and cultural background to the entire Jewish question and to the world conspiracy of Jewish social parasites seeking to drain German culture of its Aryan life-force. Published in March 1935 by the central printing offices of the NSDAP, the document is replete with *Nazideutsch*—the euphemistic language propagated at the time by National Socialists to describe their perception of Jews and others viewed as degenerate. One section, 'Der Kläger Jabès', derisively portrayed Umberto Jabès as 'der kleine jüdische Wechselagent Jabès (sprich Schabbes)'.[65] In fact, the pugnacious money changer had the audacity, according to the NSDAP document, to incite anger by staging a public protest: 'Herr Jabès, ohne persönlich angegriffen zu sein, von dem Fenster seiner über der Dresdner Bank in Kairo liegenden Wohnung aus eine Flagge hißte, die Angriffe gegen Deutschland und Hitler enthielt'.[66] According to Henri Cohen, Jabès's brother-in-law, the banner exclaimed in bold letters: 'L'ANTISÉMITISME EST UN CRIME ET IL EST LA HONTE DES PAYS CIVILISÉS.'[67]

The comment made in the Judenprozeß document has a startling parallel to a remark made by the critic Didier Cahen in the biographical section of his 1991 study of Jabès. Cahen notes that sometime during 1934–5, Jabès hung an anti-Nazi banner from his uncle's office window above the Dresdner Bank of Cairo.[68] Edmond Jabès is not named in the NSDAP document; neither is Umberto Jabès named in Cahen's book. But by reading the two accounts of the unfolding of the banner, we know that Edmond Jabès supported his uncle in the fight against racial hatred directed towards Jews.[69]

In addition to public outcries made with his uncle, Edmond Jabès was also a leading participant in youth groups against anti-Semitism. The driving ideological force behind many of these groups was Léon Castro. As noted above, he was among the most important politically committed Egyptian Jews. A wealthy lawyer, journalist, ardent Zionist and member of the Wafd (the Egyptian National Party), he was particularly well placed to fight legal and cultural battles against the growing presence of National Socialism in Egypt.[70] It goes without saying that Hitler's rise to power in January 1933 was to alter the course of twentieth-century history as no other event would. Egypt is part of that history. Castro was in an excellent position to lead the Jewish opposition to the rise of National Socialism in Egypt, and he did not fail in his task even though Egyptian anti-Semitism, inspired by the Nazis in Germany, eventually became too big a beast to defeat.

In Amsterdam in mid-1933, Castro helped inaugurate the Ligue internationale contre l'antisémitisme, for which he served as vice-president. In September 1933, in Egypt, he founded, with Simon Mani, the Ligue contre l'antisémitisme allemand, which was connected with LICA and thus formed part of the worldwide network of organizations dedicated to discrediting anti-Semitic ideology. According to Gudrun Krämer, the historian of twentieth-century Egyptian Jewry, the purpose of the LICA's activity in Egypt 'was to inform the local Jewish as well as the non-Jewish public about the objectives of National Socialism and, as far as possible, to restrict German propoganda in the region'.[71] A youth section of the LICA, the Ligue internationale scolaire contre l'antisémitisme (LISCA), was founded in September 1933. One article in the local Jewish newspaper of Cairo, *Israël*, indicates that Arlette Cohen, who knew Edmond Jabès at the time and was to marry him within two years, was a subscribing member of the Cairo section.[72] Additionally, Castro, supported by the LICA and the local lodges of B'nai B'rith, led the Jewish boycott against German products beginning in April 1933 and continuing, with varying degrees of success, until the onset of World War Two.[73]

In April 1933, at a meeting of some 400 members of the Jewish youth of Cairo held to discuss protest strategies in the face of Hitler's anti-Semitism, Edmond Jabès was among the speakers who addressed the problem and was 'vivement applaudi' by those present, including Arlette Cohen, Simon Mani, Léon Barchmann and Léon Castro.[74] Castro himself spoke at the meeting, where he proposed the immediate formation of a temporary committee whose function would be to provide the bases of a Ligue de la jeunesse juive contre l'antisémitisme allemand. Arlette Cohen and Edmond Jabès were among those immediately named to the executive committee, the former as assistant secretary, the latter as treasurer.

Jabès spoke again in May at the Maccabi (Jewish youth) sports club in Heliopolis, this time to a surging gathering of more than 1500 individuals, where he once more shared the rostrum with Castro, Mani and Barchmann. According to the newspaper report, Jabès's speech was a 'belle et émouvante page de lyrisme', mainly when he spoke about the Jewish flag whose colours were those 'd'amour et de paix'. He further reminded his audience that if they were to resist Hitler's yoke, their effort would need to be united.[75] Again, this is in May 1933.

Finally, it should be stated that Arlette Cohen was herself a vocal supporter of Zionist causes. In March 1934, she gave a speech on the 'génie créateur des Juifs' to the youth section of Cairo's Women's International Zionist Organization, in which she emphasized the Jewish contribution to science, literature and music.[76] The overt purpose for delivering the speech was to justify the presence of the Jews in the West, the Middle East and elsewhere, and, further, to explain their necessary participation in the course of human progress. The message reveals still further the outlook of Arlette Cohen and her audience. The Jews are an ancient people, distinguished from the mass of humanity but consistently contributing to its betterment. They have done nothing to deserve the treatment inflicted upon them by the Nazi party and its supporters.

Despite his participation in the fight against anti-Semitism in Egypt during the thirties, Edmond Jabès could not at the time be called a Jewish writer. While his political speeches highlighted the persecution of the Jews and the Zionist dream of an independent Jewish state, his poetry and essays from the period do not treat Jewish themes in the same manner. Certainly, he showed some interest in contemporary Jewish writers. For instance, he eagerly signed a copy of *Les Pieds en l'air* (1934) for the great French-Jewish poet André Spire, whom he had hoped to meet on his unfortunately cancelled visit to Egypt.[77]

Other francophone Jewish writers in Egypt did explore topics concerning the current Jewish problem. One such writer was Maurice Fargeon, who, in his drama *L'Eternelle Tragédie ou Israël peuple immortel* (1934), drew a parallel between the present political crisis and that under the Hasmoneans. He deplored the fact that his generation of Jews were almost completely unaware of the revolt and success of the Maccabees. Another francophone Jewish writer (originally from Palestine but active at this time in Egypt) was Elian-J. Finbert, whose *Fou de Dieu* (1932) won the Prix de la Renaissance in 1933. His book, which the Egyptian-Jewish press described as 'un roman juif', tells the story of Hillel Schwartz, a young man from Alexandria who, 'comme tant d'autres', was raised outside the Jewish tradition but who 'fait la rencontre de sa race, dans la vie des bédouins et y entend la voix d'Israël'.[78] Jabès was little interested in such literature. Rather, he sided intellectually and artistically with those Egyptian peers for whom the Zionist dream was, for the moment, but that, a dream. With the exception of his speeches against Nazi anti-Semitism delivered at the time of the Jabès–Van Meeteren affair, throughout the

Egyptian period he remained Jewish in name only, preferring to assert himself as a connoisseur of French culture while recognizing his guest status under the Egyptian monarchy. We shall see that his francophilia, and its twin, cosmopolitanism, only increased until 1957 as he immersed himself in France's modernist literature and, during the war, in Gaullist politics in exile to the point of becoming one of its standard bearers in Egypt immediately after 1945.

French culture, Egyptian residency and the Zionist aspiration mixed linguistically and socially to create a personal and communal identity replete with ambiguity that cannot, without inflicting a grotesque aberration, be reduced to any single component. The fusion is reflected in the greater Cairo Jewish community, to which Edmond Jabès belonged. In March 1933, for instance, a meeting was held at the central Ismailia synagogue to protest against Hitler's rise to power. Léon Castro, nearly always present as such gatherings, spoke, as did Simon Mani, who with Jabès founded with the Ligue de la jeunesse juive contre l'antisémitisme allemand. Mani delivered a speech in Arabic in which he paid tribute 'à l'hospitalité et à la tolérance de l'Egypte, de son Souverain et de son gouvernement envers toutes les confessions et toutes les nationalités'.[79] After giving his own speech in Hebrew, Jacob Weissman, the president of the Zionist Organization of Cairo, recited several lines from de Musset's *Nuit d'octobre*: "'L'homme est un apprenti, la douleur est son maître, Et nul ne se connait tant qu'il n'a pas souffert....'" En fait de souffrance,' he commented, 'les Juifs en savent quelque chose.' France had welcomed the Jews in their exile, and Egypt should learn its lesson from that country.

Maurice Blanchot once observed that *Le Livre des Questions* had been written 'dans l'histoire et dans l'écriture en marge de l'histoire' (*A*, 252). The remark was prescient since the catastrophe forming the book's backdrop is likewise evident throughout later works, even if it often remains unnamed and is therefore present but negatively. Is it possible to understand Jabès's Egyptian writings, or at least a portion of them, in a similar critical vein, that is, as a commentary on the political events of the day, which, we have seen, Jabès was keenly aware of? What textual evidence do we possess for such an understanding?

Jabès's earliest writings, those predating the earliest poems collected in *Je bâtis ma demeure*, can be divided into two groups: the first three books dating from 1930 to 1932, and the next three from 1934 to 1936.

This division is based on the fact that the first group (consisting of two collections of poems, *Illusions sentimentales* (1930) and *Je t'attends!* (1931), and a single poem, 'Maman' (1932)) mirrors the second group (which also consists of two collections of texts, *Les Pieds en l'air* (1934) and *Arrhes poétiques* (1935), followed by a single poem, 'L'Obscurité potable' (1936)). That Jabès did not publish any poetry in the first group that could be qualified as Jewish should come as no surprise since he did not become involved in Jewish organizations until 1933, that is, after the first poems were composed. Nevertheless, one poem of the first group, 'Solitude, me voici' from *Illusions sentimentales*, might allude to an incident of anti-Semitism. The first verse reads:

> Frère, donne-moi la main;
> contre le mauvais destin,
> vois-tu, rien d'autre à faire!

In itself, it is an expression of fraternal solidarity and suggests that Jabès had identified himself with another. That other is the playwright Georges de Porto-Riche (Bordeaux, 1849–Paris, 1930), to whom the poem is dedicated.[80] A possible basis for the identification is a fiercely anti-Semitic work which argued that since Porto-Riche was a Jew, his theatre necessarily offended French mores.[81] This, then, could be the 'mauvais destin' to which Jabès refers. On the other hand, Jabès may have been referring, simply, to Porto-Riche's advancing age,[82] an interpretation supported by the poem's final lines: 'Mourir? Non, il est trop tôt! / Vivre? Non, il est trop tard ...'

Another poem in which Jabès appears to have treated contemporary anti-Semitism is 'Moïse', which closes *Les Pieds en l'air*. The brief poem reads:

> Salamandre excitée
> vers de soie immobile [*sic*]
> mes yeux suivent quel poteau?
>
> Il y a un rat qui court dans la rue paisible ...
> Il y a un pot-à-eau raté, lié ...
> Il y a le rat qui tombe dans l'eau et qui éclabousse un ratelier ...
>
> (*Pa*, 53)

There is an undeniable verbal dexterity, for example 'rat' becomes 'raté', which is rhymed immediately after by 'lié', which in turn is followed in the final line by 'ratelier', a joining of 'raté' and 'lié'. Like many of Jabès's poems published in the early 1930s, 'Moïse' demonstrates a clever use of language, the pun, with a mixed dose of caprice and gravity to provoke a variety of emotional responses from the reader: shock, disorientation, empathy and laughter. In this way it is representative of the character of these very early poems. Reference to reality is all but abandoned—we can only guess that 'Moïse' is a metonomy evoking the Jews, that the 'rue paisible' refers to their quiet community, and that the 'rat' is a metaphor for Hitler or the National Socialists against whom Jabès was helping to organize other Egyptian-Jewish youths during the period of the poem's composition. With an eye turned to the historical moment—the decisive months following Hitler's appointment as Chancellor of the Reich—the violence of the last two lines would support such a reading. Moreover, the opposition in the first two lines, between the dynamism of the salamander and the stasis of the silkworm, connotes an emotional unease or social insecurity. What would be the outcome of the events of 1933, and of the years that followed? If there is an insufficient trace in these words of their moment in time to warrant a conclusive historical reading, then the residue of history—its burden weighing upon Jabès—would manifest itself in those writings dating from the Second World War and in those written in light of the events.

Some of the texts written after 'L'Obscurité potable' display a marked preoccupation with contemporary history and Judaism. Notable in this regard is the seven-part poem *Avec l'ombre*, which dates from the middle 1930s and early 1940s. While it was never published in its entirety, Jabès did claim that it would treat Jewish subjects, and from a biblical angle. Thus, the journalist Albert Staraselski, in his survey of French-Jewish poets in Egypt published in *Les Juifs dans les lettres françaises*, related that Jabès was at work on 'une œuvre de longue haleine, en sept volumes', whose main theme was 'que l'ombre prépare la lumière avec, pour objectif, l'homme. Qu'il nous soit permis de révéler que de ce monument heptaèdre une face sera juive, avec des transcriptions de légendes bibliques.'[83] Critically, however, the projected poem was abandoned and remains absent from the list of his completed works.[84] I shall return in Chapter 2 to the poem's significance to Jabès's output.

A final poem dating from the Cairene period in which a Jewish content is evident is the 'Chanson du dernier enfant juif', from *Chansons pour le repas de l'ogre* (1947). Like 'Moïse', the poem was composed while the Jewish question was manifestly urgent. Unlike that poem, an unambiguous association of Judaism and poetry, already made in the title, is clear enough:

> Mon père est pendu à l'étoile,
> ma mère glisse avec le fleuve,
> ma mère luit
> mon père est sourd,
> dans la nuit qui me renie,
> dans le jour qui me détruit.
>
> (*Jbmd*, 69)

The repetition of the long [i] in *glisse*, *qui* and *renie*, and of the semi-consonant [ui] in *luit*, *nuit* and *détruit*, lends the poem an unabated, verbal rhythm. But it is the unequivocal allusions in the opening line, 'Mon père est pendu à l'étoile', to a death by hanging and to the star, a Jewish star, that give the poem a Jewish shading. Moreover, the poem was dedicated to Jabès's mother-in-law, Edith Cohen, the daughter of Moïse de Cattaui; she must be taken for 'the last Jewish child'. Despite its Jewish theme, however, the 'Chanson du dernier enfant juif' does not, in its depiction of senseless violence expressed, differ from many of the other *Chansons pour le repas de l'ogre*, such as the 'Petite Chanson pour la main entêtée du soldat mort' (*Jbmd*, 71), the 'Chanson pour le sein crucifié d'une nonne' (*Jbmd*, 72), or the 'Chanson triste':

> Quand les six chevaux éventrés
> Atteignirent enfin! l'oasis,
> Dans le monde divisé,
> Plus un homme n'arrosait la joie
>
> (*Jbmd*, 73)[85]

Nevertheless, other poems in this book may very well concern the persecution of the Jews. One is the 'Chanson des arbres de la forêt noire', in which we read:

> Dans la forêt noire
> Où des pendus rient aux arbres,
> Où des soldats montent la garde,
> Un incendie éclate.
>
> (*Jbmd*, 72–3)

We do not know if the title refers to the Black Forest in Germany or if it is, rather, an allegorical setting for the poem. Perhaps Jabès meant both. Still, one line, 'La forêt est maintenant rouge', echoes another in the 'Chanson du dernier enfant juif': 'Le monde est rouge'. The colour red can signify blood, or flames: 'Un incendie éclate.' A forest or a world is in flames. The world has gone mad.

Considering that some of the poems of *Chansons pour le repas de l'ogre* were composed during Jabès's stay in Jerusalem in 1942,[86] it is remarkable that so few refer to the fate of the Jews during the war. Still more, other poems composed after the foundation of the State of Israel in 1948 (when one might expect to find further poems related to the Jews, given the revelations about the death camps) do not take up the subject. Their theme is often poetry itself, that is, the language it is written in. Many of Jabès's pre-war writings, and all of the post-war writings, belong to the tradition of anti-naturalistic verse initiated in the later nineteenth century by poets from Rimbaud to Mallarmé. They are concerned with writing, not Judaism, and as such they reflect Jabès's view of himself and the world.

A further point regarding French modernism must be emphasized. I have already noted that the Jabès family, at the turn of the century, followed the demographic trend of many Jews who had acquired the means, and moved from the medieval *haret el yahud* in the *mouski* of Old Cairo to the new villas on the outskirts of Cairo where their daily lives were taken up with the administration of law and finance in the city. Nevertheless, I noted, their education and culture had fundamentally oriented them towards France. It seems to me that the young Jabès's interests in modern French poetry and theatre ran parallel to, or, more precisely, were a result of this move. It is thus that I understand his indifference to what he perceived as antiquated Jewish learning and, hence, Jewish writing. He professed an unswerving predilection for French modernists such as Apollinaire, whose portrayal of the Jews in 'La Synagogue' would have confirmed his lack of interest in traditional Judaism. Had not Apollinaire written:

> Ils se disputent et crient des choses qu'on ose à peine traduire
> Bâtard conçu pendant les règles ou Que le diable entre dans ton père
> Le vieux Rhin soulève sa face ruisselante et se détourne pour sourire
> Ottomar Scholem et Abraham Lœweren sont en colère.[87]

For Apollinaire as for Jabès (as he understood it in Cairo), Judaism was antithetical to modernism. Jabès espoused the latter to the neglect of the former. It would have been impossible for him to do otherwise. After all, he was outside the tradition and had no extended experience of a living Judaism. I do not wish to imply that in Egypt he did not see himself as a Jew; rather, I would argue that his Jewish identity had nothing or very little to do with his self-perception as a writer. Again, Apollinaire (here from 'Zone'): 'Les aiguilles de l'horloge du quartier juif vont à rebours.'[88] On the contrary, Edmond Jabès sought to move forward in time.

Visibly, in Jabès's writings the articulation of a profound historical consciousness runs parallel to the emergence of a Jewish consciousness. As Gabriel Bounoure was to explain to him in the 1960s, 'il a fallu le malheur historique, la brisure des destins individuels pour [...] montrer l'exemplarité de l'homme-juif dans son errance et son acharnement à trouver le sens' (letter of 30 August 1964). Bounoure was writing about *Le Livre des Questions* and *Le Livre de Yukel*, and in particular about the astonishing force of Jabès's depiction of the Jew as the representative figure of the post-Auschwitz age. We have seen, however, that the expression of this Jewish consciousness in his writings came neither easily nor quickly. The clear-cut intersection of history and fiction is missing from the majority of verse composed in Egypt. Throughout the thirty-five years Jabès was writing there, the language of French modernism was stronger than that of Judaism: he was a French-speaking Egyptian writer whose cultural orientation pointed towards France. Late in his career Jabès himself acknowledged both his early and late debts to French culture and language: 'Lorsque j'évoquais, devant lui, la France dont il était devenu, par fidélité à sa culture et à sa langue, et par choix profond, l'un de ses citoyens, il se contentait de dire: "Mes premiers balbutiements étaient un hommage à la France, un hymne. Mes derniers balbutiements le seront aussi, sans doute"' (*Et*, 110). Without a doubt. As to his destiny as 'écrivain et juif', he would not assume it until after 1957. Did not Yukel Serafi, Jabès's fictional double, observe of himself: 'J'ai cru d'abord que j'étais un écrivain, puis je / me suis rendu compte que j'étais juif, puis je n'ai plus / distingué en moi l'écrivain du juif [...]' (*LQ* I, 398)? In one possible reading, and at the risk of seeming schematic, this sentence means that Jabès (or Yukel) thought of himself first as a writer and not a Jew; the period he was referring to was before his departure from Egypt. His next thought was that he was in fact Jewish, and this realization would have occurred when or shortly after he left the country, probably on his encounter with the anti-Semitic graffiti in the Odéon quarter of Paris. The third and final insight is that the writer and Jew in him were one and the same. Here, he was writing of the time after he had settled in Paris, when the constant interplay between Judaism and writing stimulated his thinking. During the Egyptian period, Jabès's perception of his Jewish identity was organized by his affiliation with the local community. It was at best peripheral, but mainly negative. He knew himself to be Jewish, but this knowledge had no transformational or functional governance over his writing. Once assumed, his Jewish consciousness would emerge as in a paroxysm, but with astounding clarity.

While he was in Egypt the expression of a Jewish consciousness in a protracted literary form had not yet been articulated. It seems, moreover, that it had not even been formulated. What occurred to Jabès after the expulsion that contributed to his sense of existential alienation, and, more importantly, how he integrated that cruel experience into his literary texts, is the subject of our discussion of the *Livre des Questions* trilogy (1963–5) in Chapter 4 below. While his Jewish roots were established in Cairo and while awareness of his Jewish identity was instilled at an early age despite his assimilated Jewish family life, Jabès did not regularly write poetry based on Jewish sources, however imaginatively, until he had emigrated to France. From a literary point of view, his Jewish awakening occurred decades later; it must be characterized as delayed but certain, or, in a word, atavistic. But here I am jumping ahead of myself. Further episodes in Edmond Jabès's Egyptian years contributed to his internal uprooting and were not explored at any length until he had definitively crossed the Mediterranean.

Notes to Chapter 1

1. Cattaui described his conversion in his interview with François-Régis Bastide, 'Rendez-vous à Paris avec les Egyptiens', *Nouvelles littéraires* 1334 (1953), 5.
2. Gudrun Krämer, *The Jews in Modern Egypt, 1914–1952* (Seattle: University of Washington Press, 1989), 8–13.
3. See *Bé* (23 Mar. 1933), 5.
4. Edmond Jabès, 'In Memoriam: Hector de Cattaoui', *Bé* (22 Feb. 1942), 2. Cattaoui is a variant spelling of Cattaui.
5. Anon., 'Un grand mariage', *I* (30 May 1935), 6.
6. See Jacob M. Landau, *Jews in Nineteenth-Century Egypt* (New York: New York University Press, 1969); and Samir W. Raafat, *Maadi, 1904–1962: Society and History in a Cairo Suburb* (Cairo: Palm Press, 1994).
7. Krämer, *The Jews in Modern Egypt*, 10, tables 1 and 2.
8. Ibid. 221.
9. See Jean-Jacques Luthi, *Introduction à la littérature d'expression française en Egypte, 1798–1945*, pref. Maurice Génévoix (Paris: L'Ecole, 1974), 13–14, and Irène Fenoglio, 'L'activité culturelle francophone au Caire durant l'entre-deux-guerres: du paradoxe à la contradiction', in *D'un Orient l'autre*, i: *Configurations* (Paris: CNRS, 1991), 457–8.
10. Fernand Leprette, *Egypte: Terre du Nil* (Paris: Plon, 1939), 191. Cf. 187.

11. The Capitulations, or nationality laws instituted in the 1880s for foreign nationals (i. e. non-Muslims whether born in Egypt or elsewhere), protected them from tax laws to which Egyptian citizens were subject. See *Dl*, 42–3, for Jabès's discussion of his own family's nationality. See also Jean and Simonne Lacouture, *L'Egypte en mouvement* (Paris: Seuil, 1956), 65–9.

12. See *Le Mondain égyptien/The Egyptian Who's Who* (Cairo: F. E. Noury et Fils, 1939). Arlette and Edmond Jabès first lived on Kasr el Nil street and then on Aziz Osman street.

13. Edmond Jabès, 'Apport à la poésie: le Logisme', *Sé* 29–30 (1932), 4.

14. See Daniel Lançon, *Jabès*, 38–9.

15. Jean Rapnouil, 'L'influence de la culture française en Egypte', in *L'Egypte nouvelle, livre d'or* (Cairo, 1938), n.p. On the universalism of the Mission laïque française, see the unsigned article 'Mission laïque française' in the *Journal d'Egypte* (11 Feb. 1937), 55–6: 'Respectueuse des traditions et des croyances de chacun, la Mission laïque s'inspire dans ses établissements des principes de neutralité qui constituent la charte même de cette institution.'

16. Interview (together with Daniel Lançon) with Cérès Wissa-Wassef (Cairo, 3 Mar. 1995).

17. Rapnouil wrote a book of verse, *Le Temps dérobé, poèmes et commentaires* (Paris: Jouve et Compagnie, 1928), which dates precisely from the years he taught Jabès.

18. Argus, 'Un grand banquet démocratique et antifasciste au Caire', *La Marseillaise* (28 July 1945), 6.

19. Anon., 'Fête annuelle du Lycée français', *Sé* 17–18 (1929), 25.

20. Anon., *I* (13 Dec. 1929), 4.

21. Anon., *I* (30 May 1930), 6.

22. *I* (6 Feb. 1931), 3.

23. *I* (28 Nov. 1930), 3.

24. *Au* 8 (1930), 37, and *La Muse française* 9 (10 Nov. 1930), 711, list *Is* among their books received. *La Muse française* 2 (15 Apr. 1932), 255, also received Jabès's second book of verse, *Jta* of 1931. The Paris-based newspaper *L'Egypte* (18 Nov. 1930), 3, gave *Is* a notice including excerpts of Egyptian critics' reviews. Several years later, *Les Humbles* 3 (1935), 10, also listed *Jta* among its books received.

25. Interview with Jason Weiss in *Conjunctions* 9 (1986), 135. The exact literary salon Jabès refers to is not known; it may be the Faubourg Léo Poldès, which Rachilde attended in the late twenties. Alternatively, an undated photograph of Rachilde at a banquet of the Amis des lettres françaises, reproduced in Claude Dauphiné, *Rachilde, femme de lettres 1900* (Périgueux: Pierre Fanlac, 1985), shows her seated in the company of Princess Bibesco and the Romanian poet Hélène Vacaresco, an early champion of Jabès (as her comments on *Is* in *Au* attest). Jabès may have met Rachilde through Vacaresco. See *Au* of 31 July 1930, 1 for the encomia of Marcel Batilliat, Frantz Jourdain, André Foulon de Vaulx, Charles Richet and Hélène Vacaresco on Jabès's first poems.

26. Adolf Shual, *Sé* 45–6 (1930), 20.

27. Lançon, *Jabès*, 79.

28. 'Déclaration', *Anthologie mensuelle* 1 (1929), n.p. The underscoring is that of the authors.

29. 'Alliance franco-égyptienne', ibid., n.p.

30. Alexandre Mercereau, 'L'Egypte nouvelle et le Droit des Peuples', *Au* 4 (1930), 20.

31. *Sé* 5–6 (1930), 20.

32. *Au* 5 (1930), 43–4. An interesting repetition of Jabès's urge to bridge the Franco-Egyptian divide occurred some fifteen years after his bid to name a street in Paris after the king of Egypt. In 1946 he wrote a letter of objection to the editor of *Pé* when Alexandria's urban planners launched a project for the 'débaptisation de la rue de France'. Rather, the street name should remain in order to 'l'embellir en hommage à tout ce que la France a fait pour nous' during the war. See that letter in *Pé* (25 Mar. 1945), 3.

33. 'L'œuvre de la Cité universitaire: son programme, son développement, son avenir', *Au* 6 (1930), 3.

34. 'Tableau', *Anthologie mensuelle* 1 (1929); 'Au clair de lune' and 'J'ai construit un châlet', *Anthologie mensuelle* 2 (Dec. 1929). The three poems are from *Is*. The following months saw the publication of other poems. The reviews of Jean Moscatelli's *Poèmes trouvés sur un banc* and François Moutran's *Soleil sous les palmiers* appeared in the issues of 28 Feb. 1930 and 31 July 1930 respectively.

35. In issue 8 of 30 Jan. 1930.

36. *Au* 9 (1930), n.p.

37. 'L'Alliance franco-égyptienne scellée au premier banquet (9 janvier 1930) de l'*Anthologie mensuelle*', *Anthologie mensuelle* 3 (1930), 1.

38. Ibid. 2.

39. Ibid. n.p.

40. Ibid. 7.

41. In 'The Noise of Time', *The Prose of Osip Mandelstam: The Noise of Time, Theodosia, The Egyptian Stamp*, trans. and intro. by Clarence Brown (Princeton, NJ: Princeton University Press, 1965), 80.

42. Stanford J. Shaw, *The Jews of the Ottoman Empire* (New York: New York University Press, 1991), 107.

43. The two books are in the collection of the Jewish Library of the Adly Street Synagogue in Cairo. A third book, the *Sefer Drash Pesach Gadol* by another Yabez, was printed in Podgorze in 1900, thus indicating the possibility of an Ashkenazic (Eastern European) branch of the Jabès family.

44. Krämer, *The Jews in Modern Egypt*, 39–41 and 78.

45. Lançon, *Jabès*, 21 ff.

46. 'Jabès, Isaac' in 'Supplément', *Annuaire des juifs d'Egypte et du Proche-Orient 1944/ 5704–5705* (Cairo: Société des éditions historiques juives d'Egypte, 1944).

47. 'Propos d'Edmond Jabès: Paris, Tel-Aviv, Jérusalem, Sdeh Boker' [5], un-published interview with David Mendelson in FEJ.

48. Anon., 'Un bon exemple à suivre', *I* (13 Jan. 1933), 4.

49. 'Le Caire quitté: conversation avec Edmond Jabès (26 juillet 1984)', interview with Jacques Hassoun and Carole Naggar, *Autrement* 12 (1985), 43–4. For a late 19th-century description of the Jewish quarter, see Sydney Montagu Samuel, ch. 1, 'The Jewish Quarter of Cairo', *Jewish Life in the East* (London: C. Kegan Paul and Co., 1881), 1–11. On the origins of the Jewish quarter with reference to the Jabès family synagogue, see Haim Nahoum Effendi, 'Communication sur les origines historiques du Ghetto (*haret el yahud*)', *Bulletin de la Société d'études historiques juives d'Egypte* 1 (Cairo: Librairie I. Moscato et Cie, 1929), 9–19. More

recently, see Jacques Hassoun (ed.), *Juifs d'Egypte: images et textes* (Paris: Scribe, 1984), 118: 'L'un des plus grands rabbins du XVe siècle qui dut s'exiler d'Espagne s'appelait Rabbi David Ibn Abi Zimra. Il fut Grand Rabbin du Caire durant 40 ans en particulier lors de la tentative avortée de sécession de Ahmed Pacha (1524). La synagogue du Reb Zimra (Radbaz) fut construite au 6 Hoch el-Souf.' A map of the *haret el yahud* produced by the Egyptian Survey Department in 1911 (sheet 38-K) confirms the address. Locating the synagogue with Daniel Lançon during a visit in the winter of 1995, I learned that it now served as a home for a poor Egyptian family. Nothing was left of it save the façade, on which two stars of David surrounded by rosettes were engraved.

50. Jabès recalled that his father regularly reserved a seat in the central Ismailia synagogue (*Dl*, 41). However, on my visit there in the winter of 1995 I was only able to locate his grandfather's seat, no. 19, inscribed 'Haïm Yabes' (*sic*).

51. David Prato, 'Etudes sur les chants de la synagogue', *I* (1 Dec. 1933), 4.

52. Three articles in *I* suffice to outline Henri Jabès's involvement in local Zionist youth circles: (1) Anon., 'Assemblée générale des sionistes', *I* (20 Jan. 1928), 3: 'Sur l'invitation du comité provisoire, les sionistes du Caire se sont réunis dans le nouveau local, 14 rue Aboul Sebaa, pour élire le comité définitif de l'organisation sioniste locale.' The members included, among others, Léon Bassan (who would contribute poetry on a Zionist theme to *I* in the next decade), Moïse Sanua and Henri Jabès. (2) Anon., 'Le Centre hébraïque de l'UUJJ', *I* (27 Jan. 1928), 3. Elected to the temporary committee were Henri Jabès, Moïse Sanua, et al. Hebrew classes given by emeritus Palestinian teachers were organized. (3) Anon., 'Organisation sioniste du Caire, appel aux anciens adhérents', *I* (10 Feb. 1928), 2–3. This article contains an open letter concerning membership, whose signatories included, among others, Ralph Harari (president), Henry (*sic*) Jabès (treasurer) and Léon Bassan (member). 'Avec la confiance dans votre attachement indéfectable à la cause sioniste, nous venons vous demander de donner encore votre appui, comme par le passé, à l'œuvre de réorganisation et de relèvement. En associant votre effort aux nôtres, [...] nous puissions participer efficacement à la reconstruction de notre vieille Eretz Israël.'

53. Anon., 'La communauté juive de Kom-Ombo possédera bientôt son temple', *I* (8 Sept. 1933), 4.

54. Ibid.

55. Anon., *I* (21 Apr. 1933), 1.

56. Krämer, *The Jews in Modern Egypt*, 131; Michael M. Laskier, *The Jews of Egypt: In the Midst of Zionism, Anti-Semitism, and the Middle East Conflict* (New York: New York University Press, 1992), 61 ff.

57. 'Préambule', *L'Antisémitisme en Allemagne*, ed. La Ligue contre l'antisémitisme allemand (Cairo and Alexandria: May 1933), 3.

58. Emmanuel Mizrahi, letter to the Editor, *I* (9 June 1933), 4.

59. Anon., 'La propagande nazie en Egypte', *I* (16 June 1933), 3.

60. Anon., 'L'Hitlérisme, dangereuse propagande du désordre social, est traîné devant les Tribunaux', *I* (30 June 1933), 6.

61. Anon., 'A l'étranger: en Egypte: une ligue contre l'antisémitisme, un procès retentissant en perspective', *Le Droit de vivre* 14 (1933), 6.

62. Cited in *I* (3 May 1935), 1. The article was written by Jean Lugol and first published in the Alexandrian edition of *Bé* (26 Apr. 1935).

63. For the Berne trial, see anon., *I* (25 May 1935), 3; for the conference organized by the Ligue contre l'antisémitism allemand, see anon., *I* (30 May 1935), 1. It is interesting to note that Edmond Jabès married Arlette Cohen on 26 May 1935, that is, in the week of the tumult over the trial. The leaders of the Egyptian Jewish community, notably Chief Rabbi Haim Nahoum Effendi pasha, were present at the wedding. See anon., 'Un grand mariage', *I* (30 May 1935), 6. It would be useful to know the contents of their speeches regarding contemporary events in the community, which may have touched on the impact of the trial on the Jewish community and on Egypt in general.

64. Wolfgang Diewerge, *Als Sonderberichterstatter zum Kairoer Judenprozeß (1933). Gerichtlich erhärtetes Material zur Judenfrage* (Munich: Zentralverlag der NSDAP, Franz Eher Nachf., 1935). Cf. Léon Castro, *Le Procès de l'antisémitisme: mémoire déposé au Tribunal Mixte du Caire pour Umberto Jabès et contre le Club Allemand au Caire* (Cairo(?): 1934).

65. Diewerge, *Als Sonderberichterstatter zum Kairoer Judenprozeß*, 24.

66. Ibid. 24–5.

67. Questionnaire prepared by Daniel Lançon and the author for Henri Cohen (Geneva, Mar. 1995).

68. Didier Cahen, *Edmond Jabès* (Paris: Belfond, 1991), 309–10. *Le Mondain égyptien/The Egyptian Who's Who* (Cairo: 1935), 106, lists Umberto Jabès's office address as 47 Kasr el Nil street, which was also the address of the Cairo branch of the Dresdner Bank.

69. Jabès returned repeatedly to the idea of the trial in his later works. He does not refer to the affair involving his uncle, but one must ask if it was not far from his mind when he concluded each of the three *LR* with a trial scene. See the three trials in *LR*: 'Le procès', 133–48; 'Le second procès', 280–1; and 'L'impossible procès', 383–7. Affinities with Kafka should not be disregarded here. Nor should Jabès's own trial before some Jewish religious groups, who found his writing heretical *vis-à-vis* rabbinic law and tradition. Cf. *LQ* I, 67–9.

70. See Krämer, 'Socioeconomic and Political Change, 1914–1948', in *The Jews in Modern Egypt*, 116–66.

71. Ibid. 130.

72. Anon., *I* (12 Apr. 1935), 19.

73. The Jewish boycott against German goods is discussed at length in Krämer, *The Jews in Modern Egypt*, 132–7, and in Laskier, *The Jews of Egypt*, 59–60.

74. Anon., 'La jeunesse juive contre l'antisémitisme allemand', *I* (21 Apr. 1933), 4.

75. Anon., 'Les Juifs d'Egypte et leurs frères d'Allemagne, manifestation contre l'antisémitisme allemand à la Maccabi', *I* (5 May 1933), 3.

76. Anon., 'A la jeune WIZO, la conférence de Mlle Arlette Cohen', *I* (23 Mar. 1934), 5.

77. The dedication reads: 'Au poète André Spire, en hommage et en admiration, ce petit livre. Edmond Jabès, Février 1934.' Jabès added, on the enclosed *carte de visite*: 'J'espère, mon cher maître, que cette plaquette vous intéressera.' The book and card are now in the possession of Marie-Brunette Spire, whom I thank for showing them to me. André Spire was to have visited Cairo in Jan. 1933, but had to cancel his visit (*I*, 13 Jan. 1933).

78. Anon., 'Un roman juif sur Alexandrie: *Le Fou de Dieu* de Elian-J. Finbert', *I* (5 May 1933), 2. Cf. 'L'hospitalité nomade' in *LH*, 79–85.

79. Anon., 'Le judaïsme égyptien et l'antisémitisme nazi: un meeting de protestation au Caire', *Bé* (30 Mar. 1933), 2.

80. The title of Jabès's first book may be an allusion to a collection of Porto-Riche's theatre pieces, *Anatomie sentimentale, pages préférées* (Paris: P. Ollendorff, 1920).

81. Henriette Charasson, *Monsieur de Porto-Riche ou le 'Racine juif'* (Paris: Siècle, 1925).

82. He died in Sept. 1930, and Jabès's poem was first published in *Au* 9 (1930), 5.

83. Albert Staraselski, *Les Juifs dans les lettres françaises* (Cairo: Henri Sas [1940]), 39–40.

84. The critic Ivo Barbitch also discussed the poem in his article 'Edmond Jabès ou la recherche de l'humain' in *Pé* (10 Mar. 1941), 7.

85. Near the end of his life, Jabès insisted that the subject of the 'Chanson du dernier enfant juif' was not specifically Jewish. See Philippe Saint-Chéron, 'Entretien avec Edmond Jabès', *NRF* 464 (1991), 66.

86. i.e. the manuscript for the 'Chanson de l'étranger', in FEJ, is dated 'Jérusalem 1942'.

87. Guillaume Apollinaire, *Alcools suivi de Le Bestiaire illustré par Raoul Dufy et de Vitam impendere amori* (Paris: Gallimard/Poésie, 1966), 96.

88. Ibid. 11.

CHAPTER 2

A Still-Born Poet

The Beginnings of Hospitality

Completed shortly before Jabès's death in January 1991, the posthumously published *Livre de l'Hospitalité* takes up the theme of
étrangeté explored in many of the texts beginning with the post-war
Cairene poetry and aphorisms collected in *Je bâtis ma demeure* and
continuing with *Le Livre des Questions* and beyond. The book is
divided into several sections, each of which recounts an illustration of
'hospitality' afforded a stranger by a series of hosts. One is theological
in nature ('L'hospitalité divine' in which humanity plays host to God
on earth) while another is a reflection on contemporary political
affairs ('Un jour de vie' in which burning questions concerning
Israeli–Palestinian relations are examined). A third bears the trace of
an incident in Jabès's life in Egypt, and it is to this incident that I
should like to turn specifically for its autobiographical content.
'L'hospitalité nomade' (*LH*, 79–85) takes the form of a dialogue
between two unnamed, elderly individuals or simply voices,
reminiscing about a nearly ill-fated desert journey:

— Je me souviens. Il y a longtemps de cela. Dans le désert du Sinaï. Nous
étions ensemble.
Toi et moi.

— Plus d'un demi-siècle s'est écoulé, depuis. (*LH*, 79)

One of the voices recalls to the other how they had just crossed the
Suez Canal en route for Palestine, Syria and Lebanon. Each adds
details to the story—the make of the car, the colour of its interior, the
five thermos flasks of iced tea on hand—when they come to a large
sand dune in which their car becomes hopelessly mired. The two face
almost certain death in the desert, but by chance a passing nomad
approaches, sparing them a wretched end.

In the summer of 1934 Jabès and another Egyptian writer, Jean

Moscatelli, did in fact begin a car journey from Cairo to Lebanon, but owing to an accident in the desert they were forced to interrupt it. They tried to negotiate the height of a sand dune, but in the end the car became caught and the two adventurers were stranded. Worse still, the thermos flasks they had prepared beforehand were shattered, so they were forced to choke down the engine's cooling fluid. After some thirty-six hours exposed to the severe desert climate the two were rescued by a Bedouin, who eventually turned them over to the military authorities. Their safe return to Cairo was assured, after they had completed the remainder of their journey.[1] In *Le Livre de l'Hospitalité* Jabès transforms the incident into a parable whose central theme is the humanity of all individuals and peoples, a theme that became increasingly important in the last third of his life as he endowed the persecution of the Jews with a universal message. Jean Moscatelli accompanied him on the doomed journey which is at the origin of 'L'hospitalité nomade', but Jabès's relationship with him goes very far beyond the dialogue in *Le Livre de l'Hospitalité*. Who, then, was his travelling companion? When did they meet, and what was the extent of their friendship?

Like Jabès, Jean Moscatelli (Cairo, 1905–Cairo, 1965) was born in Egypt and held Italian citizenship. He began publishing verse under his Italian name, Giovanni, in 1926 with the collection *Neurasthénie*, quickly followed by a succession of other books written in the vein of sentimental versifiers such as Paul Geraldy, and he was also one of the principal figures in the Franco-Egyptian arts and literary community from the late 1920s until its dissolution, taking up editorial positions in key cultural journals such as the *Semaine égyptienne* and *Images*. Jabès's professional acquaintance with Moscatelli dates from February 1930 when he reviewed Moscatelli's *Poèmes trouvés sur un banc* in the pages of the *Alliance universelle*.[2] But Jabès did not, at the time, know him personally; if he had, he would not have said rudely that the verses were 'probablement d'un adolescent'. In January 1932, Moscatelli wrote a laudatory review of Jabès's second book of poetry, *Je t'attends!*, in which he observed affinities with the German Romanticism of Heine, for the *Semaine égyptienne*.[3] Other reviews followed, including one now lost of *Les Pieds en l'air* in the satirical magazine *Goha*[4] and another of his fourth book, *Arrhes poétiques*, also in the *Semaine égyptienne*.[5]

Very early in his career, then, Jabès befriended an established literary personality in Cairo with whom he could discuss differing

ideas of poetry, art and aesthetics. Moreover, his new friend intro-
duced him to others on the Cairene cultural scene where over forty
French-language publications, such as *L'Egypte nouvelle*, *Le Flambeau*,
Un Effort and (from April 1938) the *Revue du Caire*, were in
circulation.[6] From early 1932 until the end of the Second World War,
Jabès published not infrequently in one of the most widely read
French-language cultural reviews in Egypt, the *Semaine égyptienne*, in
which Moscatelli had published since the late twenties.

   Founded in 1926 by the Alexandrian Greek Stavro Stavrinos, the
Semaine égyptienne appeared twice a month from its offices in Cairo
and Alexandria (save during the hot summer season when it appeared
only monthly) until the death of the editor in 1951.[7] Not only did
Stavrinos gather around him the most important French-speaking
Egyptian writers, including Ahmed Rassim, Albert Cossery and Gaston
Zananari, he was also in regular contact with French writers such as
Paul Valéry, Paul Eluard and André Gide, all of whom contributed
articles, letters and poems; further, Stavrinos published special volumes
dedicated to, among others, C. P. Cavafy, Goethe and Jules Romains.
And from 1930, the *Semaine égyptienne* published a series of books by
local writers. Yvonne Lauffer's collection of Arabic folktales rendered
into French, *L'Œil pour l'œil* (1930), was the first to appear.

   Edmond Jabès's first known contribution dates from March 1932
when his review of Valentin Bresle's *Le Charme poétique* and a poem,
'Syrinx', appeared; his last dates from May 1946 when his introduction
to Pierre Seghers's Cairo speech of that year was published. In all he
contributed some twenty poems, reviews and essays to the magazine.
Additionally, he published three short books through the magazine's
publishing house, Les Editions de la Semaine égyptienne: 'Maman', *Les
Pieds en l'air* and *Arrhes poétiques*. Like his first two books of poetry,
Illusions sentimentales and *Je t'attends!*, each of these books was reviewed
in the magazine's pages,[8] thus ensuring Jabès a regular presence there.

   In addition to acting as one of his first reviewers, Moscatelli
defended his friend in the wake of severe criticism that was for the
young Jabès a jarring *prise de conscience*. His early readers were
suspicious of, variously, his belated Romantic style, his obscurantism
and his self-referentiality. It is valuable to examine in some detail the
poetry of this period and the criticism that followed it because
together they illuminate how his early writings were received by the
Franco-Egyptian public, and how, perhaps more importantly, that
reception helped stimulate his fledgling creativity.

Readers in Cairo first wrote of Jabès's books with cautious enthusiasm. In late 1930, Adolf Shual said that *Illusions sentimentales* was indeed 'riche de promesses', but that readers should expect something more of the young writer.[9] In January 1932, Moscatelli wrote similarly of *Je t'attends!*: 'L'auteur de ces poésies est très jeune. Quand les lectures choisies et, surtout, la vie, dont il attend les promesses, l'auront formé, il n'est pas impossible qu'il donne une œuvre encore meilleure.'[10] But the gentle pronouncements would not last indefinitely, for Jabès was soon to come upon uncharitable critics. The focus of attention was not the first two books of poetry of 1930 and 1931, which mostly went unnoticed; rather, it was a series of articles and open letters in the *Semaine égyptienne* authored by Jabès, his supporters (such as Moscatelli) and his opponents.

In July 1932 the magazine ran Jabès's 'Apport à la poésie: le Logisme', in which he presented his then current poetics. This essay provides a detailed picture of how quickly the 20-year-old Jabès was evolving at this early stage of his development. Moreover, since the essay is the first extant view, and certainly the most extended one, of how he viewed his first books of poetry as well as the poetry and criticism of his contemporaries, the article merits close attention. For Jabès, contemporary poetry was going through a crisis. It did not take into account the revolutionary advances made in our knowledge of technology and culture. Photography was every bit as creative as painting, jazz was the unforgettable cacophony of the modern world (as the American example demonstrated) and Freud had taught us the importance of sexuality in our daily lives. The modern individual is the person who has 'la plus profonde conscience du présent' (C. G. Jung quoted at the head of the article). Poetry, Jabès argued, was too rigid in its conception and execution, and wilfully sealed off from a potentially creative impulse. 'Si la poésie d'aujourd'hui, comme dit le regretté Robert de Souza, "occupe un cabanon muré sans ouverture, entre la fosse du réalisme béante à ses pieds et le plafond du rationalisme où elle se cogne la tête", considérons ce cri comme une alarme à l'adresse du poète nouveau et retenons-y notre profit.'[11] Jabès is speaking to new poets, poets such as himself, who had not acquired much experience in writing but were envisaging fruitful careers for themselves. He is further writing from the dual perspective of an individual educated with European (or French) and Egyptian values. His failure, we shall see, consists in the overwhelming attention he gives to European values to the detriment of native Egyptian ones.

But examining native Egyptian poetry was never Jabès's stated intention. The tension between French and Egyptian writing can only be understood with critical hindsight. For instance, Jabès quotes the composer Reynaldo Hahn to the effect that: 'En Orient, comme en Occident, les exemples se succèdent et se multiplient. Là c'est la musique qui mène; ici, c'est l'essence de poésie.'[12] His purpose is not to discuss the poetry of the East or West, but rather to get at the musical essence of poetry, which goes beyond a poem's mere drama or image. For Jabès the poetic in poetry 'est le cri fort d'une foule de petits cris qui s'éparpillent pour disparaître dans le rêve. Elle est mère de haute poésie, puisque mère d'expression et de fond. Sa forme est celle de l'image ou du drame. Toute, elle est suffisante.'[13]

It is not difficult to apprehend, in reading 'Apport', an enthusiasm for theatre and the spectacle weighing on his sensibility, which is consistent with the performances he was giving in Cairo in the late 1920s and at the time of the writing of the essay. Jabès's pomposity was budding, too. More importantly, however, the essay divulges how he wished to explain the characteristic features of his model of poetry: he defines the essence of poetry as the 'cri fort d'une foule de petits cris qui s'éparpillent pour disparaître dans le rêve'—in other words, a verbal crescendo consisting of small voices rising until it vanishes into silence. Does his own poetry reflect this ideal?

Jabès applies these thoughts to his latest book of verse, published in the year preceding the article. His apologetic stand is evident. *Je t'attends!* is a recent book, true, but unfortunately it is also out of date: 'Qu'on me pardonne de revenir à une œuvre déjà classée pour moi et qui n'est que le premier pas fait dans une voie que je devais suivre pour arriver au complet épanouissement de la poétique qui me hante. Premier pas marqué non sans gaucherie.'[14] Jabès was concerned with how his poems were being received, and he refers to a review (which we have been unable to locate) of the book in which the poems are compared, to his chagrin, to hai-ku. He asserts that his poetry seeks to multiply the meanings a word has and to diversify the images it evokes. He believes the poems of *Je t'attends!*, such as these lines:

> Dans la nuit
> un cri:
> Le cri du cœur
> dans la nuit du monde.
> Dans le jour
> un cri:

> Le cri du monde
> dans la nuit du cœur
> (*Jta*, 31)

have little to do with that form. The hai-ku is but a pretext for employing a pared down style. Appealing specifically to the 'simplicité de la langue française', Jabès explains, 'je dirai que c'est bien à cause de sa simplicité que je me suis permis de tenter ce genre de poésie'.[15] In this context he refers to the critic Fernand Divoire's notion of 'simultanéisme',[16] with which he identifies his poetry, and still more to the *sage de la rue de Rome*: 'Si un Mallarmé nous avait décrit tout ce que le mot pensé dans un de ces poèmes contient de sens, d'images, d'émotions et de foule de poèmes, combien, sous sa plume, nous aurions été surpris d'avoir, livrés à nous-mêmes, et par notre seule faculté si peu trouvé.' A given line of poetry should simultaneously form differing meanings and images in the reader's intellect. Unfortunately, the reader is too often estranged from the poet's original intention, and cannot perceive the stimulus which first impelled him to compose. Consequently, says Jabès, 'Mon drame suggéré disparaît pour n'être qu'un cri et autour de lui se forment, par d'étranges remous de l'esprit, d'autres drames, d'autres images, d'autres chemins sans fin ...' which will, in the best of compositions, develop into 'le rêve qui n'est à personne', in others words, into 'le principe de vie universelle'.[17]

'Apport à la poésie: le Logisme' is followed by a long excerpt from an untitled poem. The lines demonstrate the stylistic distance covered between Jabès's first two books of poetry and the newly adopted Mallarméan poetics developed in his essay. Echoing the spilling typography of *Un Coup de dés* (1898), the poem begins:

> ... MOT — Je te parle avec des mots et mon poème, tout, serait un mot:
>   — ROUGE:
>   — Je suis rouge[18]

and goes on to analyse the materiality of the poem until a new, elevated subject gives the reader pause. That subject is love. 'Lorsque tu seras mienne, ô toi tout à fait jeune fille et qu'atrocement j'aime, je mettrai dans mes vers des marguerites fraîches et je les effeuillerai avec tendresse.' The love theme is given an enigmatic dimension that inches a step or two away from the Romantic verse of Jabès's earlier books. Because the object of his love cannot be named, the poet announces her name cryptically while deepening his investigation into the poetic and linguistic materiality with which the poem begins:

> — A:
>> A.
>> — L'initiale de son prénom.
>> Dans: 'Apport', 'A' calque la foi du premier élan ...
>> Ici, mon livre.
>> Là, neuves désillusions.
>> A — Des noms se forment sous ma plume ...
>> 'Adieu' m'apparaît, que j'écarte ...
>> A — 'Attitudes'
>> A — 'Amour'
>> A — L'initiale de son prénom.[19]

The letter 'A' is, of course, the first letter of the alphabet, but Jabès had something else in mind: it is also the first letter of the name of his girlfriend at the time, Arlette Cohen, whom he had been courting since the autumn of 1929 and whom he had not, until these verses were written, named in his poetry, although there were unmistakable references to her in previous poems:

> il faut à mon âme lassée,
> plus qu'un cœur de mère, un cœur de fiancée
> pour veiller. (*Jta*, 120)

In the space of his poetry Jabès might clandestinely visit his beloved. On the heels of his encoded declaration of love, he names himself:

> B. C. D. E.
>> — E:

that is, Edmond, or perhaps 'elle', his fiancée, at which point he pauses:

> — Je m'arrête. C'est moi que j'entrevois. L'habitude d'employer cette lettre, et je lis:
> — Elle et moi.

And off he goes again until another letter stops him in his tracks.

> F. G. H. I. J. K. L. M. N. O. P. Q. R. S.
>> — S:
>>> — J'écris:

> 'Serment'
> 'Souvenir' me hante.
>> 'Solitude.'

The poem closes on a note which shows the poet alone, physically, but in the imaginative presence of his lover:

> Mais non, mais non; je ne suis pas seul, puisque tu m'aimes et que
> je te pense.
>   Et je vois ...
>   Et je vois ...
> Et ma main dessine toute seule:
> 'Solitude.'
>
>   T. U. V. W. X. Y. Z.

For all their sentimentality, Jabès accomplishes in these verses what he had sought in the preceding essay; specifically, he distances himself markedly from the Romantic lyricism of the first books, while diving into the materiality of language. The poetry creates imagery that is multiple and meaning that is coincident; it is not 'pretext' but 'simultaneity'. The success of the exposition ought not to have been doubted.

But it was.

In the next issue of the *Semaine égyptienne*, the critic Seiffoula published a bitter analysis of the neophyte's work.[20] He accused Jabès of a snobbish erudition and, moreover, declared that the excerpts of poetry were merely 'quelques exemples de cette poésie qui fera la joie des nerfs fatigués des jeunes filles'. An acrimonious parody followed, 'écrit à la manière de M Jabès par un de ses admirateurs':

> Ecoutez, ô mes frères, la lettre R roule dans les eaux,
> Que n'est-elle sur la plage elle nous rafraîchirait
> R: Rive. Cette plage est sans air.
>   Mais voici
>   R. Ragout
>   R. Riz
>   R. Ramona
>   alors qu'en rêvant je mange au bord
>   des flots ....
> comme un HERCULE . . . . B. C. D. E.
>   E. E.
> Mais ici, je m'arrête
>   Je m'arrête un instant
>   car Edmond de Jabès ce soir a encore faim
>   E. L'initiale de mon prénom.
>   Voici un E. au plat comme un soleil anémique
>   Si les E. sont nombreux je les préfère brouillés

> Je nage depuis des mois dans un ciel chimérique
> Et en vain, depuis des mois, je cherche un R. frais.[21]

The anonymous poet takes himself for a clever punster and parodist! Drawing on Jabès's poem, written with sincerity, he transforms it into a travesty, playing on the letter 'R' and the word 'air', and on the 'E' that begins Jabès's first name and the French *œufs* (eggs).[22] Moreover, Jabès is identified (falsely) as an aristocrat, 'Edmond de Jabès'. Next, his critic compares his poetry to a book of verse in Arabic:

> *El Hadika el Mahgoura*, 'Le jardin abandonné'.
> Un titre assez banal.
> En la feuilletant je me suis demandé si elle pouvait être l'œuvre d'un homme sain.
> Mais comme la plaquette ne portait pas de nom d'auteur, j'ai compris que ce devait être un sage; car seul un fou aurait eu le courage de signer alors de pareils poèmes en Egypte.[23]

Seiffoula wonders if the Arabic poetry had been composed according to 'les théories de M E. Jabès'. After all, it is just as pretentious as his own. This comment on the anonymous Arab poet's verse is surely intended as a reflection of the naïveté of Jabès's poetry. Jabès's critic apologizes for not having on hand the book of verse in question (he recalls only its title); if he had, he would have had 'un devoir agréable de traduire quelques poèmes pour M Jabès' (he is assuming that Jabès read no Arabic). Of course, if Jabès's poems were published in an Arabic translation, 'il aurait découvert peut-être un disciple arabe, un illustre inconnu qui ignorait, sans nul doute, les théories savantes de la rhétorique moderne et tous les apports nouveaux des poètes 1930'. The critic concedes, sardonically, that despite the 'originalité artificielle' of some of Jabès's poems there are moments of true inspiration and instances of good form which have touched his 'âme blessée'. On a less disingenuous note, with which the article concludes, he admits that there are certain poems in *Je t'attends!* that genuinely moved him. 'Une âme charmante et toute en nuance. Une voix douce comme des songes innocents. Une façon personnelle de sentir la douleur. Et une précision dans le domaine des images et des MOTS.'

As mentioned, the author of the article is 'Seiffoula', which proves to be a pregnant pseudonym. The author is certainly Arabic-speaking since he uses an Arabic-language poet to parody Jabès's. That poet may very well be a fiction invented by Seiffoula; or he may be Ahmed Rassim (Alexandria, 1895–Cairo, 1958), representative of folkloric

Arabic-French letters in Egypt at the time.[24] 'Seiffoula' means 'Sword of God': the critic wanted Jabès to know that he was writing his criticism under an apparent divine authority, and with humour. Thus he wished to add a final comment on Jabès's poetry, namely, 'C'est fou là.' In other words, he encoded his pseudonym with both Arabic and French in order to demonstrate the superiority of his verbal wit across the two languages and cultures, which the *faux* French aristocrat, 'Edmond de Jabès', seemingly ignorant of Arabic verse and too entrenched in contemporary French poetry, was unable to do.

The following issue of the *Semaine égyptienne* carried a letter to the director of the publication signed by Monsieur l'Archiviste.[25] Writing in support of Jabès, the author affirms that his poetry has been composed in the tradition of Mallarmé, using words to express the limit of an idea. Nevertheless, Mallarmé's 'mathématique du Verbe, cet art de la suggestion', above all in his last poems, risks being misunderstood, or not understood at all. It necessitates 'une collaboration' with the reader 'telle que la véritable création du poème naissait de la rencontre des deux cerveaux'. Only then might the various elements in Mallarmé's (or Jabès's) poetry—the form of the verse, the typography, the white spaces and spaces between the lines—be understood.

It is tempting to entertain the thought that Jabès himself is the author of the anonymous letter, but he responded at length to Seiffoula's article in the September number of the *Semaine égyptienne* under his own name.[26] Stealthily, not once does he explicitly name his critic. As if he were intentionally mocking Seiffoula's remark that he had exhibited a snobbish erudition in the first article, Jabès again begins with a series of quotations from a number of contemporary critics and writers, including Edmond Haraucourt (who had been a member of the Alliance franco-égyptienne two years earlier and had contributed a sonnet to the pages of the organization's magazine),[27] André Gide, Jean Cocteau and Emile Bouvier, while adding footnotes to his text that give publication essentials, a scholarly convention lacking even in the first article. He employs them less to affect an air of intellectual superiority than to be ironic. Instead of responding point by point to Seiffoula's article, he simply reiterates his claim for the autonomy of the artist. If a modern poem appears incoherent to the uninitiated reader, it is because the poem was written to achieve that incoherence, and it has succeeded in doing so; the confused reader would do well to educate himself, or to study the poem with application, should he wish to seize its meaning.

Jabès's rejoinder is the first known instance in the entirety of his literary corpus in which he asserts his independence from all schools of artistic thought or practice. This is important to point out because it indicates that his self-distancing position, evident in the Parisian years, is equally apparent in the Cairene years.[28] Citing Ravel's declaration that 'La littérature est devenue une forme d'évasion',[29] Jabès concludes that since all artistic movements inevitably contradict themselves, it is better not to join them at all. Rather, the artist should 'Chercher un sentier alliciant qui invite à quitter la route primitive' and plunge himself into 'l'hallucination du mot'. (The phonetic similarity between 'alliciant', an archaic word meaning 'seductive', and 'hallucination', makes for a euphonious statement.) 'Si nous rompons avec une école,' he explains to his readers, 'c'est surtout pour rompre avec sa monotonie.' Finding himself in agreement with the physiologist and poet Charles Richet (like Haraucourt a former member of the Alliance franco-égyptienne), Jabès believes that travel is the remedy to the *ennui* of the everyday: 'Il est facile d'aller en quelques jours dans des pays étranges et splendides. Et si mes étudiants ne peuvent pas faire de coûteux voyages, au moins pourront-ils voir des paysages merveilleux se dérouler devant eux en des films excellents.'[30] Seek the unforeseen ('l'imprévu'), choose a detour ('détour'): 'il s'agit, n'est-ce pas, d'ouvrir des portes au récit.' Film is the magical vehicle in which both poet and reader travel. Adding to Richet's analogy of film as poetic adventure, of a voyage from the known to the unknown, and recalling the first word of the poem that followed his essay 'Apport à la poésie: le Logisme', Jabès says: '*j'entre* dans LE MOT, comme j'entrerais dans la vie ou dans une salle de projection, en curieux'. The spectator does not care if he disappears '*dans l'obscurité, puisque j'ai fixé mon fauteuil*' (Jabès's emphasis). In the darkness of the cinema, the poet's mind hears the voices coming from the screen, and 'Il se souvient avoir écouté de pareils [cris], il y a longtemps dans tels ou tels endroits ou dans tels ou tels moments de ma vie. ... Je note ....'[31]—the final 'Je note' obviously anticipating the 'notes' Jabès would take for the essays in his forthcoming *Arrhes poétiques*.[32]

The theoretical exposition is followed, as earlier in 'Apport', by a poetic demonstration. 'Films inflammables', like the untitled excerpts in which Jabès discreetly declares his love for Arlette Cohen, is based on a Mallarméan play on pictorial space and typesetting. Its meaning depends on Charles Richet's analogy, discussed in the preceding article, of the poet as spectator who travels to foreign lands through the medium of film. The spectator-poet is now transported to Naples where he is deeply touched by a melancholic music suffusing the air: 'A Naples, en canot, j'ai écouté d'inoubliables musiques, car la voix du chanteur se perdait dans le soir [...]. La chanson était triste et lente'.[33] In a moment of resolve that lifts him from his passivity, he thinks to himself: 'Il ne faut pas que la vie chante./Il ne faut pas que les choses parlent./Il faut parler aux choses./Il faut chanter à la vie.' And 'A LA SORTIE' of the cinema, he declares, '*Je suis le fou rêveur. / J'ai l'âme d'un ciel étoilé.*' The picture show ended, he takes away with him the memory of it:

> SOUVENIR!
> Que mon poème reste pour toi la
> vague d'une songerie ancienne, le
> dessin de cent choses vues.
> Souviens-toi. Berce-toi de tout ce
> que tu te souviens.[34]

The inspirational process of poetic creation follows this short but decisive path: past lived experience (here in the form of a song heard) is preserved as a memory; and the memory is recalled in the concrete form of the poem. The poet is he who does not abandon the source of his experience; rather, he forms his recollection of it into a lasting memorial, namely, the poem.

Thus Edmond Jabès, who had come under fire by Seiffoula earlier that summer, has moved beyond the angry, sarcastic (albeit marvellously clever) criticism of his poetry. His theory has little to do with Seiffoula's imaginary Romantic poet contemplating natural beauty, pitying himself while caressing his ailing heart. Instead of responding directly to charges of obscurity and elitism, he reaffirms his modernist aesthetic in both his theoretical exposition and his application of that theory. I do not wish to deny that Jabès was made self-conscious by Seiffoula's remarks, in particular since it is clear that 'Films inflammables' shows a distinct distancing from the first phase of his career, that of *Illusions sentimentales* and *Je t'attends!*. To be sure, Seiffoula's article was written in response to Jabès's own efforts, made public in 'Apport à la poésie: le Logisme', to move beyond the out-of-date Romantic assumptions informing his first books. Jabès was clearly hurt by the comments. In 'Films inflammables' he writes: 'Ma voix est faible, car je suis le poète mort-né'.[35] But self-pity, at this confident stage, did not last long; the sentence ends, 'à qui l'on a coupé les ailes, mais qui monte dans l'azur en déplaçant l'air de ses bras-volants et de ses pieds en cerf-volant'. Still, the criticism served as a catalyst to Jabès's poetic development. Seiffoula confirmed in him that change was necessary, and thereby spurred him on. The fact that Jabès responded to the criticism demonstrates, for his part, a mature spirit and, perhaps more importantly, a personal responsibility towards his poetry that is rooted in his readers' reception of it. Ultimately, the writer is not entirely autonomous in relation to the reader. Rather, the two are bound by an artistic contract: the poet composes good poetry, however difficult, and the reader makes a sincere effort to understand it. That Jabès had the confidence of Stavro Stavrinos and the *Semaine égyptienne* is of capital importance in this regard. In March 1932, Jabès contributed his first book review and poem to the magazine. By the summer he was permitted to contribute a lengthy essay, whose contents were not beyond criticism. The matter might have been left in the dust stirred up by the attack. Instead, the magazine published Monsieur l'Archiviste's letter and, in early autumn, Jabès's rejoinder. And as if to reassure Jabès of his faith in him, Stavrinos brought out his 'Maman' at about that time.[36] This poem is more conventional in form and more tactful in content than were his previous provocative experiments.

> reste, maman; serre moi contre toi,
> comme si j'étais tout petit ...
> ('Maman', n.p.)

'Maman' was better suited to the bourgeois taste held by Jabès's conservative Franco-Egyptian readers.[37] In the poem Jabès's older sister Marcelle who, like Sarah Schwall, died in adolescence, figures delicately, as she did in his first book of poems, which was dedicated to her memory. With 'Maman', then, it seemed as if the matter had been brought to a quiet close.[38]

However, a carefree, oppositional spirit took hold of Jabès. The experiments of the first *Semaine égyptienne* articles grew into Jabès's next book, entitled *Les Pieds en l'air*, with a preface by Max Jacob. The regressive, lonely tone of 'Maman' is largely abandoned in this publication, in which the poet's seriousness gives way to a self-sufficient voice, the voice of levity. The poetry is less self-obsessed, as it were, than it is self-possessed. The title of the collection is derived from its first poem, 'Une lettre, si tu veux'. It is hardly a *billet doux*: its tone is angry—the anger that is the result of strained love—but it reveals, at the same time, an attitude of derision that is the mark of the emotional distance necessary to produce a post-Romantic poem: 'Je suis la lumière lancée par deux phares d'automobile qui se fuit ...'. His lover mocks him, but she will have to answer for her mockery: 'Pourquoi as-tu ri si férocement avec cette bouche que j'ai tant baisée?' His feeling of love lingers, even as the love affair is finished. He must carry on. The beloved has spurned her poet-lover; even though the rejection has pained him, he finds himself with his 'pieds en l'air'. He will thus make use of queer stories ('histoires drôles') to console himself. In a literal sense, he has said his farewell to the beloved (*Pa*, 9–10).

With the appearance of *Les Pieds en l'air* in the winter of 1934 came a renewed gust of criticism. Adolf Shual wrote sarcastically of it: 'Dans une lettre préface qu'il adresse à l'auteur, Max Jacob lui déclare "Je suis tout à fait persuadé que vous irez très loin sur le chemin d'Art." Mon Dieu, s'il doit faire cette longue route avec *Les Pieds en l'air*, il faut croire que son talent tient plus de l'équilibriste que du poète, du moins, dans le sens classique que nous sommes habitués à donner à ce mot.'[39] Another critic, Zeinab, writing in the *Semaine égyptienne*, confessed: 'J'ai bien cherché à comprendre ce poète, et malgré toute ma bonne volonté je ne sais si j'y suis parvenue. [...] Jabès veut bien, de temps à autre, nous initier à son univers intime, mais il tient par dessus tout à nous ébahir. Et il réussit!'[40] Writers in Paris also noticed an undue obscurantism.[41] Jabès's new poetry, then, was a mystery to his readers, and he would have to account for it.

His 1935 collection of essays, *Arrhes poétiques*, extends the flamboyance of *Les Pieds en l'air*, and may be read as a response to some of his readers' criticisms of that book. It is divided into three dated parts, 'Arrhes poétiques' ('Les Cèdres, été 1934'), 'Discours pour s'amuser' ('Le Caire, hiver 1934'), and 'Naphtaline' ('Le Caire, Avril 1934') all preceded by an introduction, 'La Condition d'être poète'. In contrast to his previous writings, there is no verse poetry in *Arrhes poétiques*. As Jabès remarks, these are not poems but 'notes'. He has temporarily abandoned the subtlety of his verse style and instead is often writing to a specific individual or audience, most revealingly Jean Moscatelli.

In fact, the first section of *Arrhes poétiques* roughly corresponds to the summer of 1934 when Jabès and Moscatelli began the car journey across the Sinai desert to Palestine and Lebanon that would become

the source for 'L'hospitalité nomade' in *Le Livre de l'Hospitalité*. In an immediate sense, following his adventure Jabès became more confident as a poet. This was largely due to his acceptance by writers outside his immediate literary environment. For instance, in September 1934, 'Cèdres', a poem dedicated to Jabès by the Franco-Lebanese poet Hector Klat, whom Jabès and Moscatelli had visited in Lebanon, appeared in the *Semaine égyptienne*.[42] The confidence of the 22-year-old Jabès is further enhanced by his correspondence with one of the most distinguished *montparnassiens*, Max Jacob.

Just why Jabès privileged Moscatelli is explained by the close relationship the two had entertained since the early thirties. *Arrhes poétiques* is the greatest expression of their friendship. Moscatelli's line-drawing portrait of Jabès, in which he is seen smoking a cigarette and which served as the book's frontispiece, illustrates a self-assured, urbane observer of the modern, of the quotidian, who has been nursed at the teats of Baudelaire and Rimbaud. 'Au poète Edmond Jabès', reads the caption, should there be any doubt as to the occupation of the young man, 'très amicalement Jean Moscatelli'. Moreover, Jabès's dedication of the book to Moscatelli—'Au poète Jean Moscatelli'—is perhaps modelled on Baudelaire's dedication of *Les Fleurs du mal* to Théophile Gautier. As Moscatelli had referred to his colleague as 'poète' in the dedication on the portrait, so too will Jabès refer to him. The intimacy and interiority of all of the poetry before 1934 gives way to an outward-speaking voice. No longer suffering from a crushing loneliness, or no longer expressing his feeling of loneliness, Jabès floats heavenwards, he writes, 'comme un ballon, crever dans la stratosphère'. Leaving the wings of a theatre in which he sings in solitude, despite himself, histrionically, he now performs on a public stage before an audience of other poets and artists attentive to the dynamism of the cultural moment.

'Arrhes poétiques' is a manifesto, not political but artistic. It is written for would-be Franco-Egyptian poets who might wish to join the club of glorious poets. But Jabès is also addressing those artists outside Egypt, presumably in Paris, who wrongly believe that creative activity does not exist beyond the Ile de France. 'LES ARTISTES NAISSENT DE PARTOUT, MÊME DANS LE DÉSERT', exclaims Jabès: 'C'est écrire qu'en Egypte aussi, il y a des artistes ... et je veux, avant de suivre d'autres routes, m'arrêter, un instant, au seuil de leur porte. Ceux qui sont loin, ne peuvent pas comprendre pourquoi, en Egypte, on parle si peu des jeunes écrivains de ce pays qui s'expriment

en français' (*Ap*, 18). Jabès insists that there are writers of literature in French who are not French; these francophone artists (writers and visual artists alike—for *la francophonie* is a phenomenon that encompasses verbal and visual expression) are connected, and committed, to the language and culture of France even if they are far away from their source. In writing these remarks, Jabès may have had in mind the Essayistes, an intellectual youth group for francophone Egyptians, which held weekly meetings at the Conservatoire Bergrunn in the northern Cairo suburb of Heliopolis. But these young writers, he insists, do not need a literary society or 'un salon à figurines'; rather, they require 'l'AIR, de l'air de MONTPARNASSE, pour leur santé, pour la santé de leur âme. Une atmosphère respirable et non pas deux heures consacrées par journée à un quelconque devoir' (*Ap*, 19). Jabès thus pleads the case of Egyptian writers who, 'négligés comme des microbes inoffensifs' by the Parisian cultural scene, are 'presque honteux de leur condition'. Blame for the oversight does not lie entirely with the Parisians, who cannot be called upon at a moment's notice to look after their colleagues in more arid climates. The responsibility for achieving recognition belongs primarily to the Egyptian artists themselves (*Ap*, 19–20). The youth of the country must not let their shame sink them into the quagmire of artistic paralysis. Alluding to Seiffoula's criticism of him, Jabès asserts that the young poets meet informally in cafés that recall the air ('R frais') of Montparnasse. Let them nourish their souls with the bread and wine of daily life. Jabès will furnish an example of the theory of observing the poetic in the quotidian: 'Je descends de chez moi. Comme il est tôt pour aller à mon travail, je fais un détour. En route, je croise des gens et des choses déjà vues avec qui j'échange des bonjours. JE REJOINS LA POÉSIE PAR DERRIÈRE' (*Ap*, 21).

Jabès's readiness to serve as a model for other young poets took some reviewers by surprise. In April 1935, Adolf Shual observed that Jabès the private, creative spirit appeared to have little to do with the one he knew in public, the one, that is, he could meet 'dans le bureau d'un oncle célèbre', here referring to Umberto Jabès. Shual was very pleased with Jabès's 'intellectualisme raffiné [...] qui est si rare chez un homme d'Egypte'. But not all in *Arrhes poétiques*, especially what Jabès saw as humorous, was to his liking. 'Edmond Jabès revu par Laurel et Hardy, voici une réalité que nous concilions mal. Ces jongleries de l'esprit, ces calembours au Néon, ces débats où se prolonge le rêve, n'ont pourtant rien de risible, si on ne se laisse pas déconcerter par eux. Il faut aller au fond de la réalité qu'ils prétendent défier, pour se rendre compte du tourment moral qui les a inspirés.'[43] Like Seiffoula some three years earlier, Shual saw in Jabès an individual who places himself above the average Egyptian; but in his opinion there was nothing particularly negative about this attribution, which 'd'aucuns traitent de fumiste', since, after all, he was 'plus sensé et malin que nous tous'.

Jean Moscatelli's review is complimentary. He comments specifically on Jabès's particular talent for endowing the everyday with the poetic, which has an ennobling effect, and further on his use of the *fait divers*, which is entirely opposed to the 'rêve à perpétuité'. Furthermore, Moscatelli elevates Jabès by placing him in the company of several of France's most influential poets, including Tristan Derême, Cocteau, André Salmon and Max Jacob. The latter, notes Moscatelli, along with Théo Varlet, has already declared him 'comme un authentique espoir'. His is thus perplexed that Jabès should be fated 'de n'être pas, pareil en ceci aux prophètes de jadis, poète dans son pays'. If Jabès bears the onus of exclusion from certain intellectual circles in Egypt for voicing his criticism, so be it. That does not mean his poetry is facile; rather, it means that the Egyptians have not made sufficient effort to comprehend it.

It is thus that from the early 1930s Moscatelli championed Jabès, who, it may be gathered from their frequent professional contact at the time, depended on him for intellectual support in the face of sometimes hostile critics. Jabès, however, was compelled to reconsider his high opinion of his friend when, in late 1936, Moscatelli published an article in the pages of an openly Fascist journal calling Mussolini the greatest living Italian writer.[44] While Moscatelli did not denounce democratic principles in favour of Fascist politics, the gesture of vaunting Mussolini offended the independent-minded, though fundamentally francophile Jabès. In fact, only months before the article appeared, another French-speaking Egyptian writer, Georges Henein, whose contribution to modern Egyptian literature will be considered shortly, correctly understood that Jabès was 'ni futuriste, ni surréaliste, mais avant tout lui-même'.[45] Moreover, it must be recalled that by mid-1936, following the invasion of Ethiopia and his intervention in the Spanish Civil War, Mussolini had allied himself with Hitler.[46] I know of no further evidence to explain why the collaboration of Jabès and Moscatelli ended with *Arrhes poétiques*. All that is certain is that there were, henceforth, no significant points of contact—save Jabès's recollection in *Le Livre de l'Hospitalité* of the nearly disastrous desert crossing. Jabès and Moscatelli certainly remained on friendly terms; French Cairo of the 1930s, home to a small number of tightly knit intellectuals and *hommes et femmes de lettres*, was too tiny a locale for them to avoid each other entirely. Moscatelli had been important to Jabès, but by late 1936 they no longer worked together cheek by jowl.

Their differences were exacerbated after 1938 when Mussolini promulgated anti-Semitic policies in Italy. Shortly after, as the fighting of the Second World War began to touch Egyptian soil and allegiances to one government or another took on more profound implications, foreign nationals declared their loyalty to either the Allies or the Axis, or remained neutral. In the wake of Fascist Italy's entry into the war, many Italian nationals in Egypt were detained by the Egyptian government, in cooperation with the British, with the result that, in 1940, Jabès was held for a month at the Italian School of Cairo; in order to avoid further detention he proclaimed his membership of the Egyptian section of the Groupes d'action antifasciste et italiens libres, an open letter of 1941 providing physical evidence that he was an anti-Fascist activist.[47] He thereby obtained a train ticket to Palestine in July 1942 as an evacuee of the British military, who occupied Egypt at the time. Egyptian Jews and the British alike feared that should the Nazis win the battle of El Alamein, anti-Fascist and other pro-democracy activists of Egypt might be taken prisoner. Moscatelli, on the other hand, was interned for the duration of the war on account of his supposed profession of Fascism. Afterwards, he continued his writing and journalistic activities, and eventually became an editor of the popular French-language news magazine *Images*; none of his post-war poems or articles were endowed with Fascist political content. In fact, his last book of poetry, *Rubaiyat pour l'aimée*,[48] for which he received the Wacef Ghali prize in 1953, turned away from modern western poetic form (the bane of any Franco-Egyptian poet at this time of renewed Arab-Egyptian nationalism) and revealed a nostalgia for medieval Arabic poetry. It must not be forgotten that the book was published at that critical moment in modern Egyptian history when a return to Arabic language and poetic forms would have ingratiated the writer to the leaders and supporters of the National Revolution.

In summary, the most striking feature of Jabès's first publications in the *Semaine égyptienne*, reflected by their critical reception, is that they convey his wish to distance himself from the provincialism of French

Cairo. The negative criticism of his poetry bears this idea out; he was felt by many to be too un-Egyptian to be an authentic poet of the country; and in Moscatelli's view, his writings were as misunderstood or ignored by his fellow Egyptians as were the pleadings of the biblical prophets by the ancient Jews. Of course, Jabès's initial self-identification as a Franco-Egyptian writer—attested to by efforts in the Alliance franco-égyptienne and his pleas in *Arrhes poétiques* on behalf of younger Franco-Egyptian writers—cannot be disregarded. From the first, Edmond Jabès identified himself publicly as an Egyptian writer, and felt himself profoundly to be one. Nevertheless the compass needle of his first work pointed towards France and its literary institutions. It is the strange feeling of being in exile in one's native country, or the sense of internal uprooting, that best characterizes the composition and critical reception of Jabès's early publications.

Georges Henein and Surrealism's Egyptian Prospects

In the first phase of the Cairene years we observed how Edmond Jabès adhered to Romantic and Symbolist aesthetics. Their belated entry into Egypt was due to the country's provincialism in relation to France. Francophone artists and writers felt an agonizing conflict between the strong and steady pull of Parisian currents, seemingly irrelevant to local concerns, and the necessity of promulgating Egyptian culture in their own country as well as abroad. The tension between French and Egyptian culture is equally perceptible in Jabès's second phase, dating from the mid-1930s through to the end of the Second World War, as he grappled with the emergence of Parisian Surrealism in an Egyptian cultural milieu. He explained his position with regards to Surrealism in the mid-1980s when he wrote: 'Je n'ai jamais été fasciné par les peintures surréalistes'.[49] Nonetheless, he added that 'certains de mes écrits de l'époque m'ont amené à me rapprocher, un moment, de ce groupe'.[50] Which writings was Jabès referring to? Some of the very early poetry, in particular 'L'Obscurité potable' (1936), is characterized by Surrealist aesthetics:

> Je dois au rêve la puissance d'une seconde réalité ...
> Et cette autre moitié de moi où nul n'a parlé.
> Tu y as mis tes cheveux et tes yeux de non-être;
> Tandis que j'ouvrais, grande, la haute fenêtre
> Sur toi, au ciel, endormie, comme un aigle ...

Je dois au rêve l'avenir que je n'ai pas prédit,
Si dur qu'il me fut à saisir ... Les larmes versées
J'ai rêvé, une fois, que nous nous serions rêvés ...

('Op', §III)

Reality is divided betwen the physical and the psychic, and the poet
acknowledges his debt to the dream world ('Je dois au rêve'). Within
the realm of the psychic there exists a further, second realm which
would open upon the first: a dream within a dream. It is this domain
that Jabès wishes to explore. He very well might have, but his early
association with non-Surrealist writers such as Jean Moscatelli and, from
late 1933, Max Jacob bridled his interest and kept him remote from the
movement's activities. Though he knew writers such as Paul Eluard as
early as the middle thirties, he did not join the group (*Dl*, 31).

The changing political atmosphere of the mid-1930s also
contributed to his aloofness. In the previous section we saw how Jabès
parted company with local pro-Fascist writers. His disapproval of
Futurism after 1936 was in fact part of a general self-detachment from
then current artistic and literary movements. Similarly, as the National
Socialists increasingly assumed governmental control and popular
support, he was suspicious of placing his political allegiances in the
hands of the Surrealists. It is not, of course, that any member of the
group was associated with the Nazi party. However, even at the time
Jabès had spoken to friends in Paris close to the group about refugees
from Europe coming to Egypt, the imminence of war and the danger
of Hitler. They did not believe him. They thought of themselves as
revolutionary, but political reality escaped them.[51] If he was already
circumspect about the Surrealists as early as the middle thirties, the
decisive historical event that pushed Edmond Jabès away from the
movement was the Shoah. When considering his critique of and
distancing from Surrealism, it is crucial to understand that it was not
Jabès himself who was to demonstrate that Surrealist aesthetics were
irrelevant in the post-Holocaust world. Rather, it was the *events
themselves* that had invalidated Surrealist art practice. The 1947 Cairo
exhibition definitively laid to rest any interest Jabès had in the group.
'On y voyait,' he told Marcel Cohen, 'entre autres choses, des
mannequins de couturière éventrés à coup de couteau et maculés
d'encre rouge, alors que nous venions de découvrir toute l'horreur
des camps. Il me semblait qu'il y avait là une indécence inacceptable'
(*Dl*, 32).

'Le Fond de l'eau' (1947), in which the voice of the poet speaks for headless and silenced dolls, reflects this position:

> Je parle de qui je ne connais pas
> de qui je ne connaîtrai jamais que les mots
> pour toi *poupées défigurées*
>
> (*Jbmd*, 78; my emphasis)

Disfiguring dolls was grotesque, Jabès thought, in the post-Auschwitz era. A theory and practice of writing relying more on the unconscious than on consciousness to produce images was reprehensible, even if the unconscious itself was never denigrated. Detached from the reality in which they were produced, the images seemed inorganic and arbitrary and, worse, truly horrifying. The unbearable discontinuity between Surrealism and the historical moment of the pre- and post-war eras was for Jabès ever a source of tension which he sought to resolve by distancing himself from Surrealist practice. True, the stupefying power of the Surrealist image appealed to him during the 1930s and early 1940s—the years, that is, before history itself demonstrated with terrifying clarity that the literary and the plastic arts could not be produced in a vacuum if they were not to appear obscene. Even Surrealism's primogenitor, Dada, was a direct result of the horror of the Great War as experienced by Tristan Tzara, Hugo Ball and its other founders, whose *Klanggedichte* mimicked the rattling of machine guns and the fatuity of contemporary journalism. In the late 1910s this seemed like an appropriate artistic response to the irrationality of the moment. But in the galleries of the Cairo Surrealist exhibition, the ethics and aesthetics of Surrealism seemed preposterous. It is thus that the vehemence of Jabès's reaction to the movement, based both on his involvement with the group and on his observations of it from afar, necessitates a historical view of Surrealism in Egypt and of the individuals who animated its activities.

The poet and critic Georges Henein (Cairo, 1914–Paris, 1973) was for Edmond Jabès a bridge between the Cairene arts and literary communities, and the cultural centre of Paris. As an intellectual *engagé* for whom the troubling caesura between art and politics was a challenge to be met with practical initiatives, he wrote for Franco-Egyptian literary journals such as *Un Effort* and he founded art and literary groups such as Art et liberté, which had a left-wing political orientation and took Parisian Surrealism as its model. Jabès and

Henein worked closely on similar journals such as *La Part du sable* as early as 1947, and it is certain that they knew each other in the mid-1930s; nevertheless their working relationship ended in the early 1950s as their respective projects separated them professionally. But even earlier personality differences hampered an extended collaboration. Their friendship has been described as 'froide',[52] and Jabès did not contribute to the 1974 volume of tributes to Henein.[53] Despite their differences it is certain that their shared interest in the politicization of art and culture joined them in a common pursuit.

The two met in Cairo in late 1934, in all likelihood during a literary evening sponsored by the Essayistes as the Middle East was feeling the initial rumblings of National Socialist anti-Semitism and the growth of Fascism. They shared an interest in drama and poetry, and both had political aspirations. Furthermore, like those of Jabès, Henein's first publications and literary activities were greeted with some indignation by Franco-Egyptian critics. Associated with the Essayistes and their publication *Un Effort* since December 1934, Georges Henein was known as the group's *enfant terrible* for his provocative essays on literature and culture. The Egyptian journalist André de Laumois wrote against him at the time, noting that his hostile disposition contradicted the classicism of Georges Duhamel and Paul Valéry then prevalent among the members of Les Essayistes. Among the newcomers, de Laumois wrote, 'un surtout avait du talent, un talent âpre, acerbe, un style de pamphlétaire cérébral, c'est-à-dire auquel il manquait tout de même le souffle qu'un Jules Vallès cherche et trouve dans la pitié dont son cœur, si plein de haine soit-il, est rempli'. Henceforth, *Un Effort* was transformed into 'le champ d'action où s'exprime la pensée ardente, violente, corrosive (tout est relatif) de M Georges Henein et d'un ou deux de ses émules'.[54] Jean Moscatelli, himself a member of Les Essayistes, was also disturbed by Henein. He found the will-to-provoke in his *Rappel à l'ordre* (1935), co-authored with Jo Farna, insipid: 'Mais pourquoi faut-il que Georges Henein et Jo Farna se mettent en colère pour opiner? Ils sont révoltés de la condition humaine; mais croient-ils l'améliorer en frappant du poing la table ou la figure?'[55]

Despite his often madcap pronouncements, Henein shared with Jabès a genuine desire to broaden Egyptian cultural horizons, which he initiated when he decided to join the Parisian Surrealists. In January 1935, he began a correspondence with André Breton,[56] which indicates that he wished to bring *Un Effort* closer to the service of Surrealism. Instead, Breton suggested that he form a journal with a more international orientation. Ideas and impulse for the journal's inception would occur in 1939; its title would be *Art et liberté*. Meanwhile, in February 1937, Henein gave a speech in which he announced the arrival of Parisian Surrealism in Cairo—although it must be said that Franco-Egyptian artists such as Mayo, Jabès's friend from his days at the Maison des Artistes, had exhibited their Surrealist paintings in Egypt as early as late 1933.[57] Delivered at a meeting of the Essayistes and broadcast simultaneously by the Egyptian Broadcast Company, Henein's 'Bilan du mouvement surréaliste'—essentially a capsule history of Parisian Surrealism that explains its attraction as an artistic and literary movement—found supporters among many Egyptian intellectuals.[58] Jabès heard the lecture, and certainly sympathized with Henein's effort. Nevertheless, he felt slighted by Henein's deprecatory remarks about his friend and teacher, Max Jacob: 'Ranger Max Jacob parmi les Surréalistes ou à côté d'eux, c'est infliger au surréalisme un outrage qu'il n'a pas mérité. On qualifie souvent Max Jacob de fantaisiste. Un fantaisiste? Disons plutôt un clown. Et par surcroît, un mauvais clown.'[59] While no direct response to Henein's attack has been located, in a book review dating from January 1938 Jabès insinuated that any discussion of the Surrealist movement must be taken up with an 'esprit d'indépendance',[60] thereby mocking Henein's zealous loyalty to the group. The year 1936 marks the end of the British occupation in Egypt, and the following year saw the end of the Capitulations and the beginnings of Egypt's national independence. Intellectuals and artists believed, rightly, that the country was destined for a new start.[61] Henein, too, sensed the winds change. In 1938, he travelled to Paris to study literature at the Sorbonne (as had Jabès less than ten years earlier) where he became a political supporter of Trotsky. When later in 1938 he returned to Cairo, he formed an art-political movement which gathered together Egypt's leading avant-garde artists and writers, both French- and Arabic-speaking, to further the cause of Surrealism in the country.[62]

Art et liberté was founded in early 1939 by Georges Henein, Ramsès Younane, Anwar Kamil, Lutfallah Sulayman, Kamil el-Telmisany, Anwar Afifi, Zaki Salama and Fouad Kamil.[63] Its principal interests lay in the field of visual arts. Henein formed the group in response to André Breton's appeal for 'un art libre et indépendant', a call made as a reaction to National Socialism's pressure to delimit creativity.[64] Artistic creativity, then, was to be conceived of as an openly political act. If Surrealism's combination of art and politics had appealed to Georges Henein, Art et liberté, his own creation, reflected his Trotskyite political orientation as well as his Surrealist sympathies. Jabès's interests, however, lay elsewhere, and he did not become a member of the group. What, then, was he busying himself with during the first years of the war?

During the early months of 1941, the poet and critic Ivo Barbitch published a series of six portraits entitled 'Quelques poètes d'Egypte', which offer a unique, kaleidoscopic view of the literary scene's most important writers, including Arsène Yergath, Ahmed Rassim, Henein and Jabès.[65] The article on Jabès, 'Edmond Jabès ou la recherche de l'humain', summarizes only his recent achievements. *Illusions sentimentales* and *Je t'attends!* remain unmentioned, save in the remark 'Je ne veux pas parler de ses premiers vers',[66] thus continuing Jabès's own unburdening of his juvenilia. Barbitch wished to speak of Jabès's current projects, of those creative endeavours in which he attempts to bring the individual a little closer to understanding him- or herself. Writing as half of the world balanced precariously gazing into the abyss of global war while the other half had already thrown itself, or was being thrown, into it, Barbitch reflected wistfully that at its end (should it end) a historian might try to explain the meaning of the poetry of the time, which so many find so incomprehensible ('si insolite'), in terms of its humanity. Barbitch plainly placed Jabès among those writers representative of this ethical standard. His poetry seeks the human in everyday life; it is a salve to alienation in contemporary society; and it seeks to go beyond appearances and delve into the essence of things. Barbitch's view of Jabès's poetry should be understood as distinct from his own. For Barbitch, dream poetics need not be an irresponsible flight from reality, as Jabès thought it to be. Nor should it be a facile solution to social fragmentation. Rather, in Barbitch's view Jabès's recourse to the dream is an attempt to fasten the individual to lived experience. The dream is the vehicle by which heightened levels of perception may be attained. It is true that Jabès had indulged himself and his readers in a sometimes unsuccessful humour in books such as *Les Pieds en l'air*. And while in 'L'Obscurité potable' he appealed perhaps too much to Surrealism as a means of realizing his 'net désir de sortir des chemins battus', in his present work, *Avec l'ombre*, he is 'en pleine possession de ses moyens, chantant la lutte de l'Ombre et de la Lumière et suivant pas à pas l'émouvante ascension de l'homme prisonnier de son destin'.

Avec l'ombre heralds Jabès's later invention of a shattered narrative poetry, a *récit éclaté*, on a grand scale. Like *Le Livre des Questions*, it is divided into seven parts, although its subject could not, of course, anticipate the destruction of human life in the Shoah. According to Ivo Barbitch, *Avec l'ombre* tells just the opposite story, the creation of humanity. The biblical mythology of Genesis is thus central to *Avec l'ombre*, even if Jabès's use of it appears loose. The poem recounts: (1) 'la Chute de l'ombre'; (2) humanity's questioning its evolutionary progress (in 'Pour une amie de la nuit'); (3) the story of Adam and Eve; (4) how a single voice can drown out the rumble of cannon fire (in 'Ode à l'homme blanc'); (5) the onslaught of war between Light and Shadow, which is mirrored in world history (in 'Duel des ombres'); (6) the loss of human life in the war (in 'Ode à la France' and 'Ombres sacrifiées'); and, finally, (7) an assessment of human failure as a cause of war (in 'Révolution blanche'), which ends with a cry of hope for humanity.

Barbitch traces Jabès's immediate intellectual ancestry to the Surrealists. Nevertheless, he recognizes that Jabès did not always share their point of view. Like that of Jules Supervielle, for whom 'Jabès ne cache pas son admiration', Jabès's verse also bears the mark of Surrealist aesthetics. In fact, Jabès 'a fait sienne pour un moment la définition de Breton, "Dictée de la pensée, en l'absence de tout contrôle exercé par la raison, en dehors de toutes préoccupations esthétiques ou morales"'.[67] It is true that the title of Jabès's poem echoes a verse from Jules Supervielle's *Forçat innocent* (1930): 'Présences, parlez bas,/On pourrait nous entendre/Et me vendre à la mort,/Cachez-moi la figure/Derrière la ramure/Et que l'on me confonde/*Avec l'ombre* du monde.'[68] But the poet's *Fable du monde*, which recounts a Genesis-like creation, equally appears to be one of Jabès's sources. It is further important to take into account the immediate cultural context in which Jabès was composing and publishing. In particular, in June 1940 a critical article on Supervielle appeared in the *Revue du Caire* that proclaimed him, as Jabès himself wished to be perceived, 'en dehors de toute école',[69] especially Surrealism. Nonetheless, Supervielle's poetry does recall the evasive character of some of the movement's abiding poets: 'Mais, s'il s'évade, ce n'est point comme les Surréalistes pour échapper à la Terre et à l'Univers, c'est au contraire pour les mieux posséder, pour en saisir le secret et pour s'assurer qu'il n'est point seulement un somnambule au milieu des choses.'[70]

In the sense that Jabès's *Avec l'ombre* manifests an ambivalent attitude towards Surrealism, it is consistent with earlier poems such as 'L'Obscurité potable' in which the shadow of night mingles with the light of day. The verse is freer than in the earlier poem, and there is no fixed rhyme scheme. Thus,

> Je veux que ta beauté
> Ressemble à ma nuit
> D'où la lumière jaillit
> Comme d'un ventre énorme
> Coupé en deux[71]

Sexual desire, openly expressed and betraying an internal necessity, is at the centre of the human condition:

> Il me réintègre
> L'épaisse condition d'homme
> Me léguer à mon futur
> D'avoir doublé le nuage
> J'ai rapporté à la terre
> La tension du plus haut faite
> Mais je n'ai pas encore saisi,
> Ah! comment, sur mon chemin
> Mon ombre est venue à moi
> Avec son sexe, avec ma bouche.[72]

Fear, due to incertitude, has its place beside tenderness in the nocturnal imagination of the lover, who is guided by the gestures of his beloved:

> J'ai peur de la nuit
> Où nos deux têtes différentes
> Joue contre joue,
> Ne vivent pas:
> Elles attendent
> Je ne sais quoi d'attendre depuis toujours
> Lorsque ta main
> Ta fragile main le commande
> Ouvre le jour ...[73]

The discriminating reader of these lines cannot but notice that they do not appear to illustrate the creation poem described in Barbitch's article, save in some abstract, vaguely referential way (i.e. the two lovers might represent Adam and Eve, but then they might represent any amorous pair, Sarah and Yukel, for example, or *Il* and *Ile* in *Récit*, in

Jabès's later work). A reader with a more generous spirit might credit Jabès with having composed a poem that embraces a universal feeling or condition, and so forgive him the abstraction: Jabès has painted an archetypal representation of lovers. Clearly, Barbitch held the latter belief. He thought that in *Avec l'ombre* Jabès had constructed a cosmic drama reflecting the 'immense espoir d'une guerre évitée', but that that hope was then dashed in the destructive intervening years. Barbitch's analysis is singular not least because it situates Jabès in the context of world historical events and contemporary culture, both in Egypt and in France. The article is also remarkable because it describes and quotes excerpts from a poem Jabès permitted only Barbitch to publish. *Avec l'ombre*, which occupies most of his commentary, was unknown to most of Jabès's readers when the article appeared. He was awaiting 'une occasion propice' before releasing the entire poem. That moment did not arrive, and so the poem does not figure anywhere in Jabès's *œuvre*. But at the time critics such as Barbitch felt that the poem represented a turning point in Jabès's development.

Barbitch notes that *Avec l'ombre* was begun in 1935, a year before 'L'Obscurité potable' appeared. Its lengthy development is reflected in Max Jacob's letters to Jabès. Parts of an earlier version did not arouse the same enthusiasm in the great poet. In January 1938, just over two years before Barbitch's article, Jabès published four fragments without any critical commentary in another Franco-Egyptian newspaper, *Le Nil*, under the title 'Le Sens de l'ombre'.[74] The similar titles ('Le Sens de l'ombre' and *Avec l'ombre*) imply that the earlier fragments were later incorporated into the longer poem-in-progress. At about the same time that he wrote the four 'Sens de l'ombre' fragments, Jabès sent his manuscript to Max Jacob for comment. He responded shortly afterwards: 'Je te félicite de ta grande ambition: elle est de toute façon nouvelle, 1) parce que personne ne pense plus au poème fleuve, 2) parce que tu as une personnalité' (*LEJ*, 65). Generous enough, Jabès might have felt. But the encouraging note is followed by seventeen critical remarks, one of which reads: 'Les meilleurs mots sont les mots concrets table, chaise, tenailles. Hélas! il n'y en a pas un seul en 150 pages. Travaille avec sur ta table des objets: équerre, tenailles, vieilles clefs, tiroirs, etc. ... c'est très sain pour l'esprit. Descends! le ciel est en bas!' (*LEJ*, 67).[75] Although Max Jacob believed Jabès had progressed since 'L'Obscurité potable', the gratuitous reverie of the present poem left him in something of an unsought trance.

Jabès must have taken the suggestions seriously, for at least one of the very few earlier fragments we possess has been reworked. A comparison of the first two verses of the 1938 and 1941 versions establishes this fact. The early fragment reads:

> Je veux entendre ce que tu vois,
> L'oreille contre tes yeux fermés,
> Douce maison de l'obscurité,
> Où le rêve ancien, avec un autre
> Que tu fais sans le savoir ... deux hôtes
> Etrangers vêtus de blanc et d'or
> Sur les murs, abandonne où tu dors
> Le regard, qu'a refusé la mort,
> Pour le ciel, où tu cueilles des fleurs.[76]

Which can be read beside the later version:

> L'oreille contre tes yeux fermés
> Vais-je entendre ce que tu vois,
> Chaude maison de l'obscurité
> Où le rêve ancien avec un autre,
> Dans la nuit, à peine fait ... deux hôtes
> Silencieux, l'un en or l'autre en noir
> Aux murs abandonnent quand tu dors,
> Le regard refusé de la mort
> Pour le ciel où je cueille le soir.[77]

A number of phrases in the 1938 version have been modified ('Douce maison' becomes 'Chaude maison'; 'tu cueilles des fleurs' becomes 'je cueille le soir', etc.). Nevertheless, it must be admitted that Jabès has not 'come down from Heaven', as Max Jacob suggested he should. The abstractions remain, and in abundance. While it is possible that *Avec l'ombre* reflects the violence of the war in Europe and North Africa (as Barbitch claimed), it seems unlikely that readers would have associated the poem's dream imagery and biblical thematic with the devastation.

From our critical perspective, the poem is significant insofar as it marks the first time Jabès attempted to write at length about a particular moment in history. With the onslaught of war he sought to infuse his poetry with a broader historical consciousness than he had in the earlier compositions. It is the progressive awareness of the events unfolding around him that interests us most because they point to the exilic texts in which history takes on an even more brutal meaning. The reasons for Jabès's rejection of the poem are not entirely clear. It is certain that at the time Barbitch's article appeared (March 1941) he was intending to publish it. It appears that by July 1942 he had decided that it was better left 'in the shadow', as it were. As mentioned above, at that time he and other Jewish activists in Egypt were evacuated to Palestine by British occupying troops fighting Field Marshal Erwin Rommel's advancing Afrika Corps.[78] With Jabès on this transport was a young political activist and journalist, Raymond Aghion, leaving Egypt for the same reasons as Jabès, who later recalled how Jabès lent him a copy of the poem and asked for his thoughts. Aghion reports that in his opinion the poem, despite its imagery of a victorious Light in its battle with Darkness, ought to have been revised. The language and imagery of the final section, 'La Révolution blanche', troubled him. True, that section recounts the downfall of the 'Race blanche', but it could be construed as racist and should be excised from the poem, especially as foreign residents of Egypt were commonly know as 'les blancs'.[79] Jabès found the argument convincing. However, the content and wording of the poem would not be rewritten. Rather, *Avec l'ombre* was to be discarded in its entirety. It was at this point that Jabès began to compose his *Chansons pour le repas de l'ogre.*[80] Another poem, 'Quatre Mystères actuels', which was also discarded save for several fragments incorporated into a later poem, dates from this period.[81] Neither project echoes *Avec l'ombre*.

A further indication of Jabès's lack of interest in Egyptian Surrealism and Surrealism in general is his involvement in the Groupement des amitiés françaises, which, with Henri and Raoul Curiel and several others, he helped to found in the autumn of 1944.[82] Amitiés françaises professed no overt political agenda but associated itself with France libre, Charles de Gaulle's government in exile active since June 1940.[83] The Alexandrian branch of the Amitiés françaises opened shortly afterwards, headed by the great comparatist René Etiemble, who began teaching French literature at Farouk University in Alexandria in 1944, and by Etiemble's colleague at the university, Hussein Faouzi, dean of the Faculty of Sciences.[84] In his inaugural lecture of November 1944, published in the *Revue du Caire* the following month, Léon Guichard, the organization's vice-president, insisted on the universality of the French people and the French language. He observed that when Paris was liberated from the Nazis, all free-thinking people, regardless of nationality, felt, in a sense, liberated.[85] One of the two honorary presidents, Aly Chamsi pasha, reflected that 'c'est à notre mer commune, la Méditerranée—ce vieux véhicule de civilisations si diverses—où tout est à la mesure de l'homme, notre mesure!' The Mediterranean, he believed, had nurtured the many affinities indissolubly binding France and Egypt.[86] It naturally followed that the two countries, whose cultural ties had been weakened by the war, should create a centre where 'ceux qui ont fait des séjours dans notre pays [i.e. France] retrouvent ici un peu de la France qu'ils ont aimée, et [...] ceux qui ne la connaissent pas apprennent un peu à la connaître. Nous voudrions faire de ce local un petit coin de France, intellectuel, artistique, moral.'[87] The group's board members included not only Egyptians and Frenchmen, but also individuals from local ethnic communities or foreign colonies. Perhaps unawares, Amitiés françaises would become a model of tolerance towards all media of artistic expression through its frequent art exhibitions, cinematic and theatrical evenings, poetry readings and lectures on society and culture.[88] The importance of the Groupement des amitiés françaises for Jabès is that it was a distinctly Franco-Egyptian organization, but was in no way associated with the Egyptian Surrealists. Furthermore, it adhered to no political agenda other than that of maintaining and strengthening the cultural ties between Egypt and France weakened during the war.

Before Amitiés françaises closed its doors for the last time, in 1956, Jabès's responsibilities included inviting literary personalities to lecture or participate in the group's cultural life. Three of them he singled out as having met through his initiative are the writer and sociologist Roger Caillois, who lectured on 'the death of literature' in December 1948[89] and on the role of play in society in February 1956;[90] the poet Philippe Soupault, who spoke in February 1949 on the foundations of Surrealism;[91] and the poet and painter Henri Michaux, who exhibited his watercolours there in February 1956.[92] The invitations were often supported by UNESCO, as in the cases of Caillois and Soupault. The great Egyptian novelist and intellectual Taha Hussein, who repeatedly drew the cultural ties between France and Egypt to the attention of French and Egyptian publics alike, was given a dinner in his honour in 1949.[93] Some writers were asked to visit Cairo but never did or were not able to; efforts to solicit a public reading sometimes failed. For instance, in his letter of 28 January 1948 to one of the founders of modern literature, Jabès asked Tristan Tzara to grace the Egyptian capital with his presence: 'Fidèle à la poésie et à vous-même, vous demeurez, mon cher Tzara, pour nous *un exemple*. [...] Avez-vous renoncé à l'Egypte?'[94] It must be added that in the same letter Jabès reminded Tristan Tzara that he had promised (during an earlier meeting in Paris) to publish a poem from 'A l'écoute des meurtres à venir' in the *Lettres françaises*. In June 1948 the poem, 'Ressource du sujet', appeared in the journal.[95] In the sense that Jabès represented Egypt to the French, then, Tzara had not abandoned the country.

Jabès himself gave several lectures under the auspices of Amitiés françaises, including two on Max Jacob (February and May 1945) and one each on Léon Paul Fargues (December 1947), Jean Grenier (1949) and Paul Eluard (1952). If these lectures helped to strengthen the cultural ties between Egypt and France, they also contributed to advancing his literary career. Pierre Seghers's visit to Cairo in May 1946 well illustrates this point. Jabès introduced the French Resistance poet and publisher to an audience at the Lycée français, explaining that his poetry was for both the French and the Egyptians a rare source of hope during the dark war years. It is not inaccurate to say that the lecture on Seghers was decisive in the formation of Jabès's attitude towards writing: it confirmed his belief, professed since at least early 1941 when the *Avec l'ombre* fragments were published, that literature must not be detached from the history unfolding around it, nor was the poet an autonomous spirit or a carefree bohemian, as he had felt before 1934 or 1935. The terrible loss of Max Jacob and others who died during the war might somehow be compensated through an intellectual commitment, which Seghers represented to the francophone public. It was a moment in which Jabès could affirm his devotion to the image of France.[96] For his own part, Seghers ruminated in his speech on the necessity of a 'poésie engagée'.[97] Shortly afterwards he spoke warmly to an Egyptian interviewer about the commitment of Amitiés françaises to his country and to its ideals, and he added that in the coming months he would publish a collection of Jabès's poems.[98] In fact, in October 1946 he included Jabès's 'Quatre Chansons' in his literary magazine *Poésie 46*,[99] and in January 1947 he published *Chansons pour le repas de l'ogre*.

In addition to the literary evenings at Amitiés françaises, Jabès also embarked on several publishing projects. The associations formed in the course of the break-up of magazines and journals such as *Un Effort* and *Art et liberté* were solidified in *La Part du sable*, founded by Jabès and Henein in the spring of 1947. Two issues of the journal were published (number one in February 1947 and number two in April 1950), both of which were supplemented by a series of short books.

The first number of *La Part du sable* published international writers including the Romanian Gherasim Luca, the Swede Arthur Lundvist and the Frenchman Henri Pastoureau, and was illustrated by Ramsès Younane and Fouad Kamil, both contributors to *Art et liberté*. Jabès's 'Le Fond de l'eau' appeared in this number and as a booklet the following month. That poem bears the trace of the beginnings of the development of certain themes which would preoccupy him in the mature poetry, namely, the desperate cry in the space of silence, and the question and its response:

> Je parle de toi
> Une foule répond
> Des fourmis sans voix sans cris
> Et pourtant
> le silence tue comme la mort
> le silence règne seul à naître
>
> Je parle de toi
> et tu n'es pas n'as jamais existé
> Tu réponds à mes questions.
>   (*Jbmd*, 77)

It is significant that this poem departs from Breton's Surrealism of the fantastic image—it is not a demonstration of automatic writing—but it nonetheless exhibits Paul Eluard's aesthetic concerns, which were characterized by lyricism, repetition and above all a longing desire for the other to whom he amorously addresses himself.

Given Henein's and Jabès's absorption in and adaptation of Surrealist projects (each in his own way), it is not impertinent to ask if *La Part du sable* was outwardly Surrealist. Or more accurately, how Surrealist was the journal? It is prudent to avoid declaring that it was or was not Surrealist since each contributor held his own view. The reader was notified that the illustrations, for example, were the result of 'travaux automatiques'. Georges Henein himself declared that Surrealism was 'le seul projet de morale moderne (sans croquis, sans chemins tracés, sans récompenses) qui n'ait pas eu à se dégager des attaches chrétiennes—qui ait pris naissance *en état de rupture acquise*. Ceci contrairement à la morale socialiste qui, à beaucoup d'égards, se borne à transposer les valeurs chrétiennes.'[100] But by 1947 Henein had become disenchanted with the movement, and he quickly broke ranks with Breton. At the heart of Henein's disappointment was the lack of collective activity since the end of the war. While Henein did not disagree in principle with the 'positions essentielles' of Surrealism, his abandonment of Surrealist collective action indicated his wish to pursue in a spirit of independence his own literary, artistic and political activities—a position quite similar to that which we have seen Jabès hold.

Between the late forties and early fifties, several booklets appeared under the imprint of *La Part du sable*. The line-up was extraordinary. Yves Bonnefoy's *Théâtre de Douve* and Jabès's *La Voix d'encre*, Jean Grenier's *Lexique* and Philippe Soupault's *Chansons*, Henein's *L'Incompatible* and Maurice Blanchard's *Le Monde qui nous entoure* all appeared in small editions for a discriminating readership. The second issue of the journal was published in April 1950 with contributions by Grenier ('Lettre sur le tabac'), Henri Michaux ('Tranches de savoir'), René Char and Yves Bonnefoy. This issue also contained Jabès's theatrical poem consisting of several voices and an echo (it is the first of several he would compose), 'Le Rocher de la solitude', which was republished in *La Clef de voûte* (1950) and still later in *Je bâtis ma demeure*.

In January 1953 Jabès's tribute to Paul Eluard also appeared through *La Part du sable*.[101] It is a respectful acknowledgement of his indebtedness to the poet. It consists of two verse poems, 'Paysages' and an untitled one, and excerpts from a prose poem that begins: 'La mort d'un poète est une tache d'encre sur le poème. Il faut laisser aux lettres désemparées, le temps d'émerger, au papier celui de boire toute l'ombre, afin de permettre aux mots, aux hommes, de confronter leur perte.'[102] The tribute was presented at an evening sponsored by Amitiés françaises in November 1952.

The hundred or so members of the audience in the hall that evening felt, in all probability, a measure of uncomfortable tension. Present was Henein, who gave his own eulogy to Eluard. It was not as kind-hearted as Jabès's. In fact, Henein stated baldly: 'Paul Eluard a failli être un très grand poète. [...] Pourtant, dans un monde sans merci, il est le porteur de tendresse,—celui qui a voulu abréger les distances humaines.'[103] His attenuated praise irritated Jabès. The bitter memory of the inaugural speech of Egyptian Surrealism, in which he brushed aside Max Jacob[104] while vaunting André Breton's revolution in poetry, surely returned to him. By late 1952 the two were at loggerheads. As was the case with Max Jacob, the value of Jabès's friend, this time Eluard, was publicly depreciated while Breton was placed at the top of the totem-pole (even though Henein had distanced himself from the movement). Jabès's eulogy and poems written in memory of Paul Eluard were his final appearance in his joint venture with Henein. To add to his disdain for Eluard, Henein refused to publish his text under that imprint, an inappropriate venue for an unoriginal (though, in Jabès's eyes, influential) poet. Rather, he published his catty homage in a relatively minor magazine, *L'Egypte nouvelle*.

After the Eluard evening, which marks the end of the active implantation of Surrealism in Egypt, Jabès and Henein no longer worked together. Their aesthetic differences left unresolved, they had little to do with one another. In 1955 they appeared together in Jean Grenier's dedication in *Lexique*,[105] and Henein briefly referred to Jabès in his 1956 essay 'L'apport d'Albert Cossery'.[106] Afterwards they were rarely seen in print together, although they remained associated in the minds of some critics well after Jabès's departure from Egypt.[107] What, then, should be retained from their collaboration? Perhaps, simply, the following quotation from the first number of *La Part du sable*, which tersely announces the ephemeral vocation of the journal: 'Pourquoi "la part du sable" enfin? A cause de cette matière qui est en nous avant que d'être dans la nature, à la fois apaisante et égarante, conductrice et dislocatrice, plage où l'on aborde et piste déjà effacée.'

Notes to Chapter 2

1. Moscatelli recounted the story of their remarkable journey in 'Pégase 6 cylindres: pages détachées d'un cahier de route', *Sé* 31–2 (1934), 7–8, excerpts of which are discussed in Steven Jaron, 'L'amitié comme "éphémères retrouvailles"', *Portrait(s)*, 68–77.
2. *Au* 4 (1930), 39. The reviewer is not named, but is very likely to have been Edmond Jabès since he would have been the only writer for *Au* familiar with the Cairene poets, his brother Henri being more knowledgeable in theatre and Alexandre Mercereau in contemporary French letters. Furthermore, he was the magazine's Egyptian correspondent.
3. Jean Moscatelli, *Sé* 6–7 (1932), 13.
4. Moscatelli published an open letter entitled 'Pour GOHA le Simple', *Sé* 11–12 (1934), 31, in which he mentions his review of *Pa* from the pages of the magazine *Goha*. Unfortunately, a copy of that particular issue of *Goha* has never been located.
5. Jean Moscatelli, *Sé* 7–8 (1935), 15.
6. See Fenoglio, 'L'activité culturelle francophone au Caire' and in particular the appendix, 'Principales créations d'associations et d'organes de presse', 493–6.
7. Luthi, *Introduction à la littérature d'expression française en Egypte*, 83, and Lançon, *Jabès*, 94.
8. In addition to Moscatelli's reviews in *Sé* referred to above, Adolf Shual reviewed *Is* and 'Maman' in its pages in Nov. 1930 and Oct. 1932 respectively.
9. Adolf Shual, *Sé* 45–6 (1930), 20.

10. Jean Moscatelli, *Sé* 6–7 (1932), 13.
11. Jabès, 'Apport à la poésie: le Logisme', 3.
12. Ibid.
13. Ibid. 4.
14. Ibid.
15. Ibid.
16. Fernand Divoire was the author of *Stratégie littéraire* (Paris, 1928). Alexandre Mercereau of the *Au* wrote favourably of him ('Fernand Divoire') in issue 6 (30 Apr. 1930) of that magazine, and it seems probable that Jabès first came across him in its pages.
17. Jabès, 'Apport à la poésie: le Logisme', 4.
18. Ibid. 5.
19. Ibid. 6.
20. Seiffoula, 'L'apport poétique de M Edmond Jabès: "Le Logisme"', *Sé* 31–2 (1932), 12–13.
21. Ibid. 12.
22. Did Jabès have this incident in mind when he wrote, in · (*El*) (1973): 'Privé d'R, la mort meurt d'asphyxie dans le mot' (*LQ* II, 497)? If he did, he was surely not doing so with any conscious wish to take revenge on his critic; the event was forgotten, but its trace seems to have remained operative in his unconscious.
23. Seiffoula, 'L'apport poétique de M Edmond Jabès: "Le Logisme"', 12–13.
24. In his untitled review of Ahmed Rassim's *L'Ermite de l'Attaka, poème* (*Sé* 11–12 (1941), 18), Jabès wrote that 'la manière est proche de celle de Philippe Soupault et des poètes arabes ensemble'. See also Jean B. Vivante, 'Ahmed Rassim ou des résonances particulières de la langue française exprimant une pensée étrangère', *Sé* 19–20 (1942), 20–1, and the homage volume, 'Ahmed Rassim, poète arabe de langue française', *La Revue du Caire* (1959), 224–5.
25. Monsieur l'Archiviste, 'Une lettre à propos de l'apport poétique de M Ed. Jabès', *Sé* 33–4 (1932), 12.
26. Edmond Jabès, 'Réalités logistes' followed by 'Films inflammables', *Sé* 35–6 (1932), 9–10.
27. Edmond Haraucourt, 'Epithalame', *Au* 8 (1930), 1.
28. See Ch. 5, 'On Not Belonging'.
29. Jabès quotes from Marcel Arland's article in the *NRF* (1 May 1927), 429, in which Arland quotes Ravel.
30. Richet knew Jabès's first book of verse, as his praise in *Au* 9 (1930), 1, attests. Jabès is quoting from his article 'Les deux visages de l'ennui', *Revue des Deux Mondes* (15 July 1932), 313–24.
31. Jabès, 'Réalités logistes', 9.
32. See below.
33. Jabès, 'Réalités logistes', 9.
34. Ibid. 10.
35. Ibid. The still-born poet as which Jabès characterized himself reappears, at the end of the 1960s, as Yaël's still-born child. In *Elya* (1969), he seems to have challenged his readers to return to his very early writings: '*(On ne pourra jamais faire le tour de mon œuvre et si, un jour, on y parvenait, on verrait qu'un enfant mort-né en fut l'appât et le silence)*' (*LQ* II, 262–3). Cf. 'Née viable' (*LR*, 251–3).

36. Didier Cahen has noted that this poem was in fact the first authored by Jabès at the age of 16. See his 'Ecrire sa vie', ed. Jaron, *Portrait(s)*, 25. If it is so, then Jabès withheld its publication until 1932, when he was 20 years old.

37. Adolf Shual, *Sé* 41–2 (1932), 16: 'Ces courts poèmes, en vers libres, marquent un progrès sensible, sur les œuvres précédentes d'Edmond Jabès.'

38. Nonetheless, the belated Egyptian Romanticism that many found acceptable in the 1930s was deemed unacceptable by others during the next decade. Daniel Lançon kindly showed me an open letter, 'A la recherche d'un romantisme attardé', *Pé* (30 Nov. 1942), 2, signed by 'Yamile', which parodies the Romanticism of Jabès's early books: 'En écrivant ceci, je pense surtout à Monsieur Edmond. L'autre jour, je découvris par hasard ses *Confidences amoureuses*'. The title is a play on *Is*, and 'Monsieur Edmond' is Jabès.

39. Adolf Shual, *I* (29 Mar. 1934), 3.

40. 'Ed. Jabès vu par Zeinab', *Sé* 29–30 (1934), 22.

41. R. Harlong, *Gringoire* 287 (1934), 4.

42. Hector Klat, 'Cèdres', *Sé* 29–30 (1934), 2.

43. Adolf Shual, *I* (4 Apr. 1935), 5.

44. Jean Moscatelli, 'Notes italiennes', in Raoul Parme and Ivo Barbitch (eds.), *Calligrammes: art, science, littérature* 1/4–6 (1936), (n.p.): 'le plus grand écrivain de l'ère fasciste ce n'est rien moins que Benito Mussolini'. The cover reproduces the *fascio* medallion. Other contributors include Raoul Parme, Etienne Mériel, Robert Blum, Giuseppe Ungaretti, Arsène Yergath, F. T. Marinetti and Fausta Terni-Cialente. Jabès did not contribute. If Jabès renounced Futurism owing to its association with Fascism, how are we to explain his dedicating to Marinetti his two most recent books, *Pa* and *Ap*, in Apr. 1935? A possible explanation would be Jabès's wish to implant himself within the movements of the European avant-garde, and by offering his books to Marinetti he was hoping to achieve this. For the dedications, see Roger E. Stoddard, *Edmond Jabès in Bibliography*, 29–30. Both books are in the Marinetti archives in the Beinecke Rare Book and Manuscript Library of Yale University.

45. *Un Effort* 59 (1936), 22.

46. Susan Zuccotti, *The Italians and the Holocaust: Persecution, Rescue, and Survival*, intro. by Furio Colombo (Lincoln, Nebraska and London: University of Nebraska Press, 1996), 32–3.

47. Edmond Jabès, 'A mes amis grecs', *Sé* 21–2 (1941), 7. Jabès signed and dated the letter as a member of the 'Comité des groupes d'action antifasciste et italiens libres, Le Caire, le 5 Octobre 1941'.

48. With facing Arabic translation by Habib Jamati (Cairo: Aldebarah, 1952). See also Aimé Azar, 'Jean Moscatelli, poète de l'incertitude a-t-il ému le lecteur oriental?', *L'Egypte nouvelle* 429 (1952), 315–17.

49. Quoted from the catalogue to Jean Degottex's 1985 exhibition, collected in Edmond Jabès, *Un Regard*, pref. by Jean Frémon (Montpellier: Fata Morgana, 1992), 61.

50. Ibid.

51. Saint-Chéron, 'Entretien avec Edmond Jabès', 67.

52. Interview with Raymond Aghion (Paris, 25 Oct. 1994).

53. Magdi Wahba (ed.), *Hommage à Georges Henein* (Cairo: La Part du sable, 1974).

54. André de Laumois, 'Chez les Essayistes: le cénacle qui devient un club', *Bé* (7 Dec. 1934), 2. Henein retorted with 'André de Laumois' in *Un Effort* 38 (1934), 5–6.

55. Jean Moscatelli, *Sé* 15–16 (1935), 18.

56. Sarane Alexandrian, *Georges Henein* (Paris: Pierre Seghers, 1981), 17. Henein's letters to Breton, excepting those in Alexandrian's book, remain unpublished. They are in the Bibliothèque littéraire Jacques Doucet. I am grateful to Berto Farhi, Aube Elléouët and the late Elisa Breton for permission to consult them.

57. Mayo's cover illustration of *Sé* 35–6 (1933) advertises his forthcoming exhibition in Dec. 1933 in Ismailia. More than twenty years later he exhibited at Amitiés françaises. See *Bé* of 30 Apr. 1956 and *Pé* of 7 Apr. 1956 for reviews of that exhibition. Mayo further contributed four drawings to illustrate the poems of Jabès's *Pa*.

58. Henein's lecture was published in the *Revue des conférences françaises en Orient* 8 (1937), 645–54. It is reprinted in *Pleine Marge* 24 (1996), 131–48. Quotations are from this edition.

59. Ibid. 143–4.

60. This phrase comes from Jabès's untitled review essay of Paul Eluard's *Les Yeux fertiles* (Paris: Guy Lévis Mano, 1936), Philippe Soupault's *Poésie complètes, 1917–1937* (Paris: Guy Lévis Mano, 1937) and Max Jacob's *Morceaux choisis* (Paris: Gallimard, 1936) in *Sé* 3–4, (1938), 27.

61. Albert Hourani in reference to the writer Taha Hussein. See his *Arabic Thought in the Liberal Age, 1789–1938* (Cambridge: Cambridge University Press, 1983), 327.

62. See Jean-Jacques Luthi, 'Le mouvement surréaliste en Egypte', in *Mélusine* 3 (1980), 18–35; and Jaron, 'Une voix effacée d'une province limitrophe', 145–8.

63. The founding statement, printed anonymously, appeared in *Clé* 2 (1939), 12. The following month, the bulletin of *Art et liberté* 1 (1939) listed the membership.

64. Badr Eddain Abou Ghazi, *Ramsès Younane* (Cairo: Organisation égyptienne générale du livre, 1978), n.p.

65. The *Pé* articles include: 'Ahmed Rassim, poète d'Egypte et d'ailleurs' (3 Feb. 1941), 6; 'Arsène Yergath ou la magie d'enfance' (10 Feb. 1941), 2; and 'Georges Henein' (24 Mar. 1941), 5.

66. *Pé* (10 Mar. 1941), 7.

67. Ibid.

68. Quoted from Marcel Raymond, *De Baudelaire au surréalisme*, 329. My emphasis.

69. Henri Soulon, 'Jules Supervielle', *Revue du Caire* 19 (1940), 130.

70. Ibid. 131.

71. Barbitch, 'Edmond Jabès ou la recherche de l'humain', 7. The full *Avec l'ombre* and 'Sens de l'ombre' (see further below) fragments have been republished by Daniel Lançon in his *Jabès*, 11–17.

72. Ibid.

73. Ibid.

74. 'Un autre désert, le ciel' and 'Je veux entendre ce que tu vois', *Le Nil* (13 Jan. 1938), 8; and 'Seul l'aveugle prend garde' and 'Richesse qui m'est due', *Le Nil* (25 Jan. 1938), 8.

75. Max Jacob's advice, 'Descends! le ciel est en bas!', must have struck a special chord. Jabès quotes it more than twenty years later in his letter to Michel Leiris

of 4 June 1961 (in the Bibliothèque littéraire Jacques Doucet [série ms. ms 43.517]), published in Jaron, 'Repiquage poétique', 127–8.

76. *Le Nil* (13 Jan. 1938), 8.

77. Barbitch, 'Edmond Jabès ou la recherche de l'humain'.

78. See Krämer, *The Jews in Modern Egypt*, 156–7. The Central Zionist Archive, Jerusalem, file S6/3840 (13 July 1942) preserves a list of Egypt's Jewish activists to be evacuated in the possible event of a Nazi attack on Cairo and other large cities. It does *not* include Edmond Jabès or Raymond Aghion. Jabès's uncle, Umberto Jabès, is listed.

79. 'Propos d'Edmond Jabès: Paris, Tel-Aviv, Jérusalem, Sdeh Boker', [3]: 'Les "blancs", ceux qu'on appelait les étrangers, les "blancs" étaient toujours considérés comme pas tout à fait intégrés'.

80. Interview with Raymond Aghion (Paris, 25 Oct. 1994).

81. The poem, dated '1941–1943', appeared in Paul Eluard's journal *L'Eternelle Revue* 5–6 (1945), 95–7. Parts of the poem were rewritten into 'Spectacle' from *Les Mots tracent* (1951).

82. Raoul Curiel, *Bé* (19 Oct. 1944), 2, and Lançon, *Jabès*, 165–9.

83. For Henri Curiel's involvement, see Gilles Perrault, *Un homme à part* (Paris: Barrault, 1984), 108–9.

84. Stratis Tsirkas, 'Etiemble en Alexandrie (1944–1948) ou un homme des lumières dans la ville de Cavafy', in *Le Mythe d'Etiemble: hommages, études et recherches* (Paris: Didier Erudition, 1979), 276.

85. Léon Guichard, *Revue du Caire* 73 (1944), 166.

86. Ibid. 169.

87. Ibid. 168. For Jabès's recollections, see *Dl*, 38–9.

88. Ananias, 'Lettre d'Egypte', *Cahiers du sud* 322 (1954), n.p.

89. R. H., 'Mort de la littérature: la thèse de M. Roger Caillois', *Bé* (14 Dec. 1948).

90. E. C., 'Aux Amitiés françaises: "les jeux, miroir de l'homme et de la société"', *Bé* (25 Feb. 1956).

91. R. H., 'Une introduction à la lecture de "Maldoror"', *Bé* (25 Feb. 1949); and R. H., 'Les confidences d'un poète: une interview de Philippe Soupault', *Bé* (22 Feb. 1949).

92. S. G., 'Aux Amitiés françaises: hommage à Henri Michaux', *Pé* (11 Feb. 1956).

93. See, e.g., Hussein's 'France-Egypte', *Lettres françaises* 117 (1946), 5; and R. H., 'Aux Amitiés françaises: émouvant hommage au Dr Taha Hussein Bey', *Bé* (19 May 1949).

94. The letter is preserved in the Bibliothèque littéraire Jacques Doucet (TZR.C. 2.134) and is reproduced in Jaron, 'Repiquage poétique', 115–16. See n. 95 below.

95. *Lettres françaises* 211 (1948), 5. 'A l'écoute des meurtres à venir' seems to have been lost. 'Ressource du sujet', the poem from which it was apparently excerpted, was not collected in *Jbmd* but appeared (without its title) in *Le Livre de Yukel* in 1964 (*LQ* I, 221–2). A discussion of the evolution of this text appears in Jaron, 'Repiquage poétique', 115–18.

96. Edmond Jabès, 'En l'honneur de Pierre Seghers', *Sé* 15–16 (1946), 11.

97. The text of Seghers's speech was reproduced in the *Revue des conférences françaises en Orient* 10 (1946).

98. *L'Egypte nouvelle* 113 (1946), 12–13.

99. *Poésie 46* 33 (1946), 58–61.
100. *La Part du sable* 1 (1947), n.p.
101. Republished as '"La mort d'un poète est une tache d'encre sur le poème"' in Jaron (ed.), *Portrait(s)*, 10–15.
102. Ibid. 11.
103. Georges Henein, 'Paul Eluard et le surréalisme', *L'Egypte nouvelle* 447 (1953), 62.
104. Henein, 'Bilan du mouvement surréaliste', 144.
105. In the Gallimard edition. The dedication to this edition reads: 'à Edmond Jabès et Georges Henein/en souvenir reconnaissant.'
106. Georges Henein, 'L'apport d'Albert Cossery', in Raoul Parme (ed.), *Calligrammes: almanach des lettres et des arts en Egypte, 1956* (Cairo: Anis Abu Fadil, 1956), 18.
107. See, e.g., Marcel Lecomte's review of Henein's *Seuil interdit* (1956) and Jabès's *Je bâtis ma demeure* in *Le Journal des poètes* 3 (1960), 3.

CHAPTER 3

'La Patrie de l'humain'

Max Jacob, Suffering and Writing

Max Jacob (Quimper, 1876–Drancy, 1944), more than any other writer before the war, worked with Edmond Jabès to cultivate the skills necessary for composing poetry worthy of the name. And his long-term influence was far greater than that of any other, including Jean Moscatelli and Georges Henein. The difference is explained by Jabès's particular filiation with Max Jacob, a filiation that the critical literature on Jabès (and Max Jacob) has not examined in any detail. Nevertheless, there exists today sufficient material to allow, as was the case with Moscatelli and Henein, a more satisfactory reconstruction of their working relationship and, more to the point, a better understanding of its meaning for Jabès. In the second part of this chapter, Jabès's friendship with Gabriel Bounoure will also be assessed.

Edmond Jabès acknowledged his debt to the poet of the *Cornet à dés* throughout his life. The most moving avowal appears in the third, definitive edition of *Chansons pour le repas de l'ogre*, published in the second (1975) edition of *Je bâtis ma demeure*; in other words, after the seven-volume cycle of *Le Livre des Questions*, where questions of Jewish suffering across the centuries and in the previous century are paramount, had been completed:

> *A la mémoire de Max Jacob*
> ... parce qu'il y a peut-être une
> chanson liée à l'enfance qui, aux
> heures les plus sanglantes, toute
> seule défit le malheur et la mort.
> (*Jbmd*, 29)

The dedication is a memorial, an epigraph to a martyr. It is suffused with idealism: perhaps there is a song connected to childhood that might overcome the spectre of death.[1] Max Jacob repeatedly insisted on the centrality of religion in one's life—he once wrote to Jabès: 'Retourne à la foi de tes pères à laquelle tu dois d'exister encore comme race royale' (8 December 1938, *LEJ*, 75). The 'chanson liée à l'enfance' in Jabès's dedication would thus seem to indicate Judaism, the Judaism of both his and Max Jacob's childhood. In the 1988 preface to the *Lettres à Edmond Jabès*, Jabès reflected: 'Nous étions frères d'origine; compagnons de route, de vie et de mort' (*LEJ*, 18), and further: 'Tu avais raison. Dieu est bon. [...] Même pour qui n'y croit pas' (*LEJ*, 20).

In an interview with the American novelist Paul Auster, Edmond Jabès admitted that 'my first guide was Max Jacob'.[2] Once again in the new preface (1988) to Max Jacob's letters, he indicated that upon rereading them he was transported to that 'époque confuse où j'obéissais à des voix étrangères, où j'étais à l'écoute de ma propre voix', but that 'Max a guidé mes premiers pas sur la route qui ne mène nulle part mais que les mots tracent' (*LEJ*, 17 ff.). In the first volume of *Le Livre des Questions* he had reiterated his debt:

> Reb Jacob, qui fut mon premier maître, croyait à la vertu du mensonge parce que—disait-il—il n'y a pas d'écriture sans mensonge et que l'écriture est le chemin de Dieu.
>
> Reb Jacob croyait aussi à l'emphase qu'il comparait à la déchirure, avec ses faux anneaux d'eau, que fait la pierre tombée dans l'étang. La blessure se referme aussitôt. Ce sont les anneaux qui se reproduisent en s'agrandissant et qui témoignent—ô dérision—de l'ampleur du mal. (*LQ* I, 96)[3]

A certain Reb Jacob, associated with a 'parole divine' which is 'tuée aussitôt prononcée', is said to be the first master of the protagonist, Yukel Serafi, himself a writer. The statement is striking because the poet-rabbis who people *Le Livre des Questions* are said to be imaginary,[4] and yet, given the similarity to Jabès's later statements, Reb Jacob could only refer to Max Jacob.

Analysis of the earliest manuscripts of the book, in the Bibliothèque nationale de France, suggests that the name of Yukel Serafi is derived from Max Jacob's. True, Yukel's biography, insofar as it can be reconstructed, bears at least two important similarities with Jabès's and not Jacob's: both come from Egypt, and both spent the war years outside the immediate zone of conflict. In part, then, Yukel is his author's fictional double. But the BNF fragments suggest a different story. Dated to the late 1950s or at latest to the very early 1960s, they do not contain the name Yukel; 'Jacques' appears in its place. 'Yacob'

(Jacob) is Hebrew for 'Jacques', and 'Yukel' is, phonetically, an intermediary form between French and Hebrew ([y] substituting for [j]; [k] for [cq]). According to mystical tradition, a *seraph* is a burning angel, and the suffix [i] in Hebrew denotes the first person singular possessive pronoun. 'Serafi' would translate, from Hebrew into English via French, as 'my angel who burns', and the proper name of Jabès's protagonist would mean 'Jacob, my burning angel'.[5]

Jabès described his discovery of Max Jacob as 'une révélation, mais lente' (*Dl*, 28). He recognized that he was unprepared to grasp the serious meaning of his poems lurking behind the verbal disruptions and humour. Max Jacob further nurtured in the young Jabès a secure sense of independence from the artistic trends of the period. Surrealism, as we saw in the previous chapter, was the most fruitful literary and artistic trend in Cairo from the mid-1930s. Jabès admitted that he was prepared to approach the Surrealist fold at precisely that time—that is to say, during the years he composed 'L'Obscurité potable' and *Avec l'ombre*—'au moment, où, déjà, des scissions importantes avaient miné le mouvement' (*Dl*, 31). Likewise, Max Jacob was never a Surrealist. Had he aspired to join their ranks, which he did not, his Catholic faith would not have been tolerated.

Jabès's interest in Max Jacob is already obvious in 'Apport à la poésie: le Logisme' of May 1932;[6] but the more wholesome 'Maman', published later that year, bears no resemblance to Max Jacob's cubist poetry. Nonetheless it appears that Jabès met Jacob as early as 1930, through Cocteau (*LEJ*, 7). *Les Pieds en l'air*, to which Max Jacob supplied the preface (dated December 1933), is distinctly Jacobesque in its range of humour and aloofness, and in its use of the pun. The book, published in Cairo in 1934, contains poems that had appeared in *La Semaine égyptienne* as early as March 1932;[7] a mixture of styles and influences, not uncommon among the juvenile compositions, is quickly discerned. Furthermore, Jabès gave lectures and wrote critical essays on Max Jacob in the 1930s. In October 1935, the poet thanked him for one of his lectures, but that one is now lost (2 October 1935, *LEJ*, 39).[8] A single prose text by Jabès dating from Max Jacob's lifetime survives; it is a 1938 review of his *Morceaux choisis* (1937) and forms part of an essay on Paul Eluard's *Les Yeux fertiles* and Philippe Soupault's *Poésies complètes*, and it invites Egyptian readers to consider this neglected yet (in Jabès's view) important French poet.[9] Jabès quotes a recent letter from Max Jacob: 'L'avenir est à une poésie grave.

Nous vivons une époque grave qui veut qu'on lui parle son langage. A nous de ne pas être ennuyeux.' 'Ne pas être ennuyeux, voilà toute sa politique,' Jabès adds. Max Jacob's difficult salmagundi—his multisided playfulness and seriousness, his choice of spiritual and banal subjects—is a consequence of this 'policy' of avoiding terrestrial boredom: 'Mon Dieu l'affaire de la pomme,/Max est pêcheur, Max est un homme.' Jabès's attraction to Max Jacob was due to the latter's genius at deflating the solemnity of religious expression while retaining its dignity. 'Puisque Christ est un fruit et sa poutre un pressoir', quotes Jabès once more. Jabès's Egyptian readers might view the poetry of Max Jacob, who is placed in the company of Guillaume Apollinaire and André Salmon, in a similar light.

Their friendship is best revealed in the letters Max Jacob sent to Jabès between December 1933 and May 1939, collected in *Lettres à Edmond Jabès* and published posthumously in 1945 by Etiemble. They received several press notices, in Egypt and France, each of which accurately describes their significance to contemporary readers. In September 1945, the Egyptian literary and art critic Etienne Mériel explained to readers of the *Progrès égyptien* that Jabès had entered into a correspondence with Max Jacob in order to learn how to 'laisser à l'imagination toute la liberté de ses jeux'.[10] Mériel suggested that the letters be read beside Max Jacob's *Conseils à un jeune poète*, a notebook written during the last few years of his life to further the education in poetry of a young medical student identified as J. E. In April 1946, from Paris, the anonymous reviewer in *Fontaine* said that the letters were 'd'autres *Lettres à un jeune poète*'.[11] Both reviews underscored the emergent 'art of poetry' described in the letters.

In contrast to these reviews, F. Talva, writing in the *Semaine égyptienne* in December 1945, emphasized the spirituality of the last letters. Those dated between 1933 and 1936 exhibited the ludic sensibility for which Max Jacob is most often remembered, but the light tone changes after 1936, the year he took up full-time residence in the abbey of Saint-Benoît to live a semi-reclusive life of meditation, writing and painting. Max Jacob's faith interested Talva less than his sincerity and his conviction, his withdrawal from the world and his humility. Readers might think they observed a contrast between his life at Saint-Benoît and the one he led in the Montmartre of the earlier part of the century. They would be wrong, Talva suggested, because even at that time his nature was filled with 'cette même simplicité naïve, presque puérile'.[12] Talva added that the letters might have been called 'Lettres à un ami' because a master or teacher does not speak to his student with such respectful candour or deference. The parity of the two poets is not to be missed. On the one hand, their relation was understood as pedagogical; on the other, the letters attested to a firm friendship.

Jabès visited Max Jacob in Paris in June 1935 at his apartment at 17, rue Saint-Romain. Jacob was certainly susceptible to the younger poet's naïve charm. Jabès had sent him two essays (neither of which has been located) as a pretext for the visit, during which he was taken with the mixture of gravity and humour that so many contemporaries found intriguing. Eagerly he awaited the master's judgement. The great poet looked one of the texts over, and asked Jabès to come back the following day for a detailed commentary. The next day Jabès excitedly returned believing he would receive the finest reading to date of his work. The meeting was hardly what he had in mind. He recollected to Marcel Cohen how the poet seemed more interested in his horoscope, and that of his wife, than in his poetry: 'Au-dessus de sa table, des thèmes astraux fixés au mur. Il commença par m'interroger sur ma femme. A brûle-pourpoint il me demanda sa date de naissance. Connaissant la mienne, il voulait dresser notre thème commun' (*DL*, 29). But then he turned to a manuscript of poems Jabès had sent him earlier. Again, he was astonished by Max Jacob's reaction to it. 'Je l'ai bien lu,' Jabès recalled him saying, 'et, si tu le permets, je vais maintenant le déchirer pour que nous puissions en parler plus librement.' The manuscript was duly torn up and thrown into the waste-paper basket. 'C'est excellent,' the poet assured the young man, 'mais ce n'est pas toi. Tu m'imites et j'ai fait mon temps.' Now they could talk freely about poetry. 'Durant une heure et demie', Jabès related, 'il me donna la plus extraordinaire leçon de poésie. En substance, il me poussait à avoir le courage d'être moi-même, en dehors de toute mode. Il m'incitait aussi à briser les idoles et, notamment, à rencontrer Eluard—alors que les surréalistes vomissaient Max—pour mieux venir à bout d'une proximité qu'il devinait dans mes textes' (*Dl*, 29). Despite the unexpected 'close reading', Max Jacob was encouraging. After that first visit he sent Jabès a note of thanks for a 'petit volume si magnifiquement édité'— a reference to his *Arrhes poétiques*, which appeared in the spring of 1935. 'Il est comme une preuve de votre riche sensibilité et une promesse d'une grande production future' (June 1935, *LEJ*, 34–5).

The letters to Jabès are particularly important to our understanding of Jabès's perceptions of Cairo and Paris. To the young Jabès, Paris represented poetry, and modern poetry in particular. In 1934, the year before he married, he rented a two-room apartment in a building, then known as the Maison des Artistes, in a small street in the old Muslim quarter of Cairo known as the *Darb el Labbanah* ('The Milky Way'), situated between the Sultan Hussan and Ar-Rifa'i mosques and the great monument of Ottoman architecture, the Citadel. The Maison des Artistes lodged part of Cairo's bohemian set, the poets and painters who longed more for Paris's Montparnasse than for Cairo's cotton exchange. Jean Moscatelli gave a contemporary description of it, noting:

cette maison est silencieuse; mais de combien de rumeurs est fait son silence! Je les perçois mieux dans le calme où je m'emmure, comme si de n'entendre plus le brouhaha des quartiers populeux, il m'était donné d'écouter, des gens et des choses, les seuls bruits qui participent à la vie essentielle. Ils vibrent dans l'air muet en le ridant à peine. Leurs sons n'éveillent pas l'oreille assoupie. Et la solitude continue.[13]

In 1984, Jabès reflected that he too had gone there in order to take refuge from the hustle and bustle of downtown commercial life. The *Madinat el Moquattam* ('City of the Dead'), nearby, was for him a 'spectacle d'immense désolation, de ruines, la nuit surtout, au clair de lune; on était pris à la gorge. Jamais le néant ne m'avait semblé plus proche, un néant bâti sur le néant.'[14]

   Jabès wrote excitedly to Max Jacob about the *Darb el Labbanah*, the local Montparnasse. Jacob was uninterested in hearing how that corner of Paris had been refashioned in Cairo. He hoped that Jabès might appreciate Egypt not for what it lacked, but for what it so richly possessed. 'Le vrai désert d'Egypte avec chameaux et cætera est Montparnasse,' went Jacob's response of April 1935. 'Il n'y a pas d'Egypte, il n'y a pas Paris. Il y a "vous" qui êtes un peu plus qu'un espoir et même bien plus qu'un peu (à développer)' (3 or 4 April 1935, *LEJ*, 28). This advice to the aspiring poet would be among the first lessons he learned from the master, namely, not to look towards the glittering foreign country of France nor even at the monumental Pharaonic architecture of Egypt, but within himself (the inexhaustible wellspring of truth) for his poetic inspiration. It was a gentle push towards creative independence from the debilitating fantasy that Paris could be recreated in Cairo.

   Just as Edmond Jabès worked to have Max Jacob read more widely in Egypt, so too did he hope that he would promote his poetry in

Paris. He did not hesitate to ask his French correspondent if he might know of someone who could publish some of his poems. Was the request presumptuous? Max Jacob replied, on 4 June 1936: 'Tu *m'offenses cruellement* en me prenant pour un bureau de placements' (*LEJ*, 46; Max Jacob's emphasis). Nevertheless, he graciously sent some of the poems to Jean Fraysse, a friend and the editor of *Les Feux de Paris* (*LEJ*, 47). Even though the journal was printed by Guy Lévis Mano, one of the greatest publishers of private press poetry in France at the time, it did not last long; it saw but eight issues between 1935 and 1937, and then folded. Jabès's poems were nonetheless circulated and eventually noticed by Lévis Mano, the publisher of 'L'Obscurité potable'. Thus the young Egyptian was placed in the company of, among others, Philippe Soupault and Paul Eluard, both published by GLM that year.

In addition to deepening our knowledge of how Jabès perceived the Cairene cultural scene and to revealing the network by which he advanced his career abroad, Max Jacob's letters are important to our understanding of Jabès's earliest poems because they contain several comments on their composition. On reading his very early poetry, Max Jacob immediately apprehended its manifest indebtedness to earlier and contemporary masters such as Mallarmé or Apollinaire (to say nothing of Max Jacob himself). For Max Jacob, the great pre-decessors were not to be mimicked; rather, they were to be studied carefully. But it was Jabès's poetry itself that counted most. From time to time Max Jacob quotes from a poem only to offer better phrasing:

> Un poème est une orfèvrerie: la passion n'est pas le but, elle est un moyen! plus elle est contenue, plus elle anime. Un chien qui gratte un paillasson ne fait pas une peinture avec la poussière qu'il lève! Le désordre ne signifie que le désordre.
> Je vous montre une voie:
> Au lieu de commencer par: Baisers allô! j'aurais commencé par:
> ô perfection de l'amour, escarpins...
> pour annoncer le sujet.
> j'aurais mis ensuite le décor 'Arc en ciel' puis la maison, puis les bras, puis les baisers.
> (Undated letter but most likely from the summer of 1935, *LEJ*, 31–2)

He continues his critique by suggesting Jabès read Apollinaire, 'notre seul grand poète, au sujet des voyelles, des consonnes, des diphtongues' (*LEJ*, 32). But in another letter, on the subject of imitation, he tells him to avoid 'le vieux futurisme apollinarien'. Max

Jacob wished to indicate to Jabès how poetry ought to be crafted: 'Je vais te donner un bon conseil: fais des phrases en vrai, c'est dans la syntaxe que se *révèle l'individu*. Si tu n'as pas de "*forme*" de phrases dans la tête, prends-en dans Shakespeare ou bien là où il y en a: dialogues d'Aristophane' (undated though probably from late summer/early autumn 1935, *LEJ*, 37; Max Jacob's emphasis). Elsewhere he suggested that Jabès analyse Chateaubriand's prose 'pour voir comment on écrit bien avec le mot propre et comment on voit le monde de haut et de loin avec intelligence'. The object of the criticism was to bring Jabès closer to his own emerging aesthetic. 'O toi', he continued, 'qui as toutes les possibilités acquises la grandeur [*sic*] et sache que l'originalité on l'a en soi et que nous ne devons l'un ni l'autre la cultiver, ça y est ou ça n'y est pas. Tu l'as' (9 January 1937, *LEJ*, 52). The encouraging tone did not deter Max Jacob from presenting a more blunt comment: 'Tu t'évades par la fenêtre lyrique et j'attendais ce moment. Tu t'évades en creux, en bosse, en ombre, en lumière et pourtant tu restes dedans, dans le puits de la vérité. Le puits de la vérité est toute une esthétique. Tu as découvert le puits; ce puits est l'Amour' (13 February 1937, *LEJ*, 55).

After half a decade of false starts, Max Jacob himself believed that Jabès had attained a more sophisticated level of expression. Not that Jabès had matured entirely. Still, 'L'Obscurité potable' was a poem of beauty and depth. In early February 1937 Jabès sent him a copy,[15] and the master complimented him most subtly in a letter of 13 February 1937, which begins:

Là où il y a la *profondeur insondable*, je veux dire la parole qui vient des entrailles mêmes de l'homme, il y a la beauté. Ailleurs il n'y a que bibelots d'art. Cette profondeur ne peut venir que de la conviction de l'amour ou de la haine. C'est l'émotion réelle—ah oui réelle—qui donne la profondeur de l'accent et donc la beauté. Profite donc de ce que tu es amoureux pour écrire. Oui, cette fois ça y est, c'est de la poésie. (*LEJ*, 54–5; my emphasis)

Beneath the 'profondeur insondable' Max Jacob writes of there is certainly an echo of the title of Jabès's book, 'L'Obscurité potable'. But if we did not have the copy Jabès had signed over to his friend, dated only days before Max Jacob's letter, it would not be likely that we could grasp the play on words.

Until recently, it appeared that all Jabès's correspondence with Max Jacob had been lost; Jabès's letters are not reproduced in the first two editions of the *Lettres*, and it seemed that all searches for them would yield nothing. We are fortunate that at least one letter did survive. We owe the survival of the poem-letter to its having been kept, in all likelihood, with the dedicated copy of 'L'Obscurité potable'. Jabès's letter to Max Jacob is dated 4 February 1937 and it was written, as Jacob commented in his reply to him on 13 February 1937, in a mixture of verse and prose (*LEJ*, 55). Jabès recalls in his letter that Max Jacob had moved to the relative seclusion, conducive to spiritual meditation, of the abbey of Saint-Benoît in the Loire valley:

> Et pourquoi pas?
> Tu es heureux à St.-Benoît
> Je pousse, ici, ma première vie.
> Tu n'as pas d'âge et j'ai des ans.[16]

It is striking that the style here does not in the least resemble 'L'Obscurité potable', whose moderate Surrealism, which exudes a mellow beauty, contrasts with the brash rhymed couplets of the poem-letter:

> Je tente une chance en escomptant
> je plonge un œil dans le mystère.
> Si je m'éveille en m'endormant
> Je fais d'un doigt tourner la terre.

The poem-letter reveals a different voice—a still-developing voice —that in itself is of little stylistic merit. Perhaps its greatest value emerges when it is read side by side with Max Jacob's reply; it demonstrates the importance of the religious dialogue undertaken in their correspondence, which is especially significant when one considers the virtual absence of religious content in Jabès's earliest poems (the exception being a few from 1930–2 written upon the death of Marcelle Jabès). As for Max Jacob, by 1937 he had more or less finished writing cubist poetry having preferred, in general, to confine his thoughts to religious poetry, spiritual meditations[17] and letter-writing. In his poem-letter to Max Jacob, Jabès accepts the move to Saint-Benoît ('Et pourquoi pas?') and his rejection of fame. But he himself is still trying to achieve glory as a writer. Further, when he prays it is Eros who descends whereas when Max Jacob prays he is visited by angels: 'Quand tu pries/les anges descendent te regarder. Hélas!/Nul pour moi n'eut pareille idée;/seul l'amour m'a visité [...]'. Jabès's prayer is romantically amorous rather than spiritual in a theophilic sense—a point expressed, we have seen, in his poetry of this period. Max Jacob forcefully contradicts Jabès in his reply:

'C'est moi qui descendrai te regarder quand tu prieras' (*LEJ*, 55). It must be recalled that at the time the letter was written, he was a devout Catholic eager to convert his friends. From this letter, it appears he tried to encourage Jabès in this direction. Jabès, however, was not particularly sensitive to his prodding; Max Jacob's influence during the 1930s should be seen more in relation to the development of Jabès's writing than to his religious bearing. The letter in half verse and half prose shows a playful, even defiant Jabès reminiscent of the Max Jacob of *Cornet à dés* (but far less controlled than the author of the collection of 1916) rather than a dedicated spiritual seeker.

In the two or three years following the exchange around 'L'Obscurité potable', a deepening gravity appears in the letters, which corresponds to the growing Nazi threat. During this period Jacob's poetry became further infused with Christian mysticism and martyrology. He could write in all sincerity and with complete devotion lines such as 'La rivière de ma vie est devenue un lac. Ce qui s'y reflète n'est plus que l'amour. Amour de Dieu, amour en Dieu.'[18] Some of his poetry, for instance 'L'Ogre d'amour', dated early 1940, bears some resemblance to Jabès's, in particular to the collection *Chansons pour le repas de l'ogre* (begun around 1942 and completed by 1945). The 'ogre' appears in the prose poem entitled 'Chanson pour tes paupières closes':

L'ogre, en appétit, fait le vide autour de lui. Il fait la nuit. Le monde entamé n'a plus de forme. Vite, ferme les yeux. L'ogre ne mange pas ceux qui dorment. (*Jbmd*, 54)

It is clear that the 'ogre' in Jabès's poem is a threatening creature who eats those who do not sleep, small children in particular. The poet implores his interlocutor to close his eyes in order to dispel the evil ogre's destructive power. Considered in the light of the terrifying events of war, such lines do not strike the reader as out of place. But who is Max Jacob's ogre? In fact, its identity could not be more polar to Jabès's, unless it reveals some ambivalence Max Jacob might have felt towards his ogre:

Ce que tu veux ce sont les âmes, Ogre d'amour. Détache donc la mienne, mon âme de fer, pour qu'elle vole vers ton aimant.
Alors tous deux nous serons heureux, Toi, d'avoir calmé ton insatiable soif, moi de reposer sur Ta Poitrine Universelle.[19]

Max Jacob's ogre is the loving greed of the universal God for the human soul as well as, reciprocally, the mystic's thirst for God; it is not destruction and death, the abyss and night that Jabès writes of. Jacob's poetry is characterized by a mystical union of the human soul with the divine, whereas Jabès's laments the terror experienced by those caught in the maelstrom.

As in the poetry, so too in the letters. There is an intensification of religious and spiritual subjects throughout the correspondence. Questions concerning Judaism and Christianity, religious conversion, the imminence of world war and the powerlessness of the individual during a state of siege are frequently asked. In his letter of 3 (or 4) April 1935, for instance, Max Jacob writes: 'Ne dites pas du mal des prêtres parce que c'est vulgaire et c'est la seule vulgarité que vous ayez. L'Esprit est Dieu. Tout esprit est un prêtre; les grands esprits (ou doubles comme vous) ont deux pointes à la mitre comme les archevêques' (*LEJ*, 28). In January 1937, he observes: 'Nous sommes à une époque de grands changements dans l'art et je crois qu'on ne peut continuer vers l'exaspération, le brillant et l'associationisme d'idées et d'images. L'humanité prend conscience d'elle-même, il faudra lui parler son langage et le poète sera celui qui le lui parlera avec grandeur' (9 January 1937, *LEJ*, 51). Later that year, he writes (one is tempted to say, prophetically): '*D'une seconde à l'autre* les guerres peuvent être déclenchées entre tous les états du monde, les étrangers mis dans des camps de concentration, les banques fermées' (12 September 1937, *LEJ*, 60; Max Jacob's emphasis). The letter from January 1939 addresses the question of racism head on. In this letter he suggests that the Catholic Church needed to intervene in Hitler's and Mussolini's politics. He tells Jabès that he should give some good and hard thought to the idea of suffering.

Personnellement tu n'as peut-être pas réfléchi à la nécessité de faire souffrir alternativement l'Eglise et les Juifs; car la souffrance seule peut conserver une race ou une société. Il faut nous attendre dans le cours des siècles à retrouver le martyre dont le sang féconde. Quant à moi, j'y suis préparé dès longtemps et comme juif et comme catholique fervent. J'en parlais avant Hitler, j'en parlerai toute ma vie. (*LEJ*, 75–6)

Despite his efforts, however, it appears that Max Jacob viewed himself as incapable of cultivating any spiritual progress in Jabès. His final letter, dated 1 May 1939, sums up the great poet's perception of himself as Europe turned to war:

Très cher Edmond.

Je suis hors du monde

Je ne puis que subir le martyre.

Je fais un livre sur les Saintes Ecritures où j'éclaire la question du rôle biblique des juifs. Ce livre paraîtra à la N.R.F. Cela est mon rôle et mon devoir. Je ne m'en connais pas d'autre.

Je te remercie de ne pas me condamner et je suis ton ami. (*LEJ*, 77)

When Hitler invaded Poland in September 1939, the war broke out. Jabès tried to contact Max Jacob over the next few years, but their exchange was interrupted by the tangled lines of communication between Europe and Egypt. In March 1944 Jacob was arrested at the abbey of Saint-Benoît as he came out of Mass. From Orléans he was transferred to the detention camp of Drancy, just north of Paris, where he died shortly afterwards of a lung infection. 'Le dernier message que je lui avais adressé par l'intermédiaire du Vatican', wrote Jabès, 'me revint avec au dos la mention: "Décédé"' (*LEJ*, 10–11). The communiqué must have arrived in the month or two following Max Jacob's death in March, because it was only in the May 1944 issue of the *Semaine égyptienne* that Jabès, quoting the lines of Philippe Soupault that would return to haunt him late in life, published the first of his several homages to the poet:

> Monsieur Miroir marchand d'habits
> Est mort hier soir à Paris
> Il fait nuit
> Il fait noir
> Il fait nuit noire à Paris.[20]

Jabès delivered two additional eulogies, the first in Cairo in February 1945 and the second in Alexandria during May of that year.[21] Both were given under the auspices of Amitiés françaises.

'Comme Apollinaire,' wrote Jabès, 'Max Jacob demeurera, pour nous, "le poète assassiné"' (*LEJ*, 11). It goes without saying that the war was terrible enough, but the loss of a friend and mentor in the course of it, and because of his racial origins, transformed Jabès's perception of himself as a writer and as a Jew. To him, the most enduring lesson of their relationship was the appreciation of suffering in one's art and life: 'Pour les grands poètes la poésie a été une recherche dans la souffrance' (*LEJ*, 68); 'la souffrance seule peut conserver une race et une société' (*LEJ*, 76). In the course of the war and post-war years, Edmond Jabès assimilated this moral lesson and applied it when composing his own poetry, beginning with *Chansons pour le repas de l'ogre*. The lesson was fundamental, but there were still others to come. The impending Egyptian crisis of the fifties and his settling in France had personal implications for Jabès that definitively shaped his exilic cast of mind.

Gabriel Bounoure, a Pilgrim in a Strange Land

Two general features of the friendship of Jabès and Bounoure bear mentioning. First and foremost, their friendship was premissed on poetry, specifically on Jabès's compositions and on Bounoure's commentaries on them. When they met during the summer of 1952, Jabès was unknown to Bounoure, but he knew the critic's articles on many of the most important nineteenth- and twentieth-century French writers and poets, from Baudelaire to Rimbaud, from Claudel to Michaux. In other words it was the poet who was obliged to extend himself to the commentator.

That point is related to the second, the effect of the volatile political climate on Jabès. With Bounoure settled in Cairo and their relationship defined, initially at least, by poetry, they were now able to turn their thoughts to the changing political atmosphere engulfing Egypt after the Free Officers' seizure of power from the royal government of Farouk. As mentioned in the introductory chapter of this study, Jabès admitted that he had welcomed the changes the revolution made in the social and economic life of the country (*Dl*, 44).[22] He soon learned that the Free Officers revolution did not guarantee liberty to non-Egyptian nationals: with the coordinated attack on Egypt by Israel, France and Britain in late October 1956, Jabès and other non-Muslim minority residents, in particular French, British and Jewish, were placed in a position of physical and economic peril.[23] The beleaguering insecurity was by no means resolved with his arrival in France since new problems revealed themselves. It was not only the economic instability that troubled Jabès; in the months following his departure from Egypt he also had to take account of his Jewishness, a factor which seemed of greater significance than any other facet of his identity—greater than his Egyptian childhood, his Italian nationality or his eventual acceptance into French cultural life.

Jabès met Gabriel Bounoure (Issoire, Brittany, 1886–Lesconil, Brittany, 1969) in the midst of controversy. Before arriving in Cairo, Bounoure had directed the Ecole supérieure des lettres in Beirut (which he had also founded) when France was embroiled in military operations in North Africa. From Lebanon he wrote a personal letter of protest to an Egyptian friend, Abdel Hamid Badawi, the rector of the French section of Ein-Shams University in Cairo. Unbeknownst to Bounoure, Badawi published the letter so as to demonstrate publicly that not all the French agreed with the government's actions. Normally this would not have attracted notice but, as the critic Henri Bouillier recalled, Bounoure held a visible administrative position. His passport was confiscated, and he was recalled to France. Badawi felt responsible for the unfortunate turn of events, and so proposed that Bounoure assume the chair in French literature at Ein-Shams, where Jean Grenier had taught philosophy between 1948 and 1950. The French cultural attaché to Egypt, Philippe Rebeyrol, with Jabès's support, asked the French ambassador to Egypt (and honorary president of Amitiés françaises), Maurice Couve de Murville, to intervene on Bounoure's behalf in order to secure him the position in Cairo. Diplomacy succeeded, and Bounoure was in Cairo by the summer of 1952.[24]

A few words about Gabriel Bounoure's views on the study of literature are appropriate here. Bounoure viewed criticism not as a licence to dispense value judgement, but as a means of understanding a poet's personal engagement with his poem, which he conceived of as a kind of religious activity. Throughout his criticism Bounoure further sought to illuminate the processes of poetic creation, which he frequently saw as a kind of sacred interaction between the poet and the reader. He himself thought of his role as critic in humbler terms. He described the ideal literary exegete in the introduction to the single book published during his lifetime, a collection of essays entitled *Marelles sur le parvis* (1958):

Qu'il sache bien que ses jugements sont toujours conjecturaux et aventurés. Devant le porche silencieux de l'œuvre poétique, ils ne sont que jeux de marelles, essais pour conduire, en sautillant comme un boiteux, le caprice d'un palet dans un damier tracé par la raison. Le poème est cette parole contagieuse qui advient à partir d'une origine magique et met en branle un temps qui lui est propre. Mais la réflexion critique tente de déterminer cette origine et de retrouver le lieu et le tracé de cette pensée, au moyen de repères plantés sur le temps des autres, pour que ces deux opérations de sens inverse se rencontrent et coïncident.[25]

As was the case with Max Jacob, to whom Bounoure dedicated some of his final essays,[26] his seriousness was cast in light terms, hence the title of his book of essays. Again similar to Max Jacob, a sincere religious feeling pervaded his writings, but for Bounoure the feeling was a result of his study not only of the great monotheistic faiths, but also of Eastern religions. This, together with the absence of an extended theoretical reflection on literature, might well account for his neglect in French letters today. In any case, both Bounoure and Jabès understood the import of Max Jacob to their respective developments. It was a bond that they would refer to throughout their relationship.[27]

It is doubtless true that before Bounoure's arrival in Cairo there were many people close to Jabès with whom he could discuss poetry in a sustained, critical manner. One such individual is Roger Arnaldez, who was professor of German at the Lycée français of Cairo and whose 1951 essay on the Romanticism of Novalis, 'La langue et l'expression', was dedicated to Jabès.[28] In this essay Arnaldez wished to demonstrate the modernism of the Romantic poet and his relevance to contemporary poetry in general.[29] Furthermore, he was a regular member of Amitiés françaises and a contributor to *La Part du sable*. In short, he acted at times as Jabès's interlocutor, and further was close to Jabès's family, having taught his eldest daughter philosophy at the lycée and having studied Hebrew for several years with Arlette Jabès until January 1952 when Egyptian rioters burned large sections of the modern, 'European' districts of Cairo.[30]

Despite Arnaldez's close intellectual involvement with Jabès, it was Gabriel Bounoure who provided him with the most sustained camaraderie from 1952 until his death in April 1969. It is for his critical bearing on Jabès, first in his preface to *Je bâtis ma demeure* and then on the formation of *Le Livre des Questions*, that Bounoure is noteworthy. For Bounoure more than any other personality bridges Jabès's Cairo and Paris years during which his evolution is marked by the deep-seated self-doubt and the search for self-understanding that peregrination brings to the wanderer. Jabès dedicated *Le Milieu d'ombre* (1955) to his friend with the simple inscription, 'A Gabriel Bounoure.' The book concludes with a short poem, 'Le Pèlerin', which reveals a greater if subtler kinship between the two writers than the dedication does:

> Tu ne marcheras jamais assez
> pèlerin perceur fou d'horizon
> La terre apprise est une prison
> Les barreaux sont les chemins comptés
> Tu ne rêveras jamais assez

> La mer l'ennemi est déraison
> Mais le ciel le bleu ciel insaisissable
> est un murmure contenu de pierres
> amoureuses dont le temps fait des bornes
> (*Jbmd*, 277)

The pilgrim who neither walks nor dreams enough might be Bounoure or might be Jabès himself, or he might be, wrapped into the singular subject pronoun ('Tu'), both of them. Whoever he might be, however, he is a pilgrim who desires no limitations, who, despite his wish to pass beyond the horizon and through the sea, is stopped short, it appears, by that very elusive horizon.[31] And yet the final poem of *Le Milieu d'ombre* is not a simple goodbye; or if it is, then it is a farewell in which, despite the blue, murmuring heaven of which time marks the bounds, there is no stopping-point (as there are no punctuation marks in the poem): the pilgrim approaches an infinitely receding boundary.

It is of course possible to read, in the poetry, hints of Jabès's admiration of Bounoure. But there is no better material record of the critical years spanning the height of Jabès's career in Cairo and his arrival and resettlement in Paris, during which time *Le Livre des Questions* was conceived, composed and published, than their correspondence. It is significant that the first letter in the correspondence coincides with Jabès's nomination as Chevalier de la Légion d'Honneur by the French ambassador to Egypt with the support of the French cultural attaché.[32] In the following weeks Bounoure wrote Jabès a letter of congratulations, which begins:

Il y a des intersignes et des prémonitions. Samedi je vous décrivais la joie de Max Jacob, nouveau décoré, pétillant de bavardage malicieux, se promenant la boutonnière fleurie à Kemper, au pied de ce mont Frugy où le Christ lui était apparu. C'est le même ruban, j'en suis sûr, qui orne aujourd'hui votre veston. Même si l'on doit m'accuser de mythomanie, je tiendrai toujours pour certain que vous portez le même insigne que celui dont tirait orgueil notre douloureux ami. Le même ruban transmis d'un enchanteur à l'autre, par l'opération de quelque fée … Morgane ou Mélusine?

Implying that the honour had been bestowed belatedly, Bounoure goes on to say that Jabès was

déjà tout nôtre, et profondément,—pour avoir ajouté au trésor de notre poésie quelques joyaux, et des pensées d'une subtilité élégante et pénétrante sur le mystère du langage, sur ce silence étrange qui est le berceau du poème. Mais enfin il est très satisfaisant pour l'esprit qu'un petit signe éclatant comme une blessure rappelle à tous que vous êtes un de ceux qui honorez les lettres de la France. (Bounoure to Jabès, undated letter, November or December 1952)

In the eyes of the French government and in those of one of the most insightful critics of modern French poetry, Edmond Jabès, the French-speaking Egyptian poet, was now held to be a French poet and man of letters, albeit one 'à titre étranger'. Like Max Jacob's approval in 1933, the official French recognition was yet another step in Jabès's integration into French cultural life. But if the government's sanction was important to Jabès's sense of himself as a poet, it was but an administrative sanction. Bounoure, on the other hand, was attuned to Jabès's attachment to his native environment, Cairo, the setting in which he had begun to write. 'J'emportai vos livres dans ma poche, au bord du Nil durant ma promenade quotidienne ou au bout de l'Ile de Rodah près du Nilomètre [the device used to measure the water level of the Nile]', he wrote to him in 1953. And it is a feeling that was long in leaving him, as he admitted in one of his final letters while in retirement in his native Brittany: 'vos déserts sont les miens et j'y éprouve les mêmes soifs que vous' (undated letter, probably April 1969). While it was through the optic of French literature that Bounoure perceived Jabès, he understood that the peculiar combination of the Egyptian cultural and political environment of the first half of the century, with all the attendant mythologies of its barren, silent outskirts, and French culture of the same period, had fundamentally shaped Jabès's thought and writing.

The letters indicate that it was after their introduction in 1952 that Bounoure began a relaxed reading of Jabès's poetry. By early 1953 he was writing informal commentaries on that poetry written between 1947 ('Le Fond de l'eau') through Jabès's most recent book, Les Mots tracent (1951); it would be several years before the notes took the form of an essay.[33] In the meantime, Jabès continued to enjoy Bounoure's frank critical observations, such as, 'Le mystère des mots, tel qu'il se révèle au poète, contient le secret de tout, de cet univers de choses anxieuses, isolées, qui regardent vers nous et attendent que l'homme parle' (Bounoure's notes to Jabès, dated 1953). And he further brought Jabès to the attention of important publishers in Paris: 'Vu longuement [Samuel de] Sacy. Me suis donné le plaisir de lui parler abondamment de l'ami que j'ai en vous et du poète que les lettres françaises possèdent en Edmond Jabès' (23 June 1955).[34]

The relative peace of the early fifties in Egypt, followed by oncoming turmoil, decisive in Jabès's development, merits particular attention. It is at this point in time that the existential jostling, which preceded the definitive geographic rupture between Cairo and Paris, began. In February 1955, Jabès spoke with Bounoure at Amitiés françaises on Arthur Rimbaud, whose verbal profligacy and experimentation, as well as his youthful impetuosity, had inspired him since his earliest days. Jabès's text has not been located, but a reporter from the *Progrès égyptien* in attendance that evening wrote that the speaker's language was at times 'trop profonde pour des auditeurs dénués d'un sixième sens'. He too often underlined the 'mots' ('words') of Rimbaud, which caused one woman in the audience to ask what 'maux' ('evils') he was talking about![35] Bounoure's lecture is known; it was published by Jabès in May 1955 in the series 'Le Chemin des sources', founded by Jabès that year, under the title *Le Silence de Rimbaud*. The Rimbaud evening was Jabès's last moment of intellectual quietude before he left Cairo.

When considering this critical period, it is not irrelevant to speculate as to what kind of career Jabès would have had in Egypt if the force of history had not displaced him from the country. What did his activities consist of between his break with Henein in late 1952 and his departure from Egypt in June 1957? Two of them are his duties as literary adviser to Amitiés françaises and as director of 'Le Chemin des sources'. Other French writers would have stayed on in Egypt as guests of Amitiés françaises. In the meantime, Jean Grenier's *Les Grèves* appeared under 'Le Chemin des sources' imprint at the same time as Bounoure's essay on Rimbaud. In 1956 a third volume, René Char's *L'Abominable Homme des neiges*, appeared. Jabès dedicated three separate books to each of these writers.[36] Other publications were planned, including titles by Louis Guilloux, Jacques Audiberti and Jean Paulhan.[37] As to his third literary activity, composing poetry, *L'Ecorce du monde* appeared in June 1955, but to a mixed reception.[38] Two further books (*Le Milieu d'ombre* and *Du blanc des mots et du noir des signes*) and several other poems ('L'Eau du puits', 'L'Absence de lieu' and 'Le Pacte du printemps') had been completed by 1957, but they remained unpublished until *Je bâtis ma demeure* appeared.[39]

Jabès's contributions to Jean Moscatelli's monumental anthology, *Poètes en Egypte* (1955), contained no new poetry, but were representative of his growing output. A consideration of this anthology is also important to understanding how Jabès was read and published in Egypt, and it is of further interest to the history of the twentieth-century Franco-Egyptian writers active before Nasser came to power. *Poètes en Egypte* contains the work of fifty-five poets, all of whom wrote in French in Egypt during the first half of the twentieth century, and it testifies to the extensive cultural activity of French-speaking writers in Egypt. Though it was perhaps not the intention of the editor, it summarized the collective achievement of the community of French-speaking Egyptian writers.[40] Some writers included are Marie Cavadia, whose literary salon in Cairo Jabès had frequented since 1936; Andrée Chedid, who emigrated to Paris in 1946; Henry Miller's friend Albert Cossery, who also emigrated to Paris, in 1945, but is perhaps better known for his short stories and novels on Egyptian life[41] than for his poetry; Georges Henein; Joyce Mansour, much admired by André Breton; and Claude Moenis Taha-Hussein, son of the great Egyptian novelist Taha Hussein. While the anthology may be regarded as a clarion call of the crisis in francophone cultural activities in Egypt following Nasser's political success in the country, the preface and the poets' biographies contain very little in the way of political content. Rather, the object of the anthology was to introduce French readers to Franco-Egyptian poetry and, according to the editor, 'goûter cette poésie qui nous a maintes fois donné beaucoup mieux que des promesses et qui affirme avec ténacité le prestige de notre langue et de notre influence intellectuelle dans un des plus beaux pays du monde'.[42] Its contributors include not only Egyptians writing directly in French, but also Greeks, Italians, Swiss and others, but the emphasis is on Egyptian writers and the 'floraison de la langue française en Egypte'. 'Parente pauvre et ignorée, la poésie égyptienne de langue française n'a pas encore connu l'accueil réservé à Paris à la poésie belge ou canadienne. Elle illustre cependant—à sa façon qui n'est pas négligeable—une culture devenue commune. Ses accents, quelquefois originaux, ne manqueraient pas de surprendre si on les écoutait.'[43] Moscatelli emphasizes the unity of the French language used by its diverse contributors, not their political activities or affiliations, or the crisis the French cultural presence in Egypt was passing through. The absence of any discussion of current events might appear surprising since, as we have seen, Moscatelli was a committed activist in earlier years and therefore not uninitiated in politics. Instead of openly politicizing the French cause in Egypt, he more subtly insists on the value of cultural diversity and aesthetic integrity: 'je me suis laissé aller à glisser dans cette gerbe de fleurs épanouies et glanées chez autrui, des fleurettes cueillies dans mon propre jardin. Ce n'est pas, je le vois bien, la moindre des faiblesses de ce florilège'.

Jabès's selections span the years from the mid-1930s to the mid-1950s. The dates indicate that he continued to find sufficient merit in some of his earliest writings to feel that they should be included. It should be noted, however, that the bibliography does not list his first publications, *Illusions sentimentales*, *Je t'attends!* and 'Maman', the existence of which Moscatelli was aware of. Their omission was therefore intentional. If Jabès did not list these texts, after his immigration he completely dissociated himself from the earliest writings, thereby leaving the impression that his career had begun in the early 1940s (with the first poems of *Je bâtis ma demeure*) and not in the late twenties. Moscatelli's introductory note to Jabès's contribution, in which the spirit of political antagonism that stymied their friendship in the mid-thirties has disappeared, seeks to understand his poetry not only in the light of the influences of Max Jacob and Paul Eluard, but also in terms of the devastating events of the Second World War.[44]

In addition to the selections in Moscatelli's *Poètes en Egypte*, by August 1955 Jabès received proofs for 'Une chance de naître', published in October in the *Mercure de France* (Jabès to Bounoure, 27 August 1955).[45] That poem, like 'La Girafe', published in *Calligrammes*,[46] was dedicated to Bounoure. Most important of all, it was during the early months of 1956 that he first considered gathering the entirety of his post-war Cairene poetry into a single volume to be prefaced by Bounoure, who would, he hoped, act as 'le merveilleux introducteur que vous avez été pour les autres poètes que vous avez étudiés' (21 May 1956). *Je bâtis ma demeure* had been conceived, although it had neither title nor form (Jabès to Bounoure, 20 March and 21 May 1956). This leaves no uncertainty as to the supposition that the idea for the collection, which was only published while Jabès was living in Paris, had occurred to him prior to his departure.

It seems, then, that Jabès would have continued along a similar course as that he had led in the post-war years, promoting other French writers and writing his own poetry. But it was not to be. A gust of wind was blowing from quite another direction. Bounoure readied Jabès psychologically for his departure by suggesting that his true place was in France and not in Egypt. In early autumn 1956, he wrote regarding the collection of Cairene verse: 'Les poèmes qui naissent au Caire sont des exilés, des enfants perdus: ils n'ont pour témoins que le sable, les yeux vides du Sphinx, le vent du désert et l'indifférence des humains.' The collection, however, would not be still-born. Not all was lost, for in Paris, 'il y a cependant deux douzaines de demi-fous pour s'intéresser à ces orphelins, dont la patrie n'est ni le ciel, ni la terre, mais une région sans longitude, ni latitude, où toutes les forces et tous les éléments jouent et s'entrechoquent d'une façon qui révolte le bon sens'. To which he added: 'Je suis infiniment heureux que vos poèmes, quittant la vallée du Nil, s'avancent dans la littérature française, doucement favorisés par ceux qui en reconnaissent l'authenticité et la valeur.' Bounoure's insistent message to Jabès was that although his poems were composed in Egypt, they had no lasting place there. The judgement may appear severe, but it must be borne in mind that he was merely objectifying Jabès's own feeling that his native country, Egypt, had been to him a foreign land and concurrently that his destiny lay in France.

Jabès's next letter to Bounoure is astonishing for having been written the evening before the Israelis began the Sinai campaign. In the letter, dated 28 October 1956, Jabès offered his sympathy, not only to his friend, but to France, which must be wearing a shameful 'visage douloureux' on account of its military actions. Jabès's remarks are an index of his sadness at the events occurring in Egypt and, further, they are an attestation of his commitment to France:

Il est difficile—pour moi qui suis de nulle part—de vous avouer que je me sens très proche de vous en ce moment—et sans doute n'en ai-je même pas le droit. Le prendrai-je, ce droit, qu'on me le contesterait, puisque j'appartiens à cette minorité à qui on refuse, en Orient tout au moins, la parole et le cœur. Mais il ne s'agit ni de l'Orient ni de l'Europe. Il s'agit seulement d'une blessure qui est la nôtre.

In a key expression, Jabès describes himself as coming from 'nulle part'; he had become (or, imminently, would become) stateless. The seeds of passages in *Un Etranger avec, sous le bras, un livre de petit format* (1989) such as '"Ma patrie est ma langue. Aussi, le pays de ma langue est-il devenu le mien"', disait-il' (*Et*, 97), are clearly discernible in the letter of 28 October 1956. No longer having a homeland, he adopts language and writing, in the words of Adorno, as 'a place to live'. Jabès further recounts in this letter a specific event that was symptomatic of his rejection from Egypt:

Lorsque Claude Taha-Hussein, au cœur d'une séance des 'Amitiés françaises' avait proposé de changer le nom de notre groupement, parce que—

prétendait-il—'Amitiés françaises' signifie 'Amitiés dans un seul sens, dans le sens de la France', je sentais, au fond de moi-même—bien que je soutinsse le contraire, pour la forme—qu'il avait raison, et que cela je l'avais voulu au départ avec mes amis. Oui, c'était cela que nous avions voulu: affirmer au moment où la France vivait les heures les plus tragiques de son histoire, une fidélité qui n'attendait rien en retour, toute désintéressée (désintéressée n'est pas peut-être le mot, puisque nous ne supportions pas d'être privés de la France et qu'en affirmant sa présence, nous affirmions notre âme)—mais vous savez ce que je veux dire: une amitié qui n'exigeait rien de notre pays sinon de demeurer.

The tone and phrasing are noticeably similar and in some instances the same as those used, first in his open letter, 'A mes amis grecs', of October 1941—'L'Hellade demeure; vous à qui nous devons tant, vous demeurez pour vous et pour le monde. Dans cette lutte pour notre demeure et pour la demeure de tous, nous avons tous un même nom et la même voix';[47] and secondly in his introduction à Pierre Seghers's lecture in May 1946—'Durant ces tragiques dernières années où le monde fut plongé dans l'obscurité totale, nous avons tenté, ici, d'affirmer la France avec tout ce que nous gardions jalousement d'elle.'[48] In each case, Jabès was struck by the injustice and inhumanity of individual and collective action. The primary difference between the open letter and the presentation of Seghers, on the one hand, and the letter to Bounoure, on the other, is that the threat to Jabès's well-being in October 1956 assumed a reality and a proportion that had been significantly smaller in the earlier cases.

Following the meeting described in the letter to Bounoure, the name of Amitiés françaises was not changed; the organization was simply dissolved. In fact, following the coordinated attack on Egypt in late 1956 the entire intellectual climate changed dramatically, its finest cultural institutions suffering the loss of its minority animators who had left the country. Time permitting, Amitiés françaises gave farewell dinners to individuals before the respective dates of their expulsions arrived. They included Robert Blum, whose first poems appeared in the mid-1920s in Cairo and whose literary criticism and journalism were widely read in the country, and the Frenchman Fernand Leprette, who had taught in Egypt since 1920 and acted as inspector of French education in the Egyptian government. At Leprette's dinner Gabriel Bounoure recalled his extraordinary achievement in understanding the Egyptians around him while at the same time hinting at the tension filling both the room and the country: 'Autant que le tumulte collectif

d'Ataba, de Choubrah ou de boulaq, vous nous rendez sensible la marée de vie que suscite le fleuve sacré, le double mystère de la puissance végétale et de la puissance solaire,—et le grand secret de l'âme égyptienne toujours désireuse d'intégrer au même cycle inconnu de la mort et l'inconnu de la vie'.[49] 'Tout de même,' Leprette reflected in 1960, after serving the Egyptian educational institutions for some forty-five years, 'j'étais un étranger.'[50] That evening in 1956, however, he expressed his faith 'dans la valeur humaniste de la langue française, la certitude que le millier de professeurs égyptiens qui exigent le français sont à la hauteur de leur tâche, et enfin le vœu qu'il forme pour la prospérité de l'Egypte au moment où ce grand pays connaît un nouveau destin'.[51] The same thought might very well have been expressed by Edmond Jabès.

Despite Leprette's sentimental optimism, public harassment of non-Muslim minorities was endemic to Egypt from the middle 1950s. The pro-Nasser newspaper *Actualité* reviewed Robert Blum's novel *Le Signe arabe* (1956), in January 1956, and condemned the hypocrisy of all 'auteurs étrangers d'Egypte'.[52] We should read in this expression the name of Jabès. The gravity of the political situation is best summed up in Jean Grenier's diary entry of 4 April 1957: 'Etienne Mériel, Fernand Leprette à Bourg-la-Reine: expulsés d'Egypte. Aux Français et aux Anglais, on distribue des "cartes de sujets ennemis". Biens mis sous séquestre, quelquefois vendus à l'encan.'[53]

The political changes were also felt by European readers of Egyptian publications. For instance, in April 1956 the *Mercure de France* excitedly welcomed Moscatelli's *Poètes en Egypte*. The reviewer, Philippe Chabaneix, even named Jabès among the 'Egyptiens authentiques',[54] but he was not writing as a critic of the so-called foreign presence in Egypt. On the other hand, one of the hallmarks of Franco-Egyptian letters, the *Revue du Caire*, founded in 1938 by Mohamed Bey Zulficar as the organ of the Egyptian section of the Association des écrivains étrangers d'expression française (to which, it appears, Jabès himself never belonged), was reviewed negatively in Paris: 'Depuis que Nasser est monté sur l'Egypte, cette revue s'enfonce dans les sables de l'inactualité, de la non-immixation aux choses et à la vie de ce monde', wrote the critic Adrian Miatlev in *La Tour de feu* of December 1958.[55] The death knell sounded throughout the land.

'Pour moi qui suis de nulle part.'

Jabès left the country in June 1957, his role as cultural intermediary finished. His thoughts, painfully ambivalent but masterfully poised, were composed only in Paris, his mental eye having returned to the memory of the deserts of Egypt:

> J'ai quitté une terre qui n'était pas la mienne,
> pour une autre qui, non plus, ne l'est pas.
> Je me suis réfugié dans un vocable d'encre, ayant le livre pour espace;
> parole de nulle part, étant celle obscure du désert.
> Je ne me suis pas couvert la nuit.
> Je ne me suis point protégé du soleil.
> J'ai marché nu.
> D'où je venais n'avait plus de sens.
> Où j'allais n'inquiétait personne.
> Du vent, vous dis-je, du vent.
> Et un peu de sable dans le vent.
>
> (*Et*, 107)

Notes to Chapter 3

1. On the dedication, see also Steven Jaron, 'Edmond Jabès ou le fonctionnement du palimpseste', in Marc Kober, Irène Fenoglio and Daniel Lançon (eds.), *Entre Nil et sable: écrivains d'Egypte d'expression française (1920–1960)* (Paris: Centre national de documentation pédagogique, 1999), 195–9.

2. Paul Auster, 'The Book of the Dead: An Interview with Edmond Jabès', in Eric Gould (ed.), *The Sin of the Book: Edmond Jabès* (Lincoln, NB, and London: University of Nebraska Press, 1985), 9.

3. Cf. *LP*, 26: '"Le mensonge a, parfois, la limpidité de la verité," disait-il.'

4. *LQ* I, 30: 'Le roman de Sarah et de Yukel, à travers divers dialogues et méditations attribués à des rabbins imaginaires'.

5. See, further, Steven Jaron, 'Jacob, mon ange qui brûle', in Max Jacob, *Lettres à Edmond Jabès*, 3rd edn. (Pessac: Opales, 2003), 7–17.

6. 'Apport à la poésie: le Logisme', 3: 'Nous sommes tous graves, même lorsque nous faisons rire et jusque dans la fantaisie d'un Tristan Derême, dans le calembour d'un Max Jacob, dans l'extravagance d'un André Breton.'

7. e.g. 'Syrinx', *Sé* 14–15 (1932), 13; or 'Dimanche (4 décembre 1932)', *Sé* 1–2 (1932), 22.

8. Max Jacob thanks him again in an undated letter, *LEJ*, 41. Gabriel Boctor's article on 'Activités Essayistes', in *Un Effort* 57 (1935), 23, lists Jabès's forthcoming lecture on Max Jacob. Georges Henein, in a letter of Jan. 1936 to André Breton preserved in the Bibliothèque littéraire Jacques Doucet, mentions that Jabès would soon be speaking on the poet (BRT.C.943).

9. *Sé* 3–4 (1938), 27–8.

10. *Pé* (16 Sept. 1945), 5.

11. *Fontaine* 51 (1946), 676. Jacques Evrard dispelled the belief that the J. E. to whom Max Jacob had addressed his *Conseils à un jeune poète* might have been Edmond Jabès. See the introduction to the English translation of that text, *Advice to a*

Young Poet, trans. and intro. by John Adlard, pref. by Edmond Jabès, afterword by Jacques Evrard (London: Menard, 1976).

12. F. Talva, *Sé* 1–2 (1945), 24.

13. Jean Moscatelli, 'La maison du Caire', *Sé* 21–2 (1935), 2. The Maison des Artistes was immortalized by Albert Cossery in his 1947 novel, *La Maison de la mort certaine*.

14. Naggar and Hassoun, 'Le Caire quitté: conversation avec Edmond Jabès (26 juillet 1984)', 45.

15. Bibliothèque littéraire Jacques Doucet (10.902). The dedication is dated '5 février 1937'.

16. Bibliothèque littéraire Jacques Doucet (8024.402). See also Jaron, 'Repiquage poétique', 112–13. In his letter Jabès mentions a photograph of Max Jacob given to him by the poet. The photograph is reproduced in *Dl*. Before she knew of the existence of this letter, Viviane Jabès-Crasson told me her father kept this photo on his writing table throughout his life (Paris, 25 Oct. 1994).

17. See, e.g., Max Jacob, *Méditations*, ed. René Plantier (Paris: Gallimard, 1972).

18. Max Jacob, *Derniers Poèmes en vers et en prose* (Paris: Gallimard/Poésie, 1974), 196.

19. Pierre Lagarde, *Max Jacob, mystique et martyr* (Paris: Baudinière, 1944), 182.

20. Edmond Jabès, 'Hommage à Max Jacob', *Sé* 15–16 (1944), 5, republished in *Saluer Jabès: les suites du livre*, 62–4. Jabès included the same lines in his 1989 tribute to Soupault. See his 'Philippe Soupault', in *Philippe Soupault, le poète*, ed. Jacqueline Chénieux-Gendron (Paris: Klincksieck, 1992), 9–11.

21. For Cairo, see *Pé* (24 Feb. 1945), 6; for Alexandria, see *Le Journal d'Egypte* (5 May 1945).

22. Jabès was not alone in believing that the revolution would restore governmental integrity to Egypt. See Krämer, *The Jews in Modern Egypt*, 220.

23. Ibid. 221.

24. Interview with Henri Bouillier (Paris, 10 Apr. 1994). Maurice Saillet's version of Bounoure's dismissal from his position in Beirut, 'Hommage à Gabriel Bounoure', in *Lettres nouvelles* 5 (1953), 626–7, adds that the Islamic scholar Louis Massignon, a friend of Bounoure, described the incident in his inaugural lecture at the Collège de France in 1953, during which time he himself protested against the French military intervention in North Africa.

25. Gabriel Bounoure, *Marelles sur le parvis: essais de critique poétique* (Paris: Plon, 1958), 10.

26. Gabriel Bounoure, 'Magicien et martyr: une complainte mystique', *Le Monde* suppl. to no. 7523 (22 Mar. 1969), 4.

27. In the last year of his life, Bounoure referred to Max Jacob in his notes on Jabès's texts: 'Je suis de plus en plus obsédé par les chers Kabbalistes de Catalogne et d'Espagne. Max Jacob, sans le dire, allait puiser à cette source si belle, si limpide, si abondante.'

28. *Revue du Caire* 140 (1951), 21–34.

29. Many of the ideas in the essay originated in conversations between Jabès and Arnaldez. Interview with Roger Arnaldez (Paris, 22 Apr. 1995).

30. Interview with Roger Arnaldez (Paris, 22 Apr. 1995); Krämer, *The Jews in Modern Egypt*, 219–20.

31. Jabès's gesture of calling Bounoure a pilgrim seems to be echoed in Bounoure's article on Louis Massignon where he describes the great Arabist in a similar

manner: 'Il se sent, quant à lui, voué à une pérégrination sans fin et à des ascensions difficiles sur des montagnes où souffle l'Esprit de Vérité.' See Bounoure's tribute, 'L. Massignon: itinéraire et courbe de vie', *L'Herne: Massignon* (Paris, 1962), 45–54.

32. Interview with Philippe Rebeyrol (Paris, 31 Dec. 1994). The complete citation reads: 'Monsieur Edmond Jabès, de nationalité italienne, a été nommé Chevalier de la Légion d'Honneur à titre Etranger, par décret du 4 octobre 1952, pris sur le rapport du ministre des Affaires étrangères, en qualité "d'Homme de Lettres"' (letter of 24 Jan. 1995 to the author by Jean Beysset of the Grande Chancellerie de la Légion d'Honneur).

33. They are collected in Gabriel Bounoure, *Edmond Jabès: la demeure et le livre* (Montpellier: Fata Morgana, 1984).

34. Samuel de Sacy was the director of the *Mercure de France*.

35. E. S., 'Aux Amitiés françaises: hommage à Arthur Rimbaud', *Pé* (23 Feb. 1955).

36. *L'Ecorce du monde*, published in 1955 but dating from 1953–4, is dedicated to Char; as mentioned, *Le Milieu d'ombre*, dating from 1955, is dedicated to Bounoure; and *Du blanc des mots et du noir des signes*, dating from 1953–6, is dedicated to Grenier. At the time some critics remarked that the format resembled that of booklets issued by *La Part du sable*. See Etienne Mériel's review of the collection in his column, 'Lettres françaises en Egypte', *Pé* (15 June 1955), 2.

37. Printed on the verso of Gabriel Bounoure's *prière d'insérer* of the publicity announcement of the series. In his letter of 27 Aug. 1955 to Gabriel Bounoure Jabès mentions that he is expecting a text of Jean Paulhan for the collection.

38. See Etienne Mériel's review, *Pé* (1 June 1955), 2; and Pierre Oster's, *NRF* 30 (1955), 1115. Léon-Gabriel Gros's review, *Cahiers du sud* 324 (1956), 489, is more favourable.

39. 'Petites Incursions dans le monde des masques et des mots', dating from 1956, was first published in 1962 in the *Mercure de France* and later collected in the second (1975) edition of *Jbmd*, 311–18.

40. A second volume of French-Egyptian writing in which Jabès figures, *Calligrammes: almanach des lettres et des arts en Egypte, 1956*, is also a tribute to that community *in extremis*.

41. e.g. *Les Hommes oubliés de Dieu* (Paris: Charlot, 1946) and *La Maison de la mort certaine* (Paris: Charlot, 1947).

42. Jean Moscatelli (ed.), *Poètes en Egypte, anthologie* (Cairo: L'Atelier, 1955), n.p.

43. Ibid.

44. Ibid. 198. Moscatelli's text reproduces an unsigned (though obviously by Moscatelli) introductory note to excerpts from 'Trois Filles de mon quartier' published several years earlier in *Loisirs* (Autumn 1948), n.p.

45. 'Une chance de naître', *Mercure de France* 1106 (1955), 230–6.

46. 'La Girafe', *Calligrammes: almanach des lettres et des arts en Egypte, 1956*, 103.

47. *Sé* 21–2 (1941), 7.

48. *Sé* 15–16 (1946), 11.

49. 'Adresse amicale à Fernand Leprette', *Mercure de France* 1166 (1960), 367.

50. Georges Piroué, 'Un homme du Nord transplanté en terre d'Egypte', *Mercure de France* 1167 (1960), 553.

51. 'Aux Amitiés françaises: dîner d'adieux à Fernand Leprette', *Pé* (19 May 1956).

52. 'A propos de "Le Signe arabe" de Robert Blum', *Actualité* 484 (1956), 1 and 13. See also 'Les auteurs minoritaires d'Egypte: encore une trahison des clercs', ibid. These articles are in the collection of Daniel Lançon.

53. Jean Grenier, *Carnets, 1944–1971*, ed. Claire Paulhan (Paris: Pierre Seghers, 1991), 229.

54. Philippe Chabaneix, *Mercure de France* 1112 (1956), 740–1.

55. Adrian Miatlev, *La Tour de feu* 60 (1958), 112.

CHAPTER 4

Exile Confirmed

A Dwelling Built of Words

Commentators have not failed to notice that the collected Cairene poetry, beginning with its title, *Je bâtis ma demeure*, evokes an architectural structure. Jean-Luc Bayard observes that the second edition (1975), with its addition of 'Petites Incursions dans le monde des masques et des mots' (dated 1956), contains thirteen books and that the seventh book is called *La Clef de voûte*.[1] In his appreciation, Maurice Nadeau notes that if architecture were understood in a metaphorical sense, then there would be a strong relationship between dwelling ('demeure') and language: one builds a place to dwell with one's words.[2] The point is also taken up by Brooke Fredericksen, who carefully seeks textual evidence to support the claim that the principal subject of the mature Cairene poetry is exile and the problem of dwelling or inhabiting through language use.[3] While all of these critics have associated the post-war poetry with language and architecture, it is further possible to extend their range of analysis by examining the conjunction of poetry and philosophy, of language and ontology, in a philological and historical context.

The title of the collection indicates in the most immediate of terms Jabès's insistence on the architectural structure and content of the poetry. Of its four words, two—'Je' and 'ma'—are in the first person. Monad-like, the collection is subjective and indicates a high degree of self-possession. It is a declarative sentence rendered in the affirmative: 'Je bâtis ma demeure.' As the first person ('Je' and 'ma') is over-determined, so too is the idea of place doubled ('bâtir' and 'demeure'). The structure of the title has a repetitive texture: the first person ('Je') followed by a building word ('bâtis') followed again by the first person ('ma') followed once more by a building word ('demeure'). Given the combination of *bâtir* and *demeure*, it would be valuable to examine their meanings and etymologies and, further,

Jabès's particular usages of them. What, precisely, do *bâtir* and *demeure* signify?

Bâtir can mean *construire, édifier, élever* or *ériger* when it refers to material or physical objects such as a house or dwelling, a monument, theatre or bridge. To the concrete sense of *bâtir* an abstract connotation can be added, which includes *établir* or *fonder*, meaning that a fortune can be built or a theory constructed. Etymologically, *bâtir* traces its meaning to the early twelfth-century Judeo-French *bastir* ('to sew'). As to the noun *demeure*, it is derived from its verbal form, which means *rester* or *tarder*. In this sense *demeurer* means to dwell, to sojourn or to cease from travel, if momentarily. *Demeure*, then, means *domicile, foyer, gîte, habitation, logement, logis, maison, résidence* or *séjour*. In its extended sense *demeure* can also mean *tombeau*, as in 'la dernière demeure'.

It would be difficult to assert that Jabès employs the medieval meaning of the word, although the possibility that he had sewn together, as it were, the threads of memory and experience in the composition of his poetry (Greek *poiêsis* or 'making') is suggestive. It is certain that he understands *bâtir* in its various concrete and abstract meanings and that they find a place throughout his poetry, and, moreover, that the understanding reaches far into the very early poetry.[4] By *demeure* Jabès means a dwelling in the concrete sense, but his use of it is more often metaphorical. This couplet from 'L'Absence de lieu' is typical: 'Une demeure est une longue insomnie / sur le chemin encapuchonné des mines.' And in another instance, he can speak of a dwelling as 'Une somptueuse demeure' (from 'Erigées sur nos fables'). *Bâtir*, in the title of the book, means to build or erect or construct an edifice; it also means to build a reputation. Jabès builds his dwelling in a Promethean manner, as a heroic act of revolt committed against the established order governed by God-like beings.

> Avec mes poignards
> volés à l'ange
> je bâtis ma demeure
> (*Jbmd*, 99)

The verse that forms the title is from the refrain of the poem 'L'Auberge du sommeil'. The title thus functions as a synecdoche for the entire book, as a part taken for the whole. But while many of the poems examine the problem of dwelling, of one's sense of place, it will be obvious to the reader that some do not (e.g. 'Trois Filles de mon quartier', 'Les Condamnés', or 'Veines'). Nevertheless, as the title of the collection indicates, in a general way this problem envelops the poetry contained within it. The verse certainly represents it. For example, the refrain of 'Soleilland' ('*Mon amour un pays une ville une chambre un lit un mort un toit un côllier*') diminishes, word by word, until nothing, or just about nothing, is left:

> *Mon amour un pays une ville une chambre un lit un mort un toit*
> J'ai rendu le collier
> *Mon amour un pays une ville une chambre un lit un mort*
> Le toit s'est écroulé
> *Mon amour un pays une ville une chambre un lit*
> Le mort est enterré
> *Mon amour un pays une ville une chambre*
> Le lit est défait
> *Mon amour un pays une ville*
> La chambre est vide
> *Mon amour un pays*
> Quelle était cette ville
> *Mon amour notre amour*
> sans pays

(*Jbmd*, 111–12)

For what remains as the poem comes to an end is a love shared between two people—a love, the poet qualifies, that is stateless, 'sans pays'.

Dwelling nevertheless implies a sense of place, however provisional it may be. An individual dwells during or after a journey and it is in his dwelling that rest is taken or refuge sought. Woven into the meaning of dwelling, then, is the problem of ontology. Inextricably bound to the idea of dwelling in a place is, in Jabès's poetry, an unnerving dimension of rootlessness in the physical, external world. This is consistent with the age, as the post-war period knew no shortage of European-language poets and philosophers writing about the problem of dwelling. The most obvious example is that of Martin Heidegger, who, at about the same time Jabès wrote 'L'Auberge de sommeil', commented on the problem of being in a ravaged world. He spoke of how we '*mortals must ever learn to dwell*. What if man's homelessness consisted in this', he asked, 'that man still does not even think of the *real* plight of dwelling as *the* plight? Yet as soon as man *gives thought* to his homelessness, it is a misery no longer. Rightly considered and kept well in mind, it is the sole summons that *calls* mortals into their dwelling.'[5] Theodor Adorno had another way of approaching the problem, which he conceived as a result of taking refuge from war-time Germany in a foreign country. 'Dwelling, in the proper sense, is now impossible. The traditional residences we have grown up in have grown intolerable: each trait of comfort in them is paid for with a betrayal of knowledge, each vestige of shelter with the musty pact of family interests.'[6] The individual does not, *cannot* feel at home in his home. The world itself has become unhomely. Adorno recoiled from his dark prognosis: 'But the thesis of this paradox leads to destruction, a loveless disregard for things which necessarily turns against people too; and the antithesis, no sooner uttered, is an ideology for those wishing with a bad conscience to keep what they have. Wrong life cannot be lived rightly.'[7] Self-conscious souls such as Adorno cannot inure themselves to the problem of how to dwell because the circumstances of exile will not admit such a hardening of the senses. The paradox of this position is that one can neither enter a permanent dwelling nor remain outside it.

Edmond Jabès did not write philosophical treatises on the problem of dwelling and ontology; nevertheless, his poetry reveals the thought and anxieties of a man who had a protracted preoccupation with it. For it appears that Jabès's intention was to build a dwelling (taken in its extended sense) with the material of poetic language. Similar to Heidegger's evaluation of the crisis, Jabès's poetry unsettles the reader—that is to say, it displaces the reader from his or her 'dwelling'. Jabès is probably closer to Adorno, however, for it was he, as a refugee, who remained existentially suspended between two places. Further, the means by which each expressed this sense of exile was not altogether different: the aphoristic fragment rendered philosophical or poetic was their preferred means of telling how they perceived themselves in a shaken world.

As such, the opening statement of *Je bâtis ma demeure*, a quotation from Cervantes, asks the reader to engage himself in an exigent relationship with the author and his book, whose logic is uncomfortable and whose moral tone is inconvenient:

Si je vous la montre, à quoi vous servira-t-il de confesser une vérité si notoire? L'important c'est que, sans la voir, vous ayez à croire en elle, à la confesser, à l'affirmer, à la jurer et à la défendre. (*Jbmd*, 7)

The quotation, from *Don Quixote* 1.4, thus forms the epigraph to the book. Jabès, in the footsteps of Cervantes, is commenting on a well-known or notorious ('notoire') truth. And yet this particular truth is strangely invisible because it cannot or must not be represented directly: a *veritas abscondita*, it will not be readily shown nor can it be easily grasped. The moral challenge is to believe in a truth without ever seeing it. The question defies the reader by asking not only that he or she believe in this invisible truth; the reader must also admit it, affirm it, swear by it and defend it. Put in other terms, Jabès seems to be asking: 'What good would it do if the truth were to be shown?' The implicit reply is: 'It would do no good.' The point is that even should the truth be shown, it would still have to be believed in, confessed and so on.

When Jabès opened the collection of Cairene poetry with the quotation from *Don Quixote*, he introduced a theme that preoccupied his verse not only in *Je bâtis ma demeure* but in his texts for the years to come: the theme of a hidden truth that must nonetheless be affirmed. The poetic truth that defies representation, the truth that cannot be figured directly, the truth which is but a negative presentation but becomes representative of a cultural spirit—this truth is summarized in Jabès's comment on how he was to narrate Sarah's and Yukel's story: '*A conter leur tragique amour, je voulais me limiter*' (*LQ* I, 71). A barrier has been intentionally placed between the event and its representation: were the story to be recounted directly, its outline and details would be distorted. Similar to Hegel's *Aufhebung* ('sublation') and like Freud (himself writing in Hegel's shadow),[8] for whom the psychical mechanism of *Verneinung* ('negation') determines the circuitous path an individual takes in recollecting his or her past, Jabès too once observed: 'lorsqu'on écrit, on écrit pour dire quelque chose. Or, on ne dit jamais cette chose, une autre chose est dite qui est plus forte que ce que l'on voulait dire.'[9] There is no absence of truth. Rather, truth is invisible—negatively—while remaining present. It simply cannot be seen. It is incumbent upon the reader to affirm it even in its state of hiddenness. Reading with understanding, therefore, necessitates a leap of faith.

The first and last poems of *Je bâtis ma demeure*, those among the final ones he composed in Egypt, demonstrate Jabès's supplication. The opening one, 'L'Eau du puits' (*Jbmd*, 19–22), densely states and elaborates its subject: an undefinable threat to one's existence. Written in 1955 but published only with the Cairene collection in 1959, it consists of six stanzas of four unrhymed lines each. The lines have five or six syllables; some with a caesura, for instance, 'Nuit des cils. || Etre vu', and, most poignantly, 'Je vois, *verrai*. || Confiance', where the caesura follows the underscored future tense of *voir*. The poem's title is derived from the first line of the first stanza, 'Ouvre l'eau du puits'. It is significant that the first line of poetry in the entire collection is in the imperative[10] and is, additionally, in the second person singular, a grammatical form particular to close acquaintances or intimates: Jabès wishes to set the reader on equal ground with himself. He asks him or her to open the wellsprings of poetry. In fact, the first command, 'Ouvre', is followed immediately by a second one, 'Donne', and so reinforces the opening: 'Donne/à la soif un moment/de répit.' The first stanza ends with a continuation of the imperative (unrepeated) 'Donne': 'à la main/la chance de sauver'. Jabès here continues the practice of addressing the reader at or near the beginning of a collection of verse, a convention he subscribed to in his first collection of verse (i.e. 'Au lecteur' from *Illusions sentimentales*) as well as, later, in the *Livre des Questions* trilogy (*LQ* I, 11; 201; 345). Further on, the poem communicates a message of hope: life-giving, water quenches thirst, and the hand might afford protection from danger. But to save what or whom? The question is well worth asking even if it is not clear whose thirst needs to be quenched, and who needs to be saved and from whom. The imperative form implies an urgency, it is the poet's acknowledgement of the presence of an unmentioned threat. In other words, Jabès has abstracted danger to the point of invisibility. Either the threat cannot be seen, or, paradoxically, it is so well known that it need not be mentioned.

The first stanza, overdetermined in its messages of opening and hope, is followed in the second stanza and in subsequent ones by a fragmenting of the lines. The progressive fragmentation materializes the state of distress implied in the first stanza. Night is cut with light and vision: 'Nuit des cils. Etre vu./L'objet luit pour la main'; the lines become tautological and alliterative: 'Le bruit broute le bruit'; water fills the psychic space: 'L'eau cerne la mémoire.' The hope and calm of the first stanza is thus broken by the fracturing, overwhelming in effect, of the grammar and imagery in the second. The contrast is developed in the four remaining stanzas, which shuttle between two worlds, 'Le terme. L'avant-monde.' Little appears to be balanced; rather, the images rock to one side or the other, 'Dépassé le souci.'

One aspiration remains in the midst of catastrophe, yet even this glimmer of hope is tinged with ambiguity. 'Je suis,' affirms the poet; but immediately the affirmation is deflated: 'Je fus. Charnière/ longue file de fauves.' Another affirmation:

> Je vois, *verrai*. Confiance
> de l'arbre dans le fruit.

Will the poet see himself through the tragedy? Or will he be submerged by it, drowned in a deluge? Perhaps he has reason to be optimistic:

> Le mot survit au signe.
> Le paysage à l'encre.

The landscape is flooded with the water escaped from the well, but the flooding water is contained by the earth's folds and rivers. The pathways are infinite as the water courses through the landscape:

> Routes. L'infini.

The poet is comforted by the appearance of the living, a gift to behold:

> Le don du visage.
> Aux saisons, les rides.
> Au sol, les grands fleuves.

The first poem of *Je bâtis ma demeure*, then, with its theme of opening, is an appropriate overture to the collection written in the midst and aftermath of war by a poet who, while making a home in the land of his birth, was nonetheless considered by its government a foreigner and, by the end of his stay, a 'sujet ennemi'. The post-war years did not necessarily bring to Egypt the settling Europe was to know. The decade following the Second World War was an increasingly precarious time for foreign residents of Egypt and, in particular, for Egyptian Jewry. In an oblique way, as if the truth had to be hidden in order to be communicated, Jabès's poetry from this period reflects the uncertainty of the political situation in which he lived. In fact, in July 1953 he had an intermediary deliver a poem-tribute composed for the poet André Frénaud in Paris. 'Je vous l'envoie par un ami,' he explained to Frénaud. 'Ainsi il vous atteindra plus vite et surtout se dérobera à la censure qui, dans ce pays, s'exerce sur ce courrier d'une façon bien odieuse.'[11] If the poems and aphorisms are at all hopeful and humorous at times (e.g. 'Chanson pour trois morts étonnés', *Jbmd*, 33), it is because the poet saw hope and humour not as opiates or a denial of one's dependence on an untrustworthy government, but, on the contrary, as a means of coping with the social instability before him.

'L'Absence de lieu' (*Jbmd*, 23–7), the second poem in *Je bâtis ma demeure*, was written in 1956. It amplifies the theme of physical and existential uncertainty found in 'L'Eau du puits' while more baldly stating the subject in its title. (In fact, 'puits' will take on a more specific meaning in later work as Jabès's personal identity becomes focused on Judaism: 'Le *puits* où je *pui*se est en *terre juive*./Mon récit prend naissance dans le *puits*' (*LQ* I, 65; my emphasis).) 'L'Absence de lieu' is divided into seven numbered sections containing one, two or three lines of free verse. The first stanza contains but a single line—the only stanza to be so isolated. It equates a ground or land with a page: 'Terrain vague, page obsédée.' 'Vague' can mean either vague or wave, empty or waste; the phrase 'Terrain vague' therefore recalls the watery, wasted earth in 'L'Eau du puits'. The obsessed (or obsessive) page would seem to point to a nagging preoccupation with Mallarmé's Book, which Jabès will develop fully in *Le Livre des Questions*.[12] Here the terrain is transformed into the page of a book; it metamorphoses into a landscape not unlike what occurs in 'A toi, je parle', from *L'Ecorce du monde*: 'Ici, j'étale. Pages, impatient pays. Ici, je peuple, je boise, je bâtis. L'encre étanche le sol, rivière et pluie' (*Jbmd*, 213). The earth spreads before the poet like the pages of a book.

In the second verse Jabès offers a definition, quoted above, of a dwelling place: 'Une demeure est une longue insomnie/sur le chemin encapuchonné des mines.' Night mingles with day in the following line, and love—the timeless vehicle of hope in the abyss of despair—is introduced: 'Mes jours sont jours de racines,/sont joug d'amour célébré.' In further stanzas travel is evoked upon the damp earth: 'La terre baigne dans de/vaines visions de voyage.' So continues the poem, which closely follows the uncertainty of Jabès's thoughts, of his *place* in Egypt: 'Terre d'outre-nuit que le soleil arrache à/la méditation et aux épines du doute.' Finally, the poet regains his self-possession as he withdraws into the mystery of his own self and into his beloved:

> Mes secrets sont vergers.
> Le mystère est sans malice.
>
> Mon amour, une rose dans les cheveux,
> le message de l'homme et de la terre.

The earth may be soaked with a catastrophe we might call 'night' (the catastrophe remains unnamed) but the secret poetry of the imagination remains a tranquil orchard, which harbours, moreover, no resentment. As the poem comes to a close, the poet gathers himself in to his beloved; by concentrating on her, he restates the theme: man is homeless on this earth.

The concluding poem, 'Le Pacte du printemps', was also the final one to be composed. In the printed version it is dated, simply, '1957' (*Jbmd*, 319). The imprecise date does not tell us if it was completed before or after the immigration in June; fortunately, the manuscript in the Fonds Edmond Jabès indicates that it was completed in January of that year. Furthermore, the poem both reiterates the exilic theme of the previous ones and continues, literally, Jabès's engagement with language:

> Les mots se sont engagés dans
> le sentier des mines mais ont
> perdu ma voix Silence encrier
> renversé La plume est l'épave
> (*Jbmd*, 321)

The utter lack of punctuation has a disorienting effect: the reader senses the semantic breaks (signified by the capital letters dividing 'sentences') but continues, naturally, without pause or stop. None-theless, euphony lends the poem a musical quality: 'Ma plainte est celle de la plaie/ma chanson le dé du désir', a line that would suit some of the earliest poems of *Chansons pour le repas de l'ogre*. Again, the mid-1950s mark a period of tremendous turmoil in the life of Jabès and his family. The first half of 1957 was particularly trying as they endured a forced separation with Edmond detained in Cairo while Arlette and their two children took up residence in Paris. Despite the personal difficulties, the poetic form exhibits an almost perfect equilibrium: the alliteration of 'plainte' and 'plaie' is echoed by that of 'dé' and 'désir', and the two sets of alliteration are linked by 'celle' and 'chanson' in each line. Like the other late poems of *Je bâtis ma demeure*, 'Le Pacte du printemps' absorbs into verse the aphorisms on language prevalent in earlier texts. In a way comparable to 'L'Absence de lieu' and 'L'Eau du puits', the poem expresses despair at the political precariousness of life in Cairo and, on the other hand, a hope for renewal in France. It is well known that he did not find it there, although the country did shelter him in the wake of his expulsion. I should now like to turn to why he did not find it, and to show how his disappointment is reflected in his work.

Indices of Indecision

We have seen that in Max Jacob Jabès found his first demanding master of the craft of poetry and that, similarly, he found in Gabriel Bounoure an uncompromising (though not insensitive) critic who objectified in his letters to him the profound sense of rupture he was experiencing as he prepared to leave Egypt for France. When Jabès arrived in Paris in June 1957, he admitted to living 'dans une confusion intellectuelle telle que Bounoure fut pour moi une planche de salut' (*Dl*, 81). Bounoure was acutely aware of Jabès's anxiety. He understood how the historical moment—the decade-and-a-half following the war—was a period of crisis characterized by a discontinuity between poetry that valorizes 'une victoire de l'être' and poetry in which one detects 'un pouvoir inquiétant d'autonomie destructrice, au profit d'une expérience du vide et du silence'.[13] Hence, Bounoure was prepared to serve Jabès in whatever capacity was necessary to ensure his residence in France. This involved helping him obtain French citizenship and arrange the collected Cairene poetry for publication.

As to achieving the objective of becoming naturalized, the intention of which was announced as early as December 1957, Bounoure wrote an attestation of Jabès's contribution to the French Republic as defined by the ninth paragraph of article 64 of the French naturalization code: 'Peut être naturalisé sans condition de stage: [. . .] l'étranger qui a rendu des services exceptionnels à la France ou celui dont la naturalisation présente pour la France un intérêt exceptionnel': 'M Edmond Jabès,' wrote Bounoure, 'qui a quitté Le Caire en 1957, était au premier rang de ceux qui ont propagé activement en Egypte notre langue et notre culture. S'intéressant à toutes les formes de notre art et de notre pensée, il a servi l'idée française avec une activité infatigable et un dévouement passionné' (Bounoure's attestation of 6 December 1957). He further detailed Jabès's activities on behalf of France, including his insistence that the French language should not be given second importance in the Ecoles Israélites of Cairo, in particular in the free schools of the community. His founding of and participation in Amitiés françaises, 'organisation très active dont le but était de répandre dans la classe cultivée d'Egypte le goût de nos idées, l'amour de la littérature et de l'art de notre pays', confirmed his generosity towards France and the French. For his work he had been awarded the Croix de la Légion d'honneur in 1952. His poetry had interested Michaux, Char and Frénaud who 'le considèrent comme un des leurs et l'honorent de leur amitié'. And Gallimard had recently accepted his collected Cairene verse ·for publication. Jabès's case, then, was very strong. Nonetheless, despite Bounoure's letters of support he was not naturalized until 1968—but not because his contributions to the introduction and maintenance of French culture in Egypt went unacknowledged by the French authorities. Rather, it is most likely because his dossier was submitted only in 1966, that is, belatedly, ambivalently—as if something inside him, a sentiment of distrust, perhaps, had inhibited him from submitting it earlier.

As to attaining the second objective—integrating Jabès further within the French literary community—Bounoure had greater success. He helped him publish two pieces in major literary journals in February 1958; 'Soirées de concert ou les mots étrangers' appeared in the *Lettres nouvelles*[14] and 'Féminaire' appeared in the *Nouvelle Revue française*.[15] Bounoure was always encouraging. On 9 April 1958 he wrote from Cairo that he found 'Soirées de concert' especially exciting for 'toutes ces entrées de ballet qui auraient ravi notre cher Max Jacob'. Jabès, of course, tried independently to make a place for himself in the French literary community. In January 1958 he worked on four theatrical pieces, which he had first shown in draft to Bounoure on holiday in Lesconil, Brittany, in August 1957. The plays were eventually discarded from his *œuvre*, although at the time he enjoyed composing them (letter of 5 January 1958). This fact points not only to Jabès's sustained interest in drama, but to his increasingly strong feeling that he was not, like a Beckett or a Genet, a professional *homme de théâtre*; rather, the inclination towards dramatic compositions would be displaced, as it had been from time to time in Cairo, into his poetry. More important, preparations for the manuscript of *Je bâtis ma demeure* were nearly finished. On 28 November 1958 Jabès signed a contract with Gallimard for the book.[16] In June 1959, two years after his arrival in Paris, it finally appeared. That Bounoure immediately grasped the meaning of the book's title was characteristic of his critical acumen. On 16 September 1959 he wrote from Lesconil:

Une demeure! Il faut bien, sans doute, en bâtir une puisque nous n'en avons pas,—puisque nous sommes dans le temps et emportés par lui, dans l'espace et niés à tout moment par notre propre errance. Vous du moins vous avez trouvé une stabilité en perçant tous ces décors dont les portants ou les montants titubent. Votre demeure, ce n'est pas une tente qui claque au vent du désert. Vous avez choisi les matériaux les plus solides, après tout! Les mots de la poésie qui sont à la fois, par une paradoxale structure, chargés d'essence et de présence. Les vrais mots *tracent*; ils poussent leurs racines vers la vérité de l'Etre. (16 September 1959)

More than ever Jabès sought the comfort of friendship during the period when the collected Cairene poetry was appearing. To Henri Bouillier, a friend from Cairo, he penned the following inscription:

> 'J'ai marché avec le bruit involontaire
> que fait le silence dans l'herbe et dans l'air
> J'ai marché avec le vent et le vertige ancien
> des voûtes ... '

A Henri Bouillier
côte à côte,
cher compagnon et ami
Je bâtis
ma demeure
de l'exil et du chemin.
En toute affection [etc.]
[17]

—an unequivocal sign that Jabès himself understood that the poems were written 'in transit' and that they were the compositions of an individual rejected by his native environment.

The book's reviewers understood further resonances in the collection's title. Olivier de Magny believed Jabès was alluding to Hölderlin's verse, 'dichterisch wohnet der Mensch', which had recently received an influential commentary by Heidegger.[18] Robert Bréchon observed that poetry for Jabès was a 'parole irrépressible' and 'une réponse au monde' for its ever-cruel ability—really a challenge made to the poet—to silence speech.[19] Bréchon well understood that at least some of the poetry, in particular 'Le Pacte du printemps', dating from the watershed period of early 1957, was written 'au moment le plus tragique' of Jabès's life.[20] A perspicacious contemporary reader, he commented that Jabès had managed to distance himself from the literary trends of the moment, in particular Surrealism: 'Il serait faux de croire que cette écriture inspirée est "automatique"',[21] Jabès being too cerebrally active a writer to employ his word battery in a strange image formation. His poetry was characterized by a delicate balance between giving words free rein over meaning (which is how poetry is created but can also degenerate into unintelligible chaos) and restraint.[22] Lastly, Henry Amer (pseudonym of Henri Bouillier) underscored Jabès's recourse to language as a means of overcoming the political hostilities in which he had found himself.[23] From *Critique* to the *Nouvelle Revue française*, from the *Lettres nouvelles* to the *Lettres françaises* and elsewhere, the great organs of contemporary literature and thought in France assured Jabès of their interest. This support helped him to distance himself from the Cairene cultural scene, exemplified by reviews of his first books in local press organs such as *Israël*, the *Semaine égyptienne* and the *Progrès égyptien*, and to facilitate his thorough cultural repatriation.

Despite the enthusiasm of French critics during late 1959 and early 1960, Jabès continued to evince a troubling sense of displacement within the French literary community. He was on friendly terms with many of its principal personalities—from René Char to Jules Supervielle, from Maurice Nadeau to Michel Leiris[24]—and each contributed to helping him gain admission into respectable literary circles, that is, to be further confirmed in his *métier* as a poet. From a psychological point of view, however, he was unable to integrate his Egyptian past either comfortably or fully into his present life in Paris. An agonizing sense of abrupt separation between the periods of his life, again evidenced in the epistolary exchange with Bounoure, weighed upon him. Having left Cairo for a new position in Rabat, Morocco, Bounoure wrote mawkishly to Jabès on 22 December 1959 about the seven years he had spent in Egypt during which he had enjoyed his walks along the Nile and through Giza, 'quand tout l'orient devenait rouge et que le mystérieux vent du désert s'emparait des rues et des carrefours'. For Bounoure, this was poetry itself, and it was this image that he found again in Jabès's book. 'Toute cette poésie, cher ami, je la trouve dans votre livre et vous avez bâti votre maison avec des pierres vives accrochées au flanc du Moqattam et à l'aune de ces hommes participant depuis des millénaires à ces mystères de la vie et de la mort, dans la vallée sacrée. Maintenant que j'ai quitté cette terre, je la comprends, je la revois.' Jabès, too, had left the country, but unlike Bounoure he did not wish to relive the past. His reply of 7 January in the new year does not conceal his anxiety: his life in Egypt was finished, he insisted; he wanted to put the past behind him. But was his insistence perhaps too strong? Was there not something he wished to retain from his Egyptian years? Yes. It was a memory, and a very particular memory. It was the memory of endless desert, of an infinite space 'où je puisais ma perte et ma mort. Rien, rien que le sable qui, parfois, envahit les rues où je circule, engloutit la maison. Je me sens fils du sable, comme on est un enfant du terroir, de la pluie ou du vent—et même fils du vent de sable qui efface tout.' His social and professional contacts did little to ease the disquietude. And earning a living—no longer in finance, as had been his profession in Cairo, but in an entirely new area, film publicity—increased his mental exhaustion; the tedium of life in Paris, he complained to Bounoure, 'poursuit monotone et précise comme un chronomètre'.

Two of Jabès's compositions dating from the first half of 1960, each a memorial to a poet, bear out the compounding weight of his loneliness. The first, 'Les Voies lactées', is a homage to Maurice Blanchard, whose poems Jabès had published with Georges Henein in *La Part du sable* in 1951.[25] Dating from June 1960, the prose text was solicited for a memorial volume to Blanchard which had been in preparation since the poet's death several weeks earlier.[26] 'Les Voies lactées', itself an echo of a title from a poem in Blanchard's *Le Monde qui nous entoure*,[27] is a sombre tribute in which the shadow of death suffuses the prose. Its theme is the potential for poetry to regenerate a fallen spirit (perhaps its most mysterious capacity). The second tribute, dating from August 1960, was written in memory of the poet Pierre Reverdy, who died on 17 June of that year, although it was only published in January 1962.[28] 'La Demeure de Reverdy' is a verse lyric consisting of sixteen unmetered lines. Its brevity, however, should not divert our attention from its meaningfulness, as Jabès himself declared:

> Je suis entré dans la demeure de Reverdy
> sans connaître le poète,
> sans connaître l'architecte,
> sans connaître le maçon;
> mais j'ai découvert la maison
> sur ma route,
> après un carrefour, dans un chemin de crête
> à peine plus large que ses marches.
> Elle m'a paru, de l'intérieur, toute petite
> comme les paroles auxquelles on est habitué:
> une maison pour le geste et le sommeil d'un homme;
> mais elle étonne, comme la mémoire du monde,
> avec ses miroirs encastrés
> et le silence entre ses portes,
> avec ses pierres des différents âges de la pensée
> puis son étoile percée, le soir.

The poem, written after the collected Cairene poetry was published, again takes up Jabès's principal theme of dwelling in the house of poetry while reducing it to a concrete expression ('l'architecte', 'le maçon') in the form of a homage: the material ('pierres') with which the house is constructed is also the dead poet's name. Standing between *Je bâtis ma demeure* of 1959 and the first complete manuscript version of *Le Livre des Questions*, dating from December 1960, 'La Demeure de Reverdy' at once looks back at the poetry which Jabès no longer wished to relive and forward to a new project which at the time knew no definitive form.

From the two tributes it can be observed that Jabès was experiencing a psychic turmoil that only the composition of poetry might alleviate. It should be recalled, also, that the disorienting encounter with the anti-Semitic graffiti in the Odéon quarter of Paris, decisive in Jabès's perception of himself as a writer and a Jew, occurred at about this time. Poetry was for him a vital necessity ('une fatalité') by which he might remove himself from blight. It provided a modicum of renewal, albeit abstract and without any practical effect, to the real problems imposed by daily life. In fact, after he had described to Bounoure (in the letter of 7 January 1960) the fatigue of his Parisian life withering his creativity, he added, 'Pourtant, je m'y force, et *le récit* que j'ai entrepris avance sans faire de bonds' (Jabès's emphasis). Critically, the 'récit' he refers to is the first version of *Le Livre des Questions*, fragments of which Jabès previewed in a radio interview at the time, although not under that title.[29] For the moment, it is crucial to point out that, despite Jabès's wish to move forward, both the Blanchard and Reverdy homages refer to the Cairene period: if he was physically separated from Cairo, he was all the more obliged to distance himself from it in spirit.

This is not the case concerning his writings, in which the textual aggregate of the Cairene period and the first years of the Parisian period perceptible in the Blanchard and Reverdy tributes is also apparent in *Le Livre des Questions*. The long shadow of *Je bâtis ma demeure* casts itself, from the first volume onwards, in the Parisian texts. A careful reading demonstrates how the textual inweaving corresponds to Jabès's biographical upheaval:

> Etre dans le livre. Figurer dans *le livre des questions*, en faire partie; porter la responsabilité d'un mot ou d'une phrase, d'une strophe ou d'un chapitre.
> Pouvoir déclarer: 'Je suis dans le livre. Le livre est mon univers, mon pays,

mon toit et mon énigme. Le livre est ma respiration et mon repos.'

Je me lève avec la page que l'on tourne, je me couche avec la page que l'on couche. Pouvoir répondre: 'Je suis de la race des mots avec lesquels *on bâtit les demeures*', sachant pertinemment que cette réponse est encore une question, que cette demeure est menacée sans cesse. (*LQ* I, 36; my emphasis)

The wedged inscription of the two book titles in this passage forms a bibliographic continuity. The very fabric of Jabès's prose associates the diverse periods of his writing career. Their meeting ground, the angle at which they are joined, is the space of the book. The point is demonstrated incontestably if one considers the manuscript evidence, which demonstrates that the Cairene poetry was at the fore in Jabès's mind as he conceived *Le Livre des Questions*. Thus the first complete manuscript version begins with this quotation:

'Signes et rides sont questions et réponses d'une même encre.'
(*Je bâtis ma demeure*.)[30]

The texts of subsequent drafts show that Jabès agreed with Bounoure's observation that it was not possible for the reader (he was thinking *physically* as well as *metaphorically*) to enter into the new book by the gateway of the self-quotation. He suggested that the book needed 'une rampe d'accès qui invite le lecteur à venir entendre vos sages rabbins-poètes, qui ne sont pas individualisés car ils représentent une sagesse sur-historique' (undated letter, probably from the spring or summer of 1961). Jabès heeded the advice by drafting the first section of the book, 'Au seuil du livre', in fact a dialogue between two unnamed voices; the first belongs to the guardian of a door, the second to a passer-by who questions him (*LQ* I, 18–22). It is not impossible that Kafka's famous parable *Before the Law*, a tense dialogue between a man seeking entrance into 'the law' and another, the door's keeper, was in Jabès's mind. A closer model for the dialogic form might be Maurice Blanchot, to whom I shall return in the last third of this chapter. In any case, the quotation from *Je bâtis ma demeure* was subsequently dislodged, in the definitive edition, from the opening page to a later section (*LQ* I, 34).

Like his deployment of the self-quotation as a means of knitting an earlier text into a later one, Jabès referred frequently, if indirectly, in the course of the *Livre des Questions* trilogy to *Chansons pour le repas de l'ogre*. We know the significance of the 'chanson liée à l'enfance' in his 1975 dedication of the book (*Jbmd*, 29). A child's song is a *berceuse* or lullaby. The interaction of melody and infancy, Jabès believed, would act as a shield against death, or, at least, psychic despair. The *Chansons pour le repas de l'ogre*, he said, were placed at the beginning of the collected poems because, at the time of their writing, death was everywhere. Making a return to childhood, in the form of these songs, was Jabès's means of saving himself from death.[31] Correspondingly, the *chanson* is prevalent in *Le Livre des Questions*, in which death threatens to overtake Yukel's and Sarah's love. At times it takes the form of a book of lullabies:

> J'eusse aimé écrire *un livre de berceuses* pour être plus près de la parole de la huppe et du maïs.
> Mes *chants* ont la friabilité des os dans la terre. J'ai célébré, autrefois, la sève et le fruit. (*LQ* I, 206; my emphasis)

In this passage as elsewhere (*LQ* I, 392–3), the *chanson* is displaced onto the French for 'to cradle', *bercer* (or *berceau*, 'cradle', and *berceuse*, 'lullaby'). Jabès's use of it takes on the diametrically opposed meanings of tenderness and absolute terror: '"Un enfant juif a, pour berceau, la mort et, pour berceuse, la malédiction de la mort." Reb Assad' (*LQ* I, 398). In the following passage, a Torah scroll cradled lovingly in the arms of the synagogue goers is likened to a nestling child:

> 'Si tu n'as pas vu', disait Reb Yekel, 'dans la synagogue les hommes de ma race *bercer* dans leurs bras, comme un enfant, le lourd rouleau de leur passé divin dans son *écrin de bois*' (*LQ* I, 83; my emphasis)

The 'écrin de bois' designates the ornate, wooden case in which the Torah scroll is placed among Sephardic or oriental Jews. *Ecrin* takes on a further Jewish connotation in this analogy:

> 'Comme l'ombre est percée par la lumière, l'âme est percée par le cri,' écrivait Reb Seriel.
> Et Reb Lowel: 'L'âme juive est l'*écrin* fragile d'un cri.' (*LQ* I, 186; my emphasis)

Death is associated with insanity and the cradle (or wood) in the following passage from the section on Sarah's mental illness:

> La maison de la folle sommeille dans son *berceau* que des mains de nourrice balancent. La maison de la folle se balance *dans les arbres* que les feuilles dissimulent. (*LQ* I, 186; my emphasis)

There exists, then, an associative chain, neither entirely hidden nor fully disclosed, between death, childhood, the lullaby, the cradle, wood, Judaism and insanity.

In addition to maintaining the lyric presence in the prose passages of *Le Livre des Questions* through a semic distribution of the *chanson/berceuse* grouping, several verse poems also appear, and many of them are themselves 'songs':

Te souviens-tu de la première strophe de la *chanson* que composa Reb Ephraïm à la gloire de ses maîtres?

> 'Une porte comme un livre.
> Ouverte, fermée.
> Tu passes et tu lis.
> Tu passes. Elle demeure.'

(LQ I, p. 70; my emphasis)

The reader comes and goes, but the door, like the book, whether opened or closed, is eternal. Similar lyric moments abound: 'Table des saisons' ('Elle parle de miracle et pétrit le pain./L'innocence la dessine'), 'Chanson des sept bougies' ('Aïe, aïe où est ma peine?/Aïe, aïe où est ma vie?/Aïe, aïe où est ma ville/et mon Temple détruit?') (*LQ* I, 284–5), and the untitled song attributed to Reb Bertit but sung by Mansour (*LQ* I, 328), which could very well have been written for *Chansons pour le repas de l'ogre*. Plaintive Jewish songs, soothing lullabies, nightmare melodies of suffocating insanity—all find their place in *Le Livre des Questions*.

But it is the ubiquitous and nostalgic image of the Orient—of Egypt and its desert, and of the Mediterranean sea—that anchors the book. In a sense, Jabès has attempted to reintegrate the Orient into his poem. This claim requires explanation because, we have seen, around the time of the publication of *Je bâtis ma demeure* Jabès wished to place his Egyptian past behind him: 'Je ne veux plus revivre le passé; pour moi tout cela est fini', he wrote to Bounoure. But which past was he referring to? His past as a 'poète égyptien d'expression française', most likely, since as an émigré he would no longer write in Egypt, no longer as an Egyptian. Nonetheless there was a portion of his personal history that he could not easily part with: 'Je ne garde que la mémoire d'un désert illimité où je puisais ma perte et ma mort.' Henceforth his writing became obsessively nostalgic: withdrawn, surrendered, exhausted, exilic.

Jabès once stated that *Le Livre des Questions* is the 'livre de la mémoire' (*prière d'insérer* to *LQ* (1963)), a book written by a man with his gaze turned inward and towards his past. Having assumed his 'condition juive', he found a measure of existential proportion, as the

Egyptian desert gained mythic, unreal proportions:

Il s'était retrouvé, à midi, face à l'infini, à la page blanche. Toute trace de pas, la piste avaient disparu. Ensevelies. Il avait assisté, de l'intérieur de la tente qu'il avait plantée en arrivant—Comment n'avait-elle pas été emportée?—aux improvisations complexes du vent. Il l'avait entendu, soudain, rire avec le sable, danser avec le sable; l'amuser et l'irriter, s'amuser et s'irriter du nombre de ses grains jusqu'à devenir, dans son désir, un dieu de sable fou entraînant de monstrueuses créatures ailées à la conquête de l'univers. (*LQ* I, 60–1)

Egypt's deserts were the place where Jabès's imagination first nourished itself, imbibing the dry sand to draw forth its lesson of timelessness. The imagination of the author of *Le Livre des Questions* was little different. In his 'Lettre à Gabriel', he reflected that

Le Caire, où nous nous sommes connus, n'est pas la ville du sphinx et des pyramides. Les pyramides et le sphinx appartiennent au désert. Ils sont les témoins de la gloire du sable et du secret du Rien. Au delà de l'ordre des saisons, ils sont la plénitude de la saison morte dont le mystère hante le fleuve et le fruit. Où la clarté s'éclaire et ne voit pas et où le froid des ténèbres secoue de fièvre les astres, ils sont l'image et la borne de la haute splendeur et du savoir ivre de refus.

  Aux trois pyramides répondent les pyramides à degrés de Sakkarah; mais au sphinx? Chaque débris d'idole a interrogé le dieu avant de s'abolir dans l'assombrissement des sables. L'homme a dompté le monstre en s'interrogeant.

  Les oiseaux du désert méprisent la palme. La pierre est le tremplin dont ils éprouvent l'élasticité.

  Je suis allé au-delà des siècles rallumés où des rabbins auréolés m'attendaient pour me montrer le chemin.

  J'ai marché, de dune en dune, à la cadence de la voix explorée—Un nom, c'est le voyage d'une vie et la raison de la mort.

  J'ai médité d'oasis en oasis. (*LQ* I, 331–2)

The desert was a constant source of inspiration, and the recollection of his experience in it was his way, when he was disturbed by his uprooting, of re-establishing his mental equilibrium. Jabès did not evoke the political crisis, as he very well might have; an examination of early drafts of *Le Livre des Questions* shows that it was directly associated with the birth of the book.[32] On the contrary, his memory of Egypt was tender and loving. Astonishingly, Egypt was neither lost nor forsaken; it was displaced into the streets of Paris. Recalling his meetings with Bounoure along the Nile, he wrote:

Ce matin, entre la rue Monge et la Mouffe, j'ai laissé le désert, après la rue des Patriarches et la rue de l'Epée-de-Bois, où s'élève ma demeure,[33] envahir mon quartier. Le Nil n'était pas distant. Cependant, ce n'est pas sur ses berges où nous nous promenions autrefois que je vous ai conduit [...] (*LQ* I, 334)

Opposed to the desiccated land is the vibrant sea. In contrast to the destructive flooding of the land, an allusion to the Egyptian political upheaval, in many of the later poems of *Je bâtis ma demeure*, the Mediterranean (or at least its mental image, Jabès's memory of it) heals. The 'middle sea' naturally connects Egypt to Europe. It also separates Egypt from Europe. Much more important to Jabès, however, was its capacity to rejuvenate the devastated, vanquished spirit. This is made clear in 'Le Sud' (the final section of *Le Livre de Yukel*), an especially moving section in which Yukel learns of Sarah's death in the psychiatric hospital in which she had been interned for twelve years. A powerful force overcomes him, and, almost instinctively, he wishes to go south, that is, to the south of France. It is of course not the south of France that he needs to see, but the sea rolling up and back along its shorelines:

Quel impérieux désir poussa Yukel à prendre le train, quelques heures plus tard, pour le Sud?
Revoir la Méditerranée, écouter les leçons de la mer qui, par tous les temps, conserve son sel et ses couleurs? (*LQ* I, 342)

Sarah's mental breakdown had expulsed her from the realm of the living. The critical scene is the one in which, on the beach, she watches the letters of her name, which she had written in the sand, wash away, one by one, until nothing is left but her initials, S. S. (*LQ* I, 163–4; to which the final verses of 'Soleilland', *Jbmd*, 111–12, should be compared), which recall, in their horror, her persecutors. And Yukel was banished from Cairo. At the moment when all seems lost, upon learning of his beloved's death, a couplet from a long-forgotten song springs spontaneously to his mind:

Il se souvint—mais pourquoi est-ce elle et non une autre qui a surgi tout à coup de sa mémoire?—d'une phrase détachée d'un récit inconnu dont il retrouvait l'émotion, en la récitant:

> 'Père, quelle était cette ville
> dont nous étions les gardiens?'

Cette ville n'est pas Paris. Et, pourtant, Paris est la Capitale de ses sens. (*LQ* I, 339)

The song reflects Yukel's (and Jabès's) desire, impossible to satisfy, to return to the city of his childhood, 'parce qu'il y a peut-être une/chanson liée à l'enfance'. That city is Cairo: in fact, the couplet 'Père, quelle était cette ville/dont nous étions les gardiens?' echoes the final verses of a poem composed there: 'Quelle était cette ville/*Mon amour notre amour*/sans pays' ('Soleilland'; *Jbmd*, 112). The seductive attractions of Paris exercising themselves on his senses would never entirely silence the memory, however faint, of the time spent in the quarters of Cairo. Gabriel Bounoure similarly regretted the violent uprooting of the author of *Je bâtis ma demeure*. Writing to Jabès in the summer of 1962, he asked: 'Belle ville du Caire, comment as-tu pu chasser cette poésie qui était le reflet de ton âme?'

Maurice Blanchot's Deepest Question

But if the Cairene poetry had been banished from its native environment, its author, in time, learned to perceive it in an entirely new light. The salient features of Jabès's evolution from the middle fifties to the early sixties may be summarized as a creative stagnation in Cairo, interrupted by the geographical break with the city, which led to further torpor compounded by a confused creativity in Paris. Not very promising. The resolution, then? To accept himself as a Jewish exile, and in accepting the condition, to affirm it so as to produce an equilibrium between inner feeling and outer, material situation. I do not think that this is a simplification. The correspondence with Gabriel Bounoure, as always, opens an illuminating window onto this evolution. Critically, it shows that in the autumn of 1962, after the manuscript of *Le Livre des Questions* had been completed and accepted by Gallimard, and when he could finally pause to reflect, Jabès reconsidered the status of the early verse:

Si—comme le dit Blanchot dans son étude 'Etre juif' parue dans les deux derniers numéros de la *NRF*[34]—l'apport du judaïsme est *la parole* intermédiaire, médiatrice [...] mon livre [*Le Livre des Questions*] prend sa véritable signification dans la séparation et la blessure. Et des poèmes anciens comme, par exemple, 'La Soif de la mer' et 'Le Fond de l'eau' m'apparaissent, tout-à-coup, comme à la source de ce livre et profondément juifs [...].[35] (Undated letter, September or October 1962)

This is a pregnant statement, and it marks a decisive turning-point in Jabès's writings, more important still than the physical departure from Egypt. Specifically, this passage underscores how Jabès thought about his Cairene writings after they had been seemingly placed behind him. The passage from this letter to Bounoure thus helps broach two related problems: the place of the Cairene poetry and its relation to the Parisian work-in-progress (for Jabès was already at work on *Le Livre de Yukel* and *Le Retour au Livre*); and Jabès's growing interest in the writer Maurice Blanchot.

In Jabès's eyes, the Cairene poems—in which the stylistic traces of French modernism can be detected throughout—had become Jewish poems, and 'profoundly' so. True, the lines of 'La Soif de la mer':

> Il ne faut pas que tu bouges
> Il ne faut pas que tu respires
> Il faut que tu restes assise
> devant moi
> comme l'arbre avec son ombre
> comme le ciel avec la mer
>> (*Jbmd*, 113)

or those of 'Le Fond de l'eau':

> Je parle de toi
> et tu n'es pas n'as jamais existé
> Tu réponds à mes questions
>> (*Jbmd*, 77)

did not embody a Jewish theme, strictly speaking. Jabès had not previously perceived any Jewish content in their rhythms and similes. He does not say as much, but it is tempting to reconsider, in light of his statement to Bounoure, the epigraph to *Je bâtis ma demeure*, that is, the quotation from Cervantes concerning the hidden truth, as an indication of Jabès's interest in Marrano Jewry, or those Sephardic Jews who had converted to Catholicism during the Spanish Inquisition but remained, in secret, believing and in some cases observant Jews. At that time, Jabès does not seem to have regarded Cervantes as a Marrano, as he might have done. It was only at the end of his life, for example in the course of one of his last books, *Désir d'un commencement Angoisse d'une seule fin* (1991), that he discussed the Marranos, and this in reference to two previous books; in fact, there may very well be an allusion to *Don Quixote* in this text.[36] Another allusion may be to the Jabès family's Iberian origins, as discussed in Chapter 1 above. In any case, in 1962 the old poetry had been revitalized, it had been accorded a new life by the force of a retrospective interpretation. The poetry had not changed; rather, history had, and the developments in history account for Jabès's self-transformation from a Franco-Egyptian poet into an 'écrivain et juif'.

Jabès turned from a poetry based on a lyric 'Je' in *Je bâtis ma demeure* to a narrative form, grounded in the history of the Second World War yet transhistorical in its allegorical dimension, in *Le Livre des Questions*. In the process he began to re-visualize the old verse in a Jewish optic. Bounoure best summarized this radical transformation in his 1965 essay, 'Edmond Jabès: la demeure et le livre':

Au temps de ses premières chansons, Edmond Jabès n'arrêtait jamais sa pensée sur son appartenance au peuple d'Israël. Il se sentait libre de la tradition juive. Son oreille restait fermée à l'avertissement des phylactères. Les paroles des rabbins dans les synagogues lui paraissaient perpétuer, avec une obstination touchante mais vaine, une douleur, une colère et une foi sans rapport avec les appels qu'entend le poète aujourd'hui. Il ne reconnaissait pas encore pour siennes les détresses millénaires d'Israël, car 'la blessure est invisible à son commencement'. Mais un jour, le choc de l'histoire, l'iniquité incroyable des temps lui révélèrent que ses premières œuvres n'étaient que la préface d'un livre qui se cherchait lui-même. Un livre qui peut-être se perdrait lui-même dans le livre, deviendrait absence de livre, comme si l'œuvre devait finalement aboutir à l'absence d'œuvre. [...] Ainsi se découvrent d'étonnants rapports de ressemblance entre le monde du poète et l'univers transhistorique et historique du Juif.[37]

I observed above that Jabès's intellectual horizon greatly widened in the immediate post-war years. This growth was due to the necessity of distinguishing himself from poets such as Max Jacob or Paul Eluard. Similarly, concerning literary criticism, Jabès's taste was largely restricted to Marcel Raymond[38] (after he had put critics such as Robert de Souza and Fernand Divoire behind him). Bounoure, the commentator of great modernists such as Michaux, Supervielle and Jouve, was now penning notes on Jabès, which he gave him privately. Jabès was thrilled to receive them. 'Je ne vois pas d'autres critiques de la poésie, aujourd'hui, capables d'aller aussi loin. Peut-être Blanchot?' he wrote to Bounoure on 24 March 1953. The comparison was offered reservedly: 'Mais il n'a pas votre culture, car c'est cela l'important. Révélez un univers au lecteur et à l'auteur lui-même, cet univers qu'ils quittent et rejoignent ensemble, si difficile à découvrir, à délimiter.' The allusion to Blanchot indicates that Jabès was already acquainted with his criticism by 1953. Nearly ten years later, Bounoure suggested that Jabès's work-in-progress would contribute to current discussions on the Jewish question:

Car exil et dispersion, cruauté et mort, ce sont les conditions où le peuple juif plus qu'un autre est tragiquement engagé; mais le peuple d'Abraham est figure exemplaire du destin de tous les 'gentils' et s'il y a guérison du malheur et de l'exil juif, cette guérison est valable pour tous, même pour ceux qui ont l'illusion de se croire protégés par une stable demeure terrestre. Sur le plan poétique (et il y a certaines vérités qui n'apparaissent qu'à ce plan) vous complétez et enrichissez l'admirable spéculation de la pensée juive d'aujourd'hui. (Letter of 23 May 1962)

Bounoure was correct, the moment was indeed conclusive. In the months following the appearance of *Le Livre des Questions*, Jabès would no longer be considered the awkward Egyptian student of Parisian Surrealism, an identity which in any case his readers had largely forgotten. He would become, rather, the poet in a rich constellation of writers, critics and philosophers for whom the Jewish question was of capital importance as a means of understanding modern culture.

Determinative in Jabès's transformation was his reading of Maurice Blanchot. Jabès acknowledged his influence in the autumn of 1962; in fact, it was at this time that he sent him the manuscript of *Le Livre des Questions* because, he told Bounoure, 'son étude m'est très proche' (letter of 29 October 1962). Nevertheless, we must also consider the possibility that Blanchot helped to influence Jabès's recourse to writing within the parameters of mid-twentieth-century Jewish history even before 'Etre juif' had appeared in the summer of 1962. It is reasonable, it seems to me, to assume that Jabès had been particularly interested in Blanchot's essays and review articles in the *NRF* since at least the appearance of *Je bâtis ma demeure*. The subjects they treat correspond to those engaging Jabès at the time.

Such is the case with 'La question la plus profonde', a three-part article Blanchot published between late 1960 and early 1961.[39] If its very title would have been meaningful to Jabès, then its contents would have been even more so. The subject of the article is the time in which we live ('Nous nous interrogeons sur notre temps', Blanchot writes) and the necessity of continuously asking questions about it (*Ei*, 12). He observes that the current historical moment is characterized by reflection, by an intensive and interminable period of questioning:

Questionner, c'est chercher, et chercher, c'est chercher radicalement, aller au fond, sonder, travailler le fond et, finalement, arracher. Cet arrachement qui détient la racine est le travail de la question. [...] La question est mouvement, la question de tout est totalité de mouvement et mouvement de tout. Dans la simple structure grammaticale de l'interrogation, nous sentons déjà cette ouverture de la parole interrogeante; il y a demande d'autre chose; incomplète, la parole qui questionne affirme qu'elle n'est qu'une partie. La question serait, donc, [...] essentiellement partielle, elle serait le lieu où la parole se donne toujours comme inachevée. (*Ei*, 12, 13–14)

The necessity of pulling up one's roots is of the present moment. Associated with uprooting is the act of questioning. Related to the setting loose of the self is the affirmation that the self is fragmentary. Alluding to Freud, Blanchot remarks that all of our questions refer to the most profound question (*Ei*, 13), the question young children ask about where babies come from;[40] in other words, his remark was about our origins. But questioning is made impossible by the conditions of the age in which we live. All questions, he notes, are partial or incomplete. Blanchot seems to sense that he has been disingenuous here. To remain honest, he asks if he is not avoiding something fundamental regarding our existence. By describing all questions as mere fragments, he wonders if he has not taken flight before a question too essential to be asked in a complete manner. Which question is Blanchot fleeing from? What is he unable to confront directly? The question of God? The question of being?

Following 'La question la plus profonde' is a two-part article, written as a dialogue, on Emmanuel Levinas's *Totalité et infini: essai sur l'extériorité* (1961), in which two fundamental terms, the *inconnu* and the *étranger*, are introduced.[41] In Blanchot's interpretation of Levinas, speech is the necessary overture towards the unknown; we ask questions because we lack an essential item of knowledge. Similarly, we address the stranger—the person who is dispossessed of any dwelling—when confronted with the reality ('l'épiphanie') of his 'visage' (*Ei*, 77), that is, out of a responsibility to respond to his need. The relation between self and other thus necessitates an ethical posture, specifically, an ethic predicated on an impossibility: '*Nommer le possible, répondre à l'impossible*' (*Ei*, 92; Blanchot's emphasis). 'Cette réponse,' one of the voices in this dialogue says, 'cette parole qui commence par répondre et qui, en ce commencement, redit la question qui lui vient de l'*Inconnu* et de l'*Etranger*, voilà ce qui est au principe de cette responsabilité, telle qu'elle l'exprimera, par la suite, dans le langage dur de l'exigence: il faut parler' (*Ei*, 92–3; my emphasis). By speaking we are able to overcome what had impeded us previously, namely, the impossibility of replying to a given question; furthermore, speaking out of necessity has the virtue of maintaining the dialogue. But Blanchot's thoughts on necessity grow out of very precise circumstances: an individual must ask questions in the presence of the Unknown and the Stranger. Yet these terms imply absence as well. Thus, not only is the act of questioning made impossible, but it is likewise impossible to provide an answer to the question. Nonetheless, keeping our word or providing an answer is our responsibility to the Unknown or to the Stranger.

These seemingly obscure remarks are odd and perhaps even disconcerting. They are without any connection to the historical moment, and would seem to contradict Blanchot's statement in 'La question la plus profonde': 'Nous nous interrogeons sur notre temps.' What aspect of our age, then, was Blanchot referring to? While perhaps unable to articulate the thought when he wrote his early dialogue on Levinas, in a tribute to him from 1979 he did not dissociate Levinas's philosophy from history. There he recalled how Levinas had dedicated *Autrement qu'être ou au-delà de l'essence* (1974) 'A la mémoire des êtres les plus proches parmi les six millions d'assassinés par les nationaux-socialistes, à côté des millions et des millions d'humains de toutes confessions et de toutes nations, victimes de la même haine de l'autre homme, du même antisémitisme.' How was it possible to carry out a philosophical discussion when the memory of Auschwitz was fresh? Was this not obscene, an insult to the victims of anti-Semitism?[42] In the 1970s, Levinas and the question of Auschwitz were, in Blanchot's writings, necessarily associated. History had imposed itself, Levinas asserts; it obliges us to recognize the other. In 1961 and early 1962, however, it would appear that his claim that the individual is somehow answerable to the stranger had been evasive, if only because it was made without offering a concrete illustration. That inconsistency is temporary.

Blanchot's thoughts on questioning the historical moment, the post-Auschwitz age, specifically, are connected to his April 1962 review of Robert Antelme's account of his incarceration in Gandersheim and Buchenwald, *L'Espèce humaine* (1st edn. 1947).[43] In a sense these reflections remedy his previous lapses into abstraction by focusing on a specific moment. Antelme's book leads him to ask the question, 'Qui est "Autrui"?' *L'Espèce humaine* 'n'est pas seulement un témoignage sur la société des camps, il nous conduit à une réflexion essentielle. Je ne dis pas qu'il y a là, toute écrite, une réponse, mais ce qui pousse ce livre vers nous, sans tenir compte des années ni des cir-constances (tout en en tenant compte cependant), c'est ce qu'il reste

de force interrogative dans la question' (*Ei*, 191–2). Here, Blanchot would seek to question the historical moment 'sans tenir compte des années ni des circonstances'. Is that possible? Is history still mute, or rather has Blanchot kept a deaf ear to the reality of its horror? His intention would be to discuss the human being's act of questioning in the most grave of circumstances imaginable, to write about the war without mentioning it: 'Voilà ce qu'il faudrait méditer: quand l'homme, par l'oppression et la terreur, tombe comme en dehors de soi, là où il perd toute perspective, tout repère et toute différence, ainsi livré à un temps sans délai qu'il endure comme la perpétuité d'un présent indifférent, alors son dernier recours, *au moment où il devient l'inconnu et l'étranger*, c'est-à-dire destin pour lui-même, est de se savoir frappé, non par les éléments, mais par les hommes et de donner le nom d'homme à tout ce qui l'atteint' (*Ei*, 193–4; my emphasis). In *L'Espèce humaine* the need for the survivor to speak attains urgent proportions, despite (because of?) the impossibility of doing so. What most fascinates Blanchot in Antelme's book is the absolute authority the camp experience imposed on the prisoner. It is not 'seulement un témoignage sur la réalité d'un camp; ni une relation historique, ni un récit autobiographique. Il est clair que, pour Robert Antelme, et sans doute pour beaucoup d'autres, se raconter, témoigner, ce n'est pas de cela qu'il s'est agi, mais essentiellement *parler*' (*Ei*, 198; Blanchot's emphasis). While in the camps, Antelme and his fellow prisoners, more than anything else, wished to 'parler, être entendus enfin'. It was the will to communicate with the other, to speak to the other prisoners despite the prohibition on speaking, and then to speak to his present-day reader, that compelled Antelme to write. And yet a frightening paradox imposed itself: the need to speak to the other proved impossible: 'A peine commencions-nous à raconter, que nous suffoquions', wrote Antelme (quoted in *Ei*, 199). 'Pourquoi ce déchirement?' asks one of the two interlocutors of Blanchot's dialogue:

— Pourquoi cette douleur toujours présente, et non seulement ici dans ce mouvement extrême, mais déjà, comme je le crois, dans la parole la plus simple?

— Peut-être parce que, dès que deux individus se rapprochent, il y a entre eux quelque pénible formule, du genre de celle que nous avons exprimée en commençant, et ils parlent pour l'oublier ou pour la nier ou pour la représenter. (*Ei*, 200)

The constellation of ideas in this exchange are the question and its response, the possible and the impossible, the unknown and the stranger, the vital necessity of speaking in circumstances where one's voice is choked with terror. It leads to, but is not wholly crystallized in, the article that riveted Jabès to the Cairene poetry, Blanchot's 'Etre juif'.

The article is a review of three books on Judaism from that year—Albert Memmi's *Portrait d'un Juif*, André Neher's *L'Existence juive* and Charles Touati's adaptation of Isaac Heinemann's *La Loi dans la pensée juive*—and lets them serve as a foil for Blanchot's own reflections on the meaning of Jewishness. Blanchot objects to Memmi's characterization of the *être juif*, which does not differ significantly from that of a Heine or a Clara Malraux (*Ei*, 181), as essentially negative: 'Le Juif est malaise et malheur.' Sartre is also criticized for his description of the Jew as the negative to the anti-Semite's anti-Semitism. Blanchot will have none of this. He puts forth: 'Il y a une pensée, une vérité juive, c'est-à-dire qu'il y a, *pour chacun de nous*, une obligation de rechercher si, à travers cette pensée et cette vérité, un certain rapport de l'homme avec l'homme est en jeu dont nous ne pourrions nous écarter qu'en nous dérobant à une interrogation nécessaire. *Certes, cette interrogation ne sera pas, ici, accueillie comme celle d'une exigence religieuse*' (*Ei*, 182; my emphasis). While this is not apprehended as a religious prescription, Blanchot believes that it is incumbent on each individual, Jew and non-Jew, to discern what is essential in the 'vérité juive' by which we live, one neighbour next to the other. In other words, the obligation is to define oneself in relation to the other. He goes further. To Pasternak's questions, 'Que signifie être juif? Pourquoi cela existe-t-il?', Blanchot answers, 'Cela existe pour qu'existe l'idée d'exode et l'idée d'exil comme mouvement juste; cela existe, à travers l'exil et par cette initiative qu'est l'exode, pour que *l'expérience de l'étrangeté* s'affirme auprès de nous dans un rapport irréductible; cela existe pour que, par l'autorité de cette expérience, *nous apprenions à parler*' (*Ei*, 183; my emphasis). Unbound, the Jew embodies dynamism just as the nomad moves through space. The Jew exists so that we (here, the non-Jew?) understand the idea of foreignness ('étrangeté'), of actively pulling up one's roots in order to assert oneself in a new environment. The ethical lesson the Jew imparts to humanity at large is that it is necessary to speak to and for the other. The 'vérité nomade', as Blanchot calls it, is distinguished from the sedentary 'être païen', whose purpose is to 'se fixer, se ficher en terre en quelque sorte, s'établir par un pacte avec la permanence

qui autorise le séjour et que certifie la certitude du sol' (*Ei*, 183). Finally, asserts Blanchot:

Il y a une vérité de l'exil, il y a une vocation de l'exil, et si être juif, c'est être voué à la dispersion, c'est que la dispersion, de même qu'elle appelle à un séjour sans lieu, de même qu'elle ruine tout rapport fixe de la puissance avec *un* individu, *un* groupe ou *un* Etat, dégage aussi, face à l'exigence du Tout, une autre exigence et finalement interdit la tentation de l'Unité-Identité. (*Ei*, 184; Blanchot's emphasis)

In contrast to Memmi's negative position, Blanchot argues that there is a positive value to the 'être juif': to affirm one's status beyond the enclosed immediacy of a fixed space, to advance across territory without fastening roots. Knowing only the rudiments of a habitation, the 'être juif', obliged to what Blanchot calls the 'Tout' (from which, we can infer, is the absolute Other), is at liberty to displace himself, to relocate. To the Jew is opposed the pagan, master of the land. It is to the 'être païen' that the Jew must justify his sojourn in a strange land. He is subject to the good will of the host, and continuously troubled by the possibility of his caprice.

Jabès, for his part, delivers much the same message concerning uprootedness and the 'vérité de l'exil' in *Le Livre des Questions*. But he does so clearly from the perspective of one who has suffered the pain and humiliation of an uprooting. The recollection of a lived experience informs his description, in which nothing the Jew experiences or possesses can be taken for granted:

Etre Juif, c'est avoir à justifier de l'existence; c'est avoir, en commun, les mêmes nuits sans sommeil, avoir essuyé les mêmes insultes; c'est avoir cherché désespérément la même bouée, la même secourable; c'est avoir nagé, nagé nagé pour ne pas sombrer. (*LQ* I, 77)

The Jew's existence, his being, is described in terms of pheno-menological essentialism, but also as a physical condition, something that can be read on the lines of his face.

Etre Juif, c'est avoir les mêmes cernes sous les yeux, le même sourire sceptique—et, pourtant, le Juif est capable de grands enthousiasmes—; c'est avoir cligné les yeux face au soleil défendu.

The Jew is associated with an unflinching, absolute conception of justice because he himself has so often been the victim of injustice. As such, 'le Juif est l'ennemi de ceux qui fondent leur justice sur l'injustice. Gênant pour les pouvoirs absolus, il est la cible de ceux qui détiennent le pouvoir absolu; gênant parce que réfractaire.' 'Etre Juif', writes Jabès, 'c'est apprendre à se mouvoir à quelques mètres du sol qui vous est contesté; c'est ne plus savoir si la terre est d'eau ou d'air ou d'oubli.'

> Que de ruses emploie-t-il pour survivre. Quelle ingéniosité dans les moyens, quelle application dans ses métamorphoses.
> Déduire, s'adapter, tracer. On peut s'acharner sur lui, on ne réussit pas à le détruire.
> Mi-homme, mi-poisson, mi-oiseau, mi-fantôme, il y a toujours une moitié de lui qui échappe au bourreau.

For Jabès, like Blanchot, the Jew knows the experience of exile and exodus. But by seeking a positive value in Judaism, in contrast to Memmi, and by subordinating the Jew as other in relation to the non-Jew, Blanchot largely sidesteps the issue of personal suffering, which is central to Jabès's vision of being Jewish. The Jew must justify his existence, suffer injustice, and endure endless trials, and still (just how remains ultimately inexplicable) survive the executioner's attempts at annihilating him. Perhaps Memmi was correct after all: 'Le Juif est malaise et malheur.'[44] Furthermore, like Blanchot, Jabès does not, in the first books of *Le Livre des Questions*, name outright the historical referent of his poem, Auschwitz. As the absent centre of his work, it is merely suggested (presented negatively, as it were). though to tremendous effect. It was only in later works, such as *Un Etranger avec, sous le bras, un livre de petit format*, that he would write of 'Invisible Auschwitz, dans son horreur visible' (*Et*, 14).

Blanchot returned to the problem of speech inhibition and disruption, specifically in reference to *Le Livre des Questions*, about two years after his discussion of *L'Espèce humaine*. The article in which he puts forth his reading of Jabès, 'L'interruption', is divided into two parts. The first contains a reflection on the problem of interruption in the course of a conversation, which prefaces the second part, a discussion of *Le Livre des Questions*.[45] Blanchot postulates two categories of interruption. 'Dans le premier cas, l'arrêt-intervalle est comparable à la pause ordinaire qui permet le "tour à tour" d'un entretien. Alors, la discontinuité est essentielle, puisqu'elle promet l'échange' (*Ei*, 107). 'Mais il y a une autre sorte d'interruption, plus énigmatique et plus grave,' he adds (*Ei*, 108). The second category of interruption involves the separation of two individuals in conversation, not so that one may speak while the other listens, but, more profoundly, to enhance the other's foreignness, 'l'étrangeté entre nous'. 'Maintenant, ce qui est en jeu et demande rapport, c'est tout ce qui me sépare de l'autre, c'est-à-dire l'autre dans la mesure où je suis infiniment séparé de lui, séparation, fissure, intervalle qui le laisse infiniment en dehors de moi, mais aussi prétend fonder mon rapport avec lui sur cette interruption même, qui est une *interruption d'être*' (*Ei*, 108–9; Blanchot's emphasis). Being is interrupted, it is placed in suspense, in this second category of interruption. A space opens between two people in dialogue. For Blanchot, there is at once 'une exigence dialectique' at work between two individuals in conversation and 'une exigence non dialectique de la parole: la pause qui permet l'échange; l'attente qui mesure la distance infinie'. Thus there is a third category of interruption, derived from the first two. It is out of this *neutral* form of interruption that the 'acte poétique' grows forth, but other forms of 'cessation', which are 'très profondes, très perverses, de plus en plus perverses', and which postulate 'l'ambiguïté', 'le desœuvrement (peut-être la pensée)' are also present (*Ei*, 112). Blanchot confesses to having expressed himself in the abstract.[46] He therefore offers to substantiate his reflections by quoting from passages of *Le Livre des Questions*. His approach to the book is prudent, and his introduction can be characterized as almost timid: 'Du livre [...], je m'étais promis de ne rien dire. [...] Il y a ainsi des œuvres qui se confient à notre discrétion. [...] Mais vient un moment où l'espèce d'austérité qui est le centre de tout livre important, fût-il le plus tendre et le plus douloureux, le délivre de nous et rompt les liens' (*A*, 252). Blanchot gives a very dense initial description of Jabès's book before proceeding to unpack it all by analysing it in terms of his thoughts on interruption. 'Dans l'ensemble de fragments, de pensées, de dialogues, d'invocations, de mouvements narratifs, paroles errantes qui constituent le détour d'un seul poème, *je retrouve à l'œuvre les puissances d'interruption* par lesquelles ce qui se propose à l'écriture (le murmure ininterrompu, cela qui ne s'arrête pas), doit s'inscrire en s'interrompant' (my emphasis). But Jabès does not merely illustrate the force of interruption, of a poem breaking apart into a thousand shards. There is something distinctly yet enigmatically Jewish about Jabès's undertaking:

Mais ici, dans *Le Livre des Questions*—de là son insécurité et sa force douloureuse—, la rupture est non seulement enregistrée par la fragmentation poétique à ses différents niveaux de sens, mais interrogée et subie, puis ressaisie et rendue parlante, toujours deux fois et chaque fois redoublée: dans l'histoire et dans l'écriture en marge de l'histoire. Dans l'histoire où le centre de la rupture s'appelle le judaïsme. Dans cette écriture qui est la difficulté du poète, de l'homme qui veut parler juste, mais qui est aussi la justice difficile, celle de la loi juive, la parole inscrite avec laquelle on ne joue pas, et qui est esprit parce qu'elle est le fardeau et la fatigue de la lettre. (*A*, 252)

Interruption in Jabès's writings is characterized by an absent origin, but this is consistent with all writing after the smashing of the first set of Tables of the Law. All writing inscribes the condition of Jewish existence in the Diaspora: 'pas d'entente vraiment première, pas de parole initiale et intacte, comme si l'on ne parlait jamais que la seconde fois, après avoir refusé d'entendre et pris ses distances à l'égard de l'origine' (*A*, 254). The broken Tables, forever lost, are thus subject to interpretation. It is because they no longer exist in this physical world that they necessitate an act of interpretation carried out with the dignity of rabbinic tradition (*A*, 254). Interpretation thus functions as a mediation between a lost origin and a projected future, between Judaism and writing:

Les deux expériences, unies et désunies, celle du judaïsme, celle de l'écriture, qu'exprime E. Jabès et qu'il affirme l'une par l'autre, mais aussi par la patience et la générosité de sa *double vocation*, ont donc leur commune origine dans l'ambiguïté de cette rupture, rupture qui laisse intact et même révèle, par son éclat, le centre (le noyau, l'unité), mais qui est peut-être aussi l'éclat du centre, le point excentré qui n'est centre que par l'éclat de la brisure. (*A*, 256; my emphasis)

The interruption of writing and the interruption of Judaism—Jabès's 'double vocation'—are constitutive of the third form of interruption, the neutral, from which emerges the 'acte poétique'. The reader will surely find the analytical weave very tight and thus difficult to unravel. Blanchot's analysis of Jabès's book is closer to a hermeneutic juggling act than one might have wished. But it served to stimulate Jabès to further thought, to provide him with a modicum of self-understanding during a prolonged period of intense self-doubt.

From the beginning of the second half of 1962, Blanchot confirmed Jabès's own questioning of his exile and, moreover, the form of his *entretiens* validated the dialogic form of Jabès's texts. Both writers used the artifice of polyphony to explore issues close to their respective concerns. Jabès's reading of Blanchot's 'Etre juif' and related articles may have permitted him to write unself-consciously on Jewish subjects, a commitment he had not made in the first forty years of his writing career, but 'L'interruption' had the additional effect of objectifying Jabès's own articulation of his exilic condition. For Blanchot, Jabès represented the most concrete example to date in contemporary French and Jewish literature of a writer who simultaneously put into question the act of writing and the problem of being Jewish. My conviction is that Blanchot's reading of Jabès brought him closer than other writers in his move to reflecting on the era after Auschwitz, about the Jew within history, and, in particular, the question of the Jew in 'notre temps'. Blanchot first had to pass through the works of Levinas, Antelme, Memmi and others. But Jabès's book was a *récit éclaté*, a poetic narrative inventive in how it recounted a story; *Le Livre des Questions* was situated 'dans l'histoire et dans l'écriture en marge de l'histoire; dans l'histoire où le centre de la rupture s'appelle le judaïsme'. By 1964, Jabès had directed Blanchot to consider the importance of history (a step he had only partially taken in previous years) through examining the place of the Jews in it. It is true, as Blanchot noted, that the commentator who spoke with the greatest intellectual authority on the rupture-interruption caused by the breaking of the Tables was Emmanuel Levinas (*A*, 254). For Blanchot, Levinas, as contemporary philosophy's Jewish philosopher, incarnated the extreme ontological tension between thinking and Judaism in much the same manner as Jabès, contemporary literature's (Jewish) poet, did between writing and Judaism. It mattered little that Levinas, in Blanchot's view, 'se méfie des poèmes et de l'activité poétique' (*Ei*, 76).

But what of this peculiar distrust of poetry? The comment appears very curious, if one considers Levinas's 1956 essay 'Le regard du poète', a short study of Blanchot's critical essays underscoring his predilection for nomadic literature:

L'art, d'après Blanchot, loin d'éclairer le monde, laisse apercevoir le sous-sol désolé, fermé à toute lumière qui le sous-tend et rend à notre séjour son essence d'exil et aux merveilles de notre architecture—leur fonction de *cabanes dans le désert*. [...] Cabanes dans le désert. Il ne s'agit pas de revenir en arrière. Mais pour Blanchot, la littérature rappelle l'essence humaine du nomadisme.[47]

This statement resembles, in its import, another one Levinas made ten years later on the Jewish condition itself: 'La vraie vie intérieure n'est pas une pensée pieuse ou révolutionnaire qui nous vient dans un monde bien assis, mais *l'obligation d'abriter toute l'humanité de l'homme dans la cabane*, ouverte à tous les vents, de la conscience.'[48] Here, then, Levinas, in addition to having Blanchot in mind when he wrote these lines, was perhaps also thinking of Jabès, whose *Livre des Questions* trilogy had just been completed, even if he withheld public judgement on his writings for several years, until 1972.[49] Blanchot himself refers to Levinas's position regarding Jabès when he writes, 'l'on ne voit rien à répondre au critique austère, gardien de la rigueur, lorsqu'il dénonce l'affirmation poétique' (*A*, 255).[50] Furthermore, Levinas's statement in 'Le regard du poète' might be the source of Bounoure's comment on *Je bâtis ma demeure* in his letter to Jabès of 16 September 1959: 'Votre demeure, ce n'est pas une tente qui claque au vent dans le désert'—referring to the poetic language Jabès had chosen to build his dwelling.

What Blanchot found appealing in Levinas—the inclusion of a vulnerable, frail humanity when considering specifically Jewish problems —he similarly found in Jabès, whose texts further spoke of shades of Judaism and hinted at the Jewishness of non-Jews. Jabès's writings challenged readers to step beyond their narrow conceptions of Judaism by staking a claim on their doubts. Judaism was for him beyond the pale of a sometimes guilt-inducing orthodoxy, a position analagous to how he viewed himself as a writer and a Jew—as hardly one or the other, and yet quintessentially so. His wager was made modestly, with no pretence to righteousness: 'O toi qui n'es pas Juif—Je l'étais si peu. Je le suis—je t'introduis dans mes domaines; ô toi qui n'es pas écrivain—Je l'étais si peu. Je le suis—je te fais don de mes livres; ô toi qui es Juif et peut-être écrivain' (*LQ* I, 70). It is true that Jabès did not have Levinas's training as a philosopher, and that the analysis and interpretation of the Talmud, within the tradition, surpassed his knowledge; but that does not mean that he was lacking in insight into the twin conditions of being a writer and a Jew:

— Tu nous as parlé de la parole et nous avons cherché, dans tes paroles, le refuge.

Nous nous souvenons de tes paroles.

Tu nous as parlé de la liberté qui est une plante et de la difficulté d'être Juif. Tu nous as rapporté des paroles de rabbins.

— Je vous ai rapporté mes paroles. *Je vous ai parlé de la difficulté d'être Juif, qui se confond avec la difficulté d'écrire; car le judaïsme et l'écriture ne sont qu'une même attente, un même espoir, une même usure.* (*LQ* I, 136; my emphasis. Cf. *LQ* I, 398)

Writing and Judaism were inextricably bound to each other in *Le Livre des Questions* and subsequent books. As such one of Jabès's contributions to French writing and Jewish thought in the years following the Second World War was to maintain the distinction while demonstrating, at the same time, that the distinction was untenable. Maurice Blanchot was the first among Jabès's critics to bring this paradox to light, and if I have dwelt at some length on his statement, it is because he among them all articulated it with the greatest force.

Unlike Levinas, who introduced the rigorous study of Talmudic hermeneutics into the university setting and most effectively revived in the post-Holocaust era the role of the Jewish intellectual commenting on the place of the Jews, of Israel and of Jewish history in non-Jewish society, Jabès did not, as a pedagogue, guide a group of students in their return to classical Jewish sources. Unlike Blanchot, whose literary criticism ushered in a new era of textual commentary, Jabès remained outside the literary critical fold; after 1963 he published only occasional essays on his predecessors and contemporaries (gathered, mainly, in *Le Livre des Marges*). And unlike Derrida (for he must be included in this evaluation), whose *De la grammatologie* (1967) questioned the logocentric foundations of Western metaphysics and unleashed, in its wake, innumerable permutations in the domains of anthropology, literary criticism, psychoanalysis, continental philosophy and studies on gender and beyond, Jabès cannot be considered the initiator of a new critical apparatus. His contribution to contemporary thought was much more modest, and yet it seems quite likely that Derrida was including himself among those for whom, in the ten years since the first volume of *Le Livre des Questions* appeared, 'rien ne s'est formé qui n'ait son précédent quelque part dans le texte de Jabès'.[51] Jabès, then, was at once at the centre and the periphery of critical thinking in the 1960s and subsequent years.

Levinas and Blanchot discussed the Jabésian text at various times in brief critical articles devoted to the subject, the most valuable of which are gathered in the 1972–3 issue of the *Nouveaux Cahiers* published on the occasion of an assessment of Jabès's place in contemporary writing and thought. In his contribution, Levinas defined the true poet as he who '*perd sa place*'. In fact, his poetry is an 'opening in space'. In contrast to minor Jewish poets, who merely make references to Jewish history or classical sources as a means to developing a theme, Jabès's texts merit the distinction of authenticity because 'ils tournent encore dans le vertige qui vient de ce qu'il appelle "le lieu vertigineux du livre"'.[52] It is thus that Jabès was placed on a par with writers such as S. Y. Agnon, Martin Buber and Paul Celan,[53] who held an interrogation of the metaphysical dimensions of language to be central and who opened the path of the Self towards the Other.

Blanchot defined Jabès's writings (indeed, he goes so far as to assert the same for all writing after the Shoah) in relation to the fact of the death camps and the extermination of the Jews.[54] Specifically, Jabès embraces at least two paradoxes, the first of which has to do with the tension between returning and moving forward and the second, between remaining in place and wandering:

Le 're' du retour [i.e. *Le Retour au Livre*] s'inscrit comme l''ex' de l'exil, ouverture de toute extériorité: comme si le retour, loin d'y mettre fin, marquait le commencement en son recommencement d'un mouvement qui ne peut savoir s'il est l'exode. Revenir, ce serait en venir de nouveau à s'ex-centrer, à errer. Israël, pour autant qu'il affirme la loi du retour non seulement n'existe que par l'exil, en rapport avec l'exil qu'il voudrait et à bon droit faire disparaître, mais est lui-même un appel à un nouveau exil, exil au lieu même et par le lieu où celui-ci s'achève. Seule *demeure* l'affirmation *nomade*.[55]

Jabès's writings, then, enshrine a dialectic of return and exile, of dwelling and nomadism, which reflect not only the millennial history of the Jews (and, most recently, in the State of Israel's legislation that any diaspora Jew may immigrate unimpeded to the country) but also the most important contemporary poetry whose subject is the war years, as the allusion to Char's *Seuls demeurent* (1938–44) suggests.

To recapitulate, there was a clear if troubled reciprocity between Jabès and Blanchot. In the early sixties, Jabès's existential exile, his Jewish condition, was confirmed by the latter; while a reading of Jabès, in conjunction with his interests in Levinas, Antelme and the others, further sensitized Blanchot to the presence of the other in his midst, of his essential truth and of his lived history. Jabès was conscious of their shared inclinations. But it was only in the course of a brief dialogue in *Un Etranger avec, sous le bras, un livre de petit format* that he proffered a view of their odd interdependence, or what Blanchot understood as a 'friendship' but Jabès preferred to call an 'alliance' ('pacte'; *Et*, 49). In this dialogue, two nameless voices converse; the first is perhaps a journalist who asks the questions, the other is in all likelihood Jabès:

— Comment est née votre amitié?
— C'est une longue histoire.
— Lui as-tu écrit?
— Il m'a dit qu'il possédait quelques lettres de moi.
— Alors?
— Eh bien. Elle est née de l'intérêt croissant porté à ses ouvrages; de la distance accentuée, au fur et à mesure de mes lectures, avec moi-même, inévitable conséquence de ma proximité avec lui. Répéter ses gestes, ses mots; épouser ses fantasmes, surmonter ses déceptions [...] (*Et*, 48)

Notes to Chapter 4

1. Jean-Luc Bayard, 'La demeure ou les trois temps du livre', *Quinzaine littéraire* 582 (1991), 15.
2. Maurice Nadeau, 'Pour Edmond Jabès', *Quinzaine littéraire* 582 (1991), 13. Originally in *Instants* 1 (1989), 9–12.
3. Brooke Fredericksen, 'Dwelling in Words: The Early Poetry of Edmond Jabès', *French Forum* 3 (1993), 335–54.
4. Cf. 'J'ai construit un chalet', *Is*, 24: 'J'ai construit un chalet au milieu d'un jardin/où j'ai mis mon âme afin qu'elle soit heureuse;/ce chalet, c'est un rêve éclos sur mon chemin;/ce jardin c'est un vers où s'attarde, flirteuse,//la nymphe Hamadryade.'
5. Martin Heidegger, 'Building Dwelling Thinking' (1951), in *Poetry, Language, Thought*, trans and intro. by Albert Hofstadter (New York: Harpers, 1971), 161; Heidegger's emphasis.
6. Adorno, *Minima Moralia*, 38.
7. Ibid. 39.
8. See Jean Hyppolite's 'Commentaire parlé sur la *Verneinung* de Freud', in Jacques Lacan, *Ecrits* (Paris: Seuil/Le Champ freudien, 1966), 879–87. André Green has further explored Freud's relationship to Hegel in 'Hegel et Freud: éléments pour une comparaison qui ne va pas de soi', in *Le Travail du négatif* (Paris: Minuit/Critique, 1993), 43–72.
9. Saint-Chéron, 'Entretien avec Edmond Jabès', 67.
10. Dominique Combe, 'Citation de Jabès', *Temps modernes* 538 (1991), 171.
11. The letter, dated 'Le Caire, 9 Juillet 1953', is in the Fonds André Frénaud of the Bibliothèque littéraire Jacques Doucet (Ms. 49.526). See also Jaron, 'Repiquage poétique', 119.
12. See Serge Meitinger, 'Mallarmé et Jabès devant le livre: analyse d'une divergence culturelle', in Stamelman and Caws (eds.), *Ecrire le livre autour d'Edmond Jabès*, 133–45; and Eric Benoit, *Ecrire le cri: 'Le Livre des Questions' d'Edmond Jabès, exégèse* (Bordeaux: Presses Universitaires de Bordeaux, 2000), 33, 42, 46 n., 68–9, 78, 88, 91 and 179 n., as well as his *De la crise du sens à la quête du sens: Mallarmé, Bernanos, Jabès* (Paris: Cerf, 2001).
13. Gabriel Bounoure, introduction to *Marelles sur le parvis*, 4.
14. *Lettres nouvelles* 57 (1958), 200–7.
15. *NRF* 62 (1958), 360–2. An excerpt from the introduction to Bounoure's *Marelles sur le parvis* appeared in the following issue: *NRF* 63 (1958), 414–28.

16. Letter in FEJ.

17. In the collection of Henri Bouillier, whom I thank for allowing me to reproduce the dedication.

18. Olivier de Magny, 'Le pouvoir de féerie', *Lettres nouvelles*, NS 23 (1959), 30–1. The French translation of Heidegger's essay ('L'homme habite en poète'), by André Préau, appeared in *Cahiers du sud* 344 (1958), 49–66, that is, in the year preceding de Magny's review.

19. Robert Bréchon, 'Edmond Jabès ou la foi poétique', *Critique* 153 (1960), 123.

20. Ibid. 124.

21. Ibid.

22. Ibid. 124–5.

23. Henry Amer, *NRF* 81 (1959), 523.

24. In 1952 Char published Jabès in *Le Temps de la poésie* 6 (1952), 28–30, which appeared through GLM. All of the contributions (save Char's introduction) were unsigned. Jabès contributed an excerpt from 'Veines' (*Jbmd*, 177–9, beginning 'Chevaliers qui renonciez à dire' and ending 'Chevaliers aux chansons de bourgeons et de sable/le visage dans les médaillons de rosée'). See also Char's five letters to Jabès written between 26 Feb. 1963 and 25 Sept. 1972, in *Nouveaux Cahiers* 31 (1972–3), 54–5. Further, Char's poetry is a strong intertextual presence in Jabès's dating from the late 1940s; see Jaron, 'Edmond Jabès ou le fonctionnement du palimpseste', 194–5. Jabès and Leiris knew each other as early as 1961; see Jaron, 'Repiquage poétique', 126–9. Nadeau recounted his first meeting with Jabès in 'Pour Edmond Jabès', 11. Supervielle wrote to Jabès upon the publication of *Jbmd*. His letter of 31 Aug. 1959 is in the Gabriel Bounoure–Edmond Jabès correspondence dossier.

25. Maurice Blanchard, *Le Monde qui nous entoure*, in *Les Barricades mystérieuses*, pref. by Jean-Hugues Malineau (Paris: Gallimard/Poésie, 1994), 93–107.

26. Apparently for *Tel quel*, to have been edited by Noël Arnaud. However, that volume never appeared, and the tribute remains unpublished. See Pierre Peuchmaurd, *Maurice Blanchard* (Paris: Seghers, 1988), 218. The typescript is now in FEJ.

27. Blanchard, *Les Barricades mystérieuses*, 106.

28. Edmond Jabès, 'La Demeure de Reverdy', *Mercure de France* 1181 (1962), 148. Bounoure's text, 'Pierre Reverdy et sa crise religieuse de 1925–1927', along with other tributes to the poet, appeared in the same volume.

29. On 21 Feb. 1960 Alain Cuny featured Jabès in an RTF radio programme, 'Poésie vécue', during which Jabès read from an untitled poem which begins: 'Je te cherche./Le monde où je te cherche est un monde sans arbres.' The poem was worked into *Le Livre des Questions* (*LQ* I, 48–9). The interview itself reflects the premature 'tearing away' of Jabès from his native environment. Among his notes for this interview, in FEJ, we read: 'J'ai mis je crois trois heures à composer oralement ce poème. Trois heures, c'est peu et c'est beaucoup pour un poème de quelques minutes ... peu parce qu'il a fallu l'arracher à moi ... beaucoup parce qu'en général je mets moins de temps pour les écrire. *Un poème doit mûrir. On ne peut pas arracher à l'arbre son fruit sans risquer de saigner dangereusement la branche*' (my emphasis). Another text dating from this period that echoes the above poem and 'La Demeure de Reverdy' appears in *Sens plastique* 28 (1961), n.p. It is a short critical piece on the Egyptian artist Simone Picciotto (b. 1929), part of which

reads: 'Simone Picciotto peint *comme on ouvre une porte ou une fenêtre* mais tout son être participe à *ce geste. Le seuil* une fois franchi ou les volets enfin poussés, elle nous donne à partager, à aimer, dans un ordre souverain, les images fixées par le pinceau de ses rencontres, de *ses découvertes.* Que *l'arbre*, que l'oiseau ou *la pierre* aient répondu à ses sollicitations et qu'elle ait su les écouter au point de les recréer' (my emphasis). Unlike 'porte', 'arbre', 'pierre' and 'découvertes', 'seuil' does not appear in the previous tributes, but it recurs throughout *Le Livre des Questions.*

30. The aphorism first appeared in 'Les rames et la voile' in *Du blanc des mots et du noir des signes (Jbmd*, 301). A second aphorism from Cairo, first published in 'Spectacle' (in *Les Mots tracent, Jbmd*, 174), appears in *Le Livre de Yukel (LQ* I, 290): 'Une petite fille souffle sur ses joues. Le visage est découvert.' The manuscripts are in FEJ. See also Combe, 'Citation de Jabès', 174.

31. Saint-Chéron, 'Entretien avec Edmond Jabès', 67. Jabès expressed this regressive movement very early on, in 'Maman', in which the poet seeks refuge in his mother's arms following the death of his sister. See Ch. 2 above.

32. See Jaron, 'La "matrice cachée" du *Livre des Questions*', 96–101.

33. In May 1961 the Jabèses moved to the rue de l'Epée-de-Bois (fifth arrondissement) from the rue de Condé (sixth arrondissement), their first residence in Paris.

34. Maurice Blanchot, 'Etre juif', *NRF* 116 (1962), 279–85; 'Etre juif (fin)', *NRF* 117 (1962), 471–6 (both in *Ei*, 180–90).

35. For 'La Soif de la mer', see *Jbmd*, 113–20; for 'Le Fond de l'eau', see *Jbmd*, 75–84. The expression 'La Soif de la mer' was replaced, in *LQ*, by 'la soif de la terre': 'L'eau délimite les oasis. D'un arbre à un arbre, il y a toute la soif de la terre' (*LQ* I, 30).

36. Edmond Jabès, *Désir d'un commencement Angoisse d'une seule fin* (Montpellier: Fata Morgana, 1991), 22: 'Au Moyen-Age, en Espagne, sous l'Inquisition, certains "juifs repentis", que l'on désignait sous le nom de "marrannes" et dont la plupart avaient accepté la conversion pour éviter le châtiment suprême ou l'expulsion, portaient, dans une poche appropriée, bien dissimulée dans la doublure de l'une des amples *manches* de leurs vêtements—en général, celle de gauche—*un livre de petit format*, recueil de commentaires de la Thorah ou de prières d'enfance' (my emphasis). The use of 'manches' would refer, in this reading, to *don Quijote de la Mancha.* The two earlier books in question are *Le Petit Livre de la subversion hors de soupçon* (1982) and *Un Etranger avec, sous le bras, un livre de petit format* (1989).

37. Bounoure, 'Edmond Jabès: la demeure et le livre', in *Edmond Jabès: la demeure et le livre*, 33–4.

38. See the introductory note to Edmond Jabès, '"La mort d'un poète est une tache d'encre sur le poème"', in Jaron, *Portrait(s)*, 10. Marcel Raymond is also mentioned in Jabès's review essay of Eluard, Soupault and Max Jacob, *Sé* 3–4 (1938), 27, and in his 1944 'Hommage à Max Jacob', in Cahen, *Saluer Jabès*, 63.

39. Maurice Blanchot, 'La question la plus profonde', *NRF* 96 (1960), 1082–6; 'La question la plus profonde (II)', *NRF* 97 (1961), 85–9; and 'La question la plus profonde (III)', *NRF* 98 (1961), 282–91 (all republished in *Ei*, 12–34). There are often several differences between the versions of an essay Blanchot published in a review and its final form in a book. As most of the changes in the articles I refer to are minor, with the exception of one, discussed below (see n. 46),

I quote from the final versions of Blanchot's essays as they appeared in *Ei* and *A*. Nevertheless I also note the sources of the articles as they first appeared.

40. Freud discusses this problem in *Three Essays on Sexuality* (first published 1905), in *The Standard Edition of the Complete Psychological Works of Sigmund Freud*, vii, ed. James Strachey et al. (London: Hogarth Press, 1953), 196.

41. Blanchot, 'Connaissance de l'inconnu', *NRF* 107 (1961), 1081–94; 'Tenir parole', *NRF* 110 (1962), 290–8. These essays were republished in *Ei*, 70–9.

42. Maurice Blanchot, 'Notre compagne clandestine', *Textes pour Emmanuel Levinas*, ed. François Laruelle (Paris: Jean-Michel Place, 1980), 86–7.

43. Blanchot and Antelme met in 1958. See Christophe Bident, *Maurice Blanchot: partenaire invisible, essai biographique* (Seyssel: Champ Vallon, 1998), 368 ff.

44. Derrida would seem to agree with Memmi, except that his reference is to Hegel. According to Derrida, 'La conscience juive est bien la conscience malheureuse et *Le Livre des Questions* en est le poème; inscrit en marge de la phénoménologie de l'esprit' (*Ed*, 104).

45. Blanchot, 'L'interruption'. The essay was republished in two parts: 'L'interruption comme sur une surface de Riemann', *Ei*, 106–12; and as a section of 'Traces', *A*, 252–8.

46. This is true only for the version of the essay printed in the *NRF*, as a comparison of the two versions of the opening paragraph shows. The first version reads: 'Ces réflexions ['L'interruption comme sur une surface de Riemann', which immediately precedes this paragraph] sont abstraites. Mais je propose, à qui voudrait les animer, de lire un livre dont le souvenir—la lecture en sa réminiscence—m'a accompagné, tandis que j'essayais de les articuler dans une forme générale. De ce livre, je m'étais promis de ne rien dire. Il y a ainsi des œuvres qui se confient à notre discrétion' (*NRF* 137 (1964), 875). Whereas the second begins: 'Du livre, des livres d'Edmond Jabès, je m'étais promis de ne rien dire (même penchant au silence à l'égard de certains ouvrages austères, voire retirés, mais prématurément ébruités, saisis par une bizarre renommée et ainsi réduits à une signification de classe, de groupe ou d'usage). Il y a ainsi des œuvres qui se confient à notre discrétion' (*A*, 252). The second version does not refer to 'L'interruption comme sur une surface de Riemann', as that essay appeared not in *A* but in *Ei*. Further, the second version is preceded by essays on Jacques Dupin and Roger Laporte, these two, with that on Jabès, bearing the collective title 'Traces' (*A*, 246–58). Lastly, in the second version Blanchot refers to all of the preceding books of Jabès, not only to *LQ* ('Du livre, des livres d'Edmond Jabès'); this is explained by the fact that only *LQ* (1963) had been published when Blanchot's essay first appeared, whereas the second version appeared in 1971.

47. Emmanuel Levinas, 'Le regard du poète', first published in *Le Monde nouveau* 98 (1956); quoted here from *Sur Maurice Blanchot* (Montpellier: Fata Morgana, 1975), 23–4. My emphasis.

48. 'Sans nom' (1966), in *Noms propres* (Montpellier: Fata Morgana/Biblio Essais, 1976), 144–5. My emphasis.

49. 'Edmond Jabès' first appeared in *Nouveaux Cahiers* 31 (1972–3) and was republished in *Noms propres*, 73–5.

50. Similarly, Derrida appears to have wished to provoke Levinas into making a statement about Jabès's writings when he wrote, in 'Violence et métaphysique:

essai sur la pensée d'Emmanuel Levinas': 'Levinas souscrirait-il à cette phrase infiniment ambiguë du *Livre des Questions* d'E. Jabès: "Tous les visages sont le Sien; c'est pourquoi IL/n'a pas de visage"?' (*Ed*, 166).

51. Jacques Derrida, in *Nouveaux Cahiers* 31 (1972–3), 56.
52. Emmanuel Levinas, ibid. 59.
53. Levinas's tributes to these writers are gathered in his *Noms propres*.
54. Maurice Blanchot, in *Nouveaux Cahiers* 31 (1972–3), 51.
55. Ibid. 52. Blanchot's emphasis.

CHAPTER 5

On Not Belonging

One of the hazards of Edmond Jabès's exile is that, far from the centre of literary activities, he adhered strictly throughout the Cairene period to that very centre. Just where Jabès belonged was for many of his readers a subject of confusion. His attachment to France worked against him insofar as some thought his Egyptian writings were too close to those of the Surrealists or post-Surrealists, to an Eluard or a Char,[1] while for others the hand of Max Jacob was unmistakably present.[2] Alternatively, the poetry of *Je bâtis ma demeure*, whose leitmotifs are water, sand and sun, could only have been written by someone hailing from the Mediterranean.[3] Thus, readers were divided between those who saw Jabès as solidly grounded in his native environment and others who believed he had written a kind of alien, artificial verse. To a certain degree, it must be said that Jabès himself contributed to the confusion. A remark to Marcel Cohen is particularly revealing in this regard. '[R]evendiquer ma culture française au Caire', he said, 'me tenait presque lieu de filiation réelle. Reconnaître une filiation, c'était m'amputer de moi-même' (*Dl*, 80). In other words, the confusion his readers perceived was a due to a split, an amputation, at the heart of his own approach to poetry, itself the result of what I have called an internal uprooting. This confusion was exacerbated once Jabès had settled in Paris, where he tried to give the impression that he was a poet trained in the school of French modernism: he could then blend in, as it were, with other poets of the *NRF* or those published by GLM, those such as Jules Supervielle, André Frénaud or Maurice Blanchard. The critical problem, however, was that Jabès's resemblance to them was only partial and, in fact, fundamentally mistaken: his experience of life was uniquely his own. This seemed only natural. He, and he only, was a political refugee; and only he had to come to terms with his Judaism. At bottom was the essential question of how Jabès was to position himself in relation to Egypt, French culture and Judaism; in other words, his self-

examination had to take into account what he was to call his 'appartenance', or his adhesion, to these three terms. As he told Cohen, this
period of reflection had begun by the time the early parts of *Le Livre
des Questions* were being drafted. At that time, he said, 'j'ai eu
l'impression que la culture sur laquelle je m'étais reposé jusque-là se
lézardait brutalement' (*Dl*, 78). The culture he was referring to was
French, and as it broke apart, in his mind, the level of his anxiety shot
up. He was forced to admit that the poetry of French culture did not
correspond to his existential condition, and this was undeniably painful
to him. French modernism was no longer the comfortable refuge it had
been. Only shortly before beginning work on the book Jabès had been
cast out of Egypt, and now France hardly made any sense to him. The
intuition that he did not belong anywhere, from a political viewpoint
if not from the point of view of being, produced in him an undying
resolve. 'N'ayant plus d'appartenance, je pressentais que c'est à partir
de cette non-appartenance qu'il me fallait écrire' (*Dl*, 78).

Despite his anxiety, or perhaps because of it, Jabès found the
rupture with Egypt and France wholly liberating. With Bounoure's
constant guidance, he transformed his artistic uncertainty into a
salutary creativity. Henceforth, his writing would take on an absolute
heterogeneity. Cognizant of the multiform character of his writings,
Jabès described the problem of attributing a specific genre to them in
this dialogue from his 'Lettre à Gabriel' in *Le Retour au Livre*:

— J'ai, entre mes mains, *Le Livre des Questions*. Est-ce un essai?
— Non. Peut-être.
— Est-ce un poème aux puits profonds?
— Non. Peut-être.
— Est-ce un récit?
— Peut-être.
— Dois-je en déduire que tu aimerais qu'il fût reçu comme le récit de tes
rivières, de tes récifs?
— Livre étranger comme le vocable et comme le Juif, inclassable parmi les
livres, comment l'appeler? (*LQ* I, 332)

Neither Jabès nor Bounoure knew what to call it. In the opinion of
its author, *Le Livre des Questions* would defy generic classification: it
was neither an essay nor a poem nor a narrative, or perhaps it was all
of them at once. Like its author in relation to Egypt and France, in an
absolute sense it was foreign to these categories. It would not conform
to any single genre because it would contain them all—but in
fragments. The new work could only be characterized as 'inclassable'.

Jabès's appreciation of the heterogeneous text was not unique at the time. He is not far from Michel Leiris, for instance, who wrote in his diary on 26 September 1966 that his project would be: 'Un livre qui ne serait ni journal intime ni œuvre en forme, ni récit auto-biographique ni œuvre d'imagination, ni prose ni poésie, mais tout cela à la fois. Livre conçu de manière à pouvoir constituer un tout autonome à quelque moment que (par la mort, s'entend) il soit interrompu.'[4] Leiris's book would be completed at death; as such, it would be posthumous. More to the point, it would include between its pages a variety of genres, and so it would be defined negatively: 'A book which would be neither ... nor ...': in other words, Leiris's book (as he then projected it) would be neither this nor that, but all.

Writers such as Jabès and Leiris seeking to investigate the concept of the autonomous book trace their immediate intellectual origins to Mallarmé, who in 1895 wrote, famously, 'tout, au monde, existe pour aboutir à un livre'.[5] In Jabès's view, the world Mallarmé referred to was 'peut-être le monde dans la totalité première'. However, the world as book in its initial, total state differed from Jabès's conception of the analogy. For him, on the contrary, 'le monde qui aboutit à un livre est un monde qui a rejoint le Rien à partir duquel s'écrit le livre'.[6] To Mallarmé's 'totalité première', then, is opposed Jabès's 'Rien'. This is a crucial point because for Jabès writing is born out of nothingness, or death. Thus, Jabès wondered if Mallarmé's project might somehow have been self-limiting:

Vouloir ramener tous les livres à un seul; dominer toutes les lectures que l'on pourrait en faire, n'était-ce pas, au départ, priver ce livre unique de ses innombrables prolongements et de ceux, surtout, échappant à l'auteur lui-même? Le prolongement d'un livre est ce qui dépasse sa propre tentative; ce qu'un livre ultérieur et le lecteur sont appelés à combler. C'est la vie même du livre. Comment l'auteur pourrait-il l'intégrer à son projet? (*Dl*, 119)

In aspiring to animate his books with the material of the world so as to capture the life of the word, Jabès did not complete, as Mallarmé had hoped to do, a book in which all the world would be contained. Such a book would be reductive, he thought; it would lack the vitality necessary for it to be infinitely extensible. Jabès saw himself as butting his head against an aporia. Not only was *Le Livre des Questions* to defy the assumption that it would be limited to a single genre, but, further, it would require a shape that enabled it to surpass the conventions of authorship: Jabès had conceived his book as transcendental in relation to its author. He wished to place it into the hands of others. Moreover, his 'livre étranger', as he described it, would resemble neither Mallarmé's nor Leiris's because it was characterized as Jewish. If an impasse concerning both genre and authorship had been reached, then, the egress by which Jabès would remove himself was grammatical.

The solution he proposed was ingenious. For Jabès, the French verb tense that best connotes a message of deferral is the past conditional. By putting off answering a question, or defining a term, Jabès was able to extend the writing of his book. This he did grammatically. As such, the past conditional is central to the entirety of Jabès's Parisian *œuvre*. For instance, he uses it in *Le Livre des Questions* to introduce an identification that is then negated ('J'aurais pu être cet homme. J'ai partagé son ombre', *LQ* I, 86; see also *LQ* I, 82 and 96): 'I would have been ... if I had ....' The verb tense is similarly found throughout the later Parisian writings:[7]

> *(Il faudra que je m'explique, un jour, sur cette appartenance du mot devenu non-appartenance au mot; ou, plutôt, sur cette non-appartenance devenue appartenance: mon itinéraire juif.*
> *— Etes-vous juif?*
> *— L'aurais-je été; mais comme le vide est le tourment du vide?) (LR,* 198–9)

As this passage from *Le Soupçon le Désert* (1978) hints, the past conditional is related to the principle of *non-appartenance*, translated into English as 'not belonging' but conceived as the affirmation of a proposition and its subsequent negation. The past conditional is closely related to the interrogative mode of Jabès's writings, to the belief that, to quote him quoting one of his imaginary rabbis, '"Seule la créature sans appartenance connaît l'exil divin, car elle est étrangère à son propre exil"'(*LR*, 198). *Non-appartenance* became the means by which Jabès achieved an extreme liberty. The closing passage of the first volume of *Le Livre des Questions* does not come to a full stop— 'As-tu vu se faire et se défaire un royaume?/As-tu vu se faire et se défaire le livre?' (*LQ* I, 197)—nor can it because contingency and despair impregnate each page that precedes it. Nonetheless despair is, as he wrote in Cairo, the necessary condition for hope: 'Amoureuse retrouvée avec le livre ouvert' (*Jbmd*, 218), here echoing Eluard.[8] Similarly, the third volume of *Le Livre des Questions* concludes—Jabès employs the Mallarméan 'aboutissement'—with the 'insertion de la page porteuse des trois questions essentielles' (*LQ* I, 438). Jabès's book

is forever a 'livre ouvert', it is always to be fathomed. 'Qu'importe où je crois aller, si toute démarche est le fatal retour aux origines' (*LQ* I, 438), at which point he observes: 'Seul existe le monde à travers Dieu et l'homme dans le livre ouvert' (*LQ* I, 438).[9] Which origins was he referring to? To Egypt? Yes, albeit the country had for him become mythic. To Judaism? Yes, but that too was in many ways mythic. To France, or rather to the French language? That, still more, Jabès had always possessed.

Edmond Jabès repeatedly used the expression *non-appartenance* to describe his sentiment of cultural, religious and domestic *étrangeté*. 'Not belonging' was more than the stylistic expression of an aesthetic aspiration; it was an epistemological, as a form of knowing, and, even more, an ontological goal. Maurice Blanchot could write (in reference to Georges Bataille), 'à l'homme, tel qu'il est, tel qu'il sera, appartient un manque essentiel d'où vient ce droit de se mettre lui-même et toujours en question' (*Ei*, 305). It was in this spirit that Jabès put himself and his writings into question; as a stranger, he possessed the 'manque essentiel' of which Blanchot wrote. In the final analysis, Jabès found in this absence the place, *le Livre*, where parallel lines meet. There, all of his ambiguities, contradictions and questions could be at home. Again, Blanchot: 'Le livre est désormais sans appartenance; c'est ce qui le consacre comme livre' (*A*, 252). In the infinite space of the Open Book, Jabès freely fixed his francophone-Egyptian roots, his 'Judaïsme après Dieu' (as he came to call his relationship to Judaism, *LQ* II, 201–2), and his ambivalence towards living in France after 1957. Read as a whole, his complete works encompass the idea of the hazard of exile, of moving away from any stylistic or cultural association or definition and towards a negative presentation, detached from the hinges of time and space, in which the particular is subsumed in the universal, the essential in the accidental, and the immanent in the transcendental.

The principle of *non-appartenance* was useful to Jabès as a justification for maintaining his position as a writer outside generic categories and, further, as a rationalization of his status as a Jew who did not adhere to the conventions of rabbinic prescriptions. Why reduce Judaism to a time-bound, relative truth? For Jabès, what counted was the eternal—the eternal, that is, with sufficient suggestive references to historical time to anchor the narrative so that the reader would not become lost in abstraction.[10] Jabès wished to place himself at a remove from groups that would define themselves by a name. Against nominalism, he distanced himself from the central

agency's headquarters. 'J'ai toujours préféré les situations en marge, pour cette position de recul qu'on leur doit et qui nous permet de juger, d'imaginer, d'aimer, de vivre dans l'instant et hors de l'instant, libre mais de cette liberté de l'esclave qui en rêve' (*LQ* I, 333). This explains how he had, early on,

> rêvé d'une œuvre qui n'entrerait dans aucune catégorie, qui n'appartiendrait à aucun genre, mais qui les contiendrait tous; une œuvre que l'on aurait du mal à définir, mais qui se définirait précisément par cette absence de définition; une œuvre qui ne répondrait à aucun nom, mais qui les aurait endossés tous; une œuvre d'aucun bord, d'aucune rive; une œuvre de la terre dans le ciel et du ciel dans la terre [...]
>
> *Livre, objet d'une inépuisable recherche; n'est-ce pas ce que voit la tradition juive dans le Livre?* (*LQ* II, 343; my emphasis)

It is true, then, that Jabès associated an interminable, searching drive with the Jewish classical tradition. In fact, an early rabbinic compilation, redacted in the second or third century, has Ben Bag Bag say, 'Ha'foch ba v-ha'foch ba, d'cho'lah va', meaning that we should delve into the Torah, and we should look into it yet again, for everything is contained in it.[11] Even with age Jabès's *élan vital* did not diminish. It is precisely in questioning, in the search for answers and in the necessity of answerability, that Jabès viewed himself as a Jew and, further, as a writer:

> '*Questionner, c'est être sans appartenance*; c'est, le temps de la question, être dehors, de l'autre côté de la ligne', avait noté reb Koyré.
>
> Reb Haïm lui écrivit: 'J'ai fait de la question, ma vie. N'ai-je donc pas été Juif?' (*LR*, 210–11; my emphasis)
>
> *Appartenir à ce qui, par essence, récuse toute appartenance*—l'universel; voilà la vraie vocation juive: son devenir déferré.

> 'Qu'est-ce qu'être juif? Je suis tenté, pour ma part, de répondre que c'est celui à qui cette question s'adresse et celui qui, soi-même, se pose tout bas la question', écrivait Yukel. (*LR*, 319; my emphasis)

The Jew is the object of the questioning of others, but is further the one who asks questions, thus putting the other into suspension. But Jabès posits more. For him, the Jew embodies a paradoxical social position: the Jew belongs to a group that challenges the viability and necessity of belonging to a group. Upon reflection, this thought gives rise to some concern. After all, how can one belong to a group defined by its opposition to all groups? A fundamental problem, then, emerges from the assertion of such a proposition: Has not Jabès sawn the branch on which he sits from the trunk to which it is connected? Is it possible to reject all forms of belonging without, ultimately, claiming adhesion to one particular group, to that group whose membership consists exclusively of outsiders?

In the course of a speech given at the Fondation du Judaïsme Français in 1982, Jabès developed his view of his position on the French literary scene across his career: 'Si, depuis toujours, je suis rivé à la langue française, la place que j'ai conscience d'occuper dans la littérature de notre pays n'en est pas, à proprement parler, une. Elle est moins la place d'un écrivain que celle d'un livre qui n'entre dans aucune catégorie' (*LM*, 179). Jabès believed that the heterogeneous nature of his books authorized him to claim a position defined by negative presentation, a 'lieu d'un non-lieu', among contemporary French writers. He felt that his books could only be compared to 'paroles de sable': 'un bref instant audible, visible: parole d'une écoute extrême et d'une mémoire très ancienne' (*LM*, 180). Ancient in their history, provisional in their genesis, ephemeral in their life, Jabès's books arose out of an 'expérience du désert', which was, for him, at once 'celle du lieu de la Parole—où elle est souverainement parole— et celle du non-lieu où elle se perd à l'infini' (*LM*, 180). In Egypt, 'le désert' was, he admitted, 'le lieu privilégié de ma dépersonnalisation' (*Dl*, 32 ff.). As early as 1931 he was conscious of how it denuded him:

> Je m'étire sur le sable
> comme dans un bain chaud,
> et m'abandonne
>
> (*Jta*, 100)

as these lines from *Je t'attends!* attest, although the image of the desert was not central to his writings at the time. But, as I argued in Chapters 3 and 4 above, with his forced departure from Egypt there gushed an urgent nostalgia. An irremediable distance separated Jabès from his native country. In order to return to this lost place, he had to write *consciously* of his country from the perspective of exile, and to make exile his stated theme.

Jabès's characterization of the desert as the 'lieu d'un non-lieu' is itself a description of his paradoxical status as a writer and a Jew: 'A la question: "Vous considérez-vous comme un écrivain juif?" j'ai toujours répondu: "Je suis écrivain et juif"; réponse, a priori, déconcertante mais qui relève du souci majeur de ne pas réduire l'un et l'autre à ce que je pourrais en dire en les confondant' (*LM*, 181). It is thus that Jabès denied himself the false comfort of the widely used designation *écrivain juif*, and stubbornly insisted on bifurcating into the separate terms, *écrivain* and *juif*. Consistent with his assertion that his books were not reducible to any single genre, he felt it inaccurate to emphasize their writerly quality to the detriment of their Jewish quality, and vice versa. He sensed an inevitable yet burdensome relation between the two designations, and that they shared a common denominator. The common denominator he was alluding to was his very person: ' *"Face à l'impossibilité d'écrire qui paralyse tout écrivain et à l'impossibilité d'être Juif, qui, depuis deux mille ans, déchire le peuple de ce nom l'écrivain choisit d'écrire et le Juif de survivre"* ', observed Yukel, to which Reb Kabri added: '*Nous sommes liés par l'impossible*' (*LQ* I, 253–4). The writer writes, and the Jew survives. Writing was a means, perhaps *the* means, of surviving. But what, in Reb Kabri's remark, was 'impossible'? The 'impossible' refers to the act of interrogation, the ceaseless questioning both the writer and the Jew engage themselves in. What can be called a 'community of the impossible', the one whose membership consists of writers and Jews, seems distinctly possible. For Jabès, this union is based on an aporia, an impossibility. But the impossibility is a shared condition: the writer is unable to write and the Jew is unable to be a Jew. In his speech of 1982, Jabès further admitted that once he had asserted himself as a writer (presumably, this would date back to the late 1920s), he began to feel the stirrings of his Jewish consciousness. His explanation for his awakening as a writer and a Jew was that both shared the same history, 'l'histoire du livre dont ils se réclament'. 'Ce sont mes interrogations d'écrivain qui m'ont permis d'aborder, dans sa gravité, le questionnement juif; comme si le devenir juif, à un moment donné, n'était plus qu'un devenir-écriture' (*LM*, 181).[12] What was important to Jabès was the notion of *becoming*, of how a Jewish person evolves as a Jew and of how a writer evolves as a writer. In other words, process and means were valued more than results and endings. The former were associated with questioning, whereas the latter were associated with answers.

But if writing and Judaism were at once impossibly knotted and separated by the act of questioning, then why not identify oneself simply as a *Jewish writer*, as one who produces a *Jewish writing*? It seems that Judaism and writing are one and the same. Jabès did admit the existence in history of Jewish writing. But, it must be conceded: 'Un thème juif, non, ne suffit pas à faire un livre juif. Le récit juif est bien moins dans l'anecdote, dans l'aveu, dans la peinture d'un milieu, que dans l'écriture. On ne raconte pas Auschwitz. Chaque mot nous le raconte' (*LM*, 182). Regardless of his origins, the moment in history summarized by Jabès in the word Auschwitz obliged him to write as a Jew, that is, from the sources of what Blanchot would call 'Jewish being'. Fundamentally, this is where Jabès parts company with the symbolism of Mallarmé. While both were engrossed by the meaning of writing and how writing could be contained in the space of a book, Auschwitz opened up a historical chasm that, of course, Mallarmé could not know.

I would further argue that Edmond Jabès separated writing from Judaism in order to account for the two distinct periods in his career, the Cairene (1929–57) and the Parisian (1957–91). In asking himself what it meant to be a writer, he came to know what it meant to be a Jew. For the writer and the Jew, each new book renews their respective adventures. The renewal is infinite because there is always something left unsaid in the previous work: 'Il y a, pour le Juif et pour l'écrivain, un perpétuel commencement—qui n'est pas un recommencement—, un même étonnement face à l'écrit, une même foi dans ce qui reste encore à lire, à dire' (*LM*, 182), although, as Leiris asserted, death marks an end point: 'Livre conçu de manière à pouvoir constituer un tout autonome à quelque moment que (par la mort, s'entend) il soit interrompu.' True, each of Jabès's books marks the starting-point for the next, which explains how the first *Livre des Questions* (1963) grew into the second and third volumes (1964 and 1965) and, further, how those books were followed by an additional four volumes (1967, 1969, 1972 and 1973), and how the septology initiated further series of books, including *Le Livre des Ressemblances* (1976, 1978 and 1980). But why, I would ask, is it necessary to include his first works, dating from the late 1920s, in his corpus? If we are to believe Jabès's statement, 'J'ai tenté, dans mes ouvrages, de rendre sensible le mouvement auquel obéit la parole et qui s'étend du *silence antérieur* qu'elle rompt au silence qu'elle inaugure en se taisant' (*LM*, 183; my emphasis), then his corpus ought to be extended to take into consideration even those very early texts typically dismissed by its author and most commentators. Jabès himself seems to be suggesting that his very early poetry is shrouded in a kind of 'prior silence'. This poetry is estranged in relation to the works comprising *Je bâtis ma demeure*, it constitutes the negative presentation of that writing which Jabès considered as belonging to his corpus. It is his *membra disjecta*, what was unacceptable to him and the great majority of his readers during his years of renown. And yet even he seemed to intimate—as when he quoted Kafka, 'Ce qui dépend de nous est d'accomplir le négatif; le positif est déjà donné' (*LQ* II, 468)[13]—that our very task should be to bring these rejected works to light. It is perhaps out of the necessity of affirming the stranger in Jabès—that foreign element in his being—or of recognizing the existence of those distant, silent works that do not figure in the bibliography he envisaged for himself after the death of Max Jacob, when all preceding *Chansons pour le repas de l'ogre* (1947) were negated, that he draws his greatest force as a writer. The books that do not belong to the bibliography, in other words, those books which are so marginal that they may only be commented on through reference to the principle of *non-appartenance*, are, I have tried to demonstrate, the bedrock of everything that was to follow. Each early book and poem shares with the later works a singular and irreducible sound—a cry of desperation, a cry of love, a language of nothingness, a '*tourment du vide*'.

Jabès's letter of 1 November 1946 to the journalist and critic Louis Parrot further illustrates the hazard of expressing his exile, and his abiding sense of loneliness and melancholy. From the office of his apartment in Zamalek, the poet informed his French correspondent that he had read the issue of *L'Eternelle Revue*, edited by Parrot with Paul Eluard, in which his 'Quatre Mystères actuels' appeared.[14] He also indicated that Pierre Seghers, who had visited Egypt in the spring of 1946, would soon be publishing his *Chansons pour le repas de l'ogre* and that Parrot would receive a copy when the book appeared. Having thus detailed his latest activities, the tone of the letter becomes more serious, pensive. Jabès speaks in earnest to Parrot: 'Il y a longtemps que je voulais vous écrire, mais il est difficile, de si loin, de se faire connaître. Comment parler de soi, de son œuvre? J'attendrai une occasion.'[15] One possible way of interpreting Jabès's question is to see it as a means of arousing, in Parrot, further curiosity about his correspondent's poetry so that he might one day read him carefully and speak of him to other influential personalities on the Parisian literary scene.[16] I think that that reading is not incorrect, but surely the words express something more. This question could only have been asked by a foreigner, by an individual far from the heart of activity. The resonance with Maurice Blanchot's key terms, the 'stranger' and the 'unknown', is not irrelevant to our understanding of how Jabès lived and worked in Egypt. The letter, then, indicates that Jabès, during this period, was already writing from the perspective of an outsider, as a foreigner who was intimate with the language—now French, now the idioms of modern poetry—of the majority and yet was still not integrated into the scene where that language was current.

A passage from a later statement on the hazard of self-expression, here from *Le Livre des Questions*, parallels Jabès's question to Louis Parrot:

> Comment s'expliquer, ah, comment? Il ne l'a jamais su. Le verbe en lui, ça fait deux. C'est un silencieux. Il a tant de choses à dire qu'il n'a jamais formulées; des choses simples comme bonjour et qui feraient plaisir à certains; des choses auxquelles on ne pense plus, que l'on a peut-être oubliées. Des choses qui feraient honte à d'autres.
>
> Maintenant, il est trop tard, trop tard. (*LQ* I, 54)

If anything is expressed here, it is Jabès's sense that he had somehow failed to communicate, that he had missed the opportunity to do so. It was not for lack of subjects that he had failed. Rather, a different obstacle prevented him from asserting himself. The word (*le verbe*) was cracked, wounded: 'ça fait deux'. It was thus Jabès himself who was painfully absent, or, rather, negatively present in relation not only to French literature but to his own writing: he was a 'writer' and a 'Jew'.[17] When he asked Parrot, 'Comment parler de soi, de son œuvre?', he was in fact circumscribing the fundamental problem that would preoccupy him throughout his life.

The elemental focus in Jabès's career, from his student days to the mid-1960s and still after, was the interpretation of his material and existential situations. Writing might ameliorate a bitter state. The act of interpretation could be understood, in a sense, as the rectification of a misdeed: the poet would restore the fallen, encourage the belittled or return the exiled. The interpretations were put forth by one who considered himself a stranger, an unknown. It mattered little if his sense of estrangement remained unfelt, to a degree, by his interlocutor: the necessity of expressing the hope for renewal remained, and, in expressing his hope for renewal, he was alleviating his sorrow and loss. Perhaps faintly echoing the observation of Max Jacob that 'Pour les grands poètes la poésie a été une recherche dans la souffrance' (*LEJ*, 68), Edmond Jabès obstinately held to the belief in the '*mission de l'écrivain*' who carried within him the weight of '*sa souffrance et son espoir*' and, fundamentally, whose poems gave '*un sens profond à sa vie*' (*LQ* I, 64). If the origin of poetry was a wound, a separation or a displacement, then its composition might be a soothing balm.

Notes to Chapter 5

1. See, e.g., Henry Amer's review of *Jbmd* in *NRF* 80 (1959), 522–34, Alain Bosquet's in *Combat* 4/692 (1959), 6, and Robert Marteau's in *Esprit* (NS, Dec. 1959), 792.

2. Unsigned review in *Culture française* 5 (1959), 38.

3. Jean Baumier in *Europe* 367–8 (1959), 291–2. See also Pierre Berger in *Carrefour* (30 Sept. 1959), 21, and the editor's note to the excerpt of Gabriel Bounoure's preface to *Jbmd* in *Etudes méditerranéennes* 6 (1959), 134.

4. Michel Leiris, *Journal, 1922–1989*, ed., with intro. and notes, Jean Jamin (Paris: Gallimard, 1992), 614.

5. Stéphane Mallarmé, 'Le livre, instrument spirituel', in *Igitur, Divagations, Un Coup de dés*, pref. by Yves Bonnefoy (Paris: Gallimard/Poésie, 1976), 267. Leiris had been rereading Jacques Scherer's 1957 edition of Mallarmé's *Le 'Livre'* since at least June 1966.

6. 'Dialogue avec Edmond Jabès' in *Ecrire le livre*, 311.

7. Cf. his use of the *futur antérieur*: 'J'aurai donc été juif par le trajet' and 'J'aurai donc été juif par légitime légèreté de plume' (both quotations *LQ* II, 201).

8. The remark was made in reference to Paul Eluard's *Le Livre ouvert, 1938–1944* (Paris: Gallimard/Poésie, 1974). On the occasion of his tribute to Paul Eluard given at Amitiés françaises in Dec. 1952, Jabès explained: 'Le livre ouvert est une île qui hante, avec les amants et les chercheurs de trésors, les mots lyriques au large col de pêcheur.' See Jabès, '"La mort d'un poète est une tache d'encre sur le poème"', 12.

9. Cf. Derrida in 'Ellipse' (the closing essay in *Ed*, dedicated to Gabriel Bounoure): 'Si la clôture n'est pas la fin, nous avons beau protester ou déconstruire, "Dieu succède à Dieu et le Livre au Livre"' (*Ed*, 429).

10. There is an important historical echo in his use of the expression *non-appartenance*. Under the Vichy government, discussion took place among officials as to how, administratively, non-Jews and Jews should be designated. Parting from the ideological standards of the time, *certificats de non-appartenance à la race juive* were issued to those deemed non-Jewish. See Michael R. Marrus and Robert O. Paxton, *Vichy France and the Jews* (New York: Basic Books, 1981), 93–4. As the immediate historical setting of *LQ* is Paris in the war years, it seems probable that Jabès's understanding of *non-appartenance* refers, bitterly, ironically, to its use by officials under Vichy.

11. *Pirkei Avot* 5.26, *The Complete Artscroll Siddur: Weekday, Sabbath, Festival*, trans. and notes by Rabbi Nosson Scherman (Brooklyn, NY: Mesorah Publications Ltd, 1984), 579.

12. The questioning continued in later books, notably in *Le Parcours* (1985), whose last section is entitled 'Judaïsme et écriture'.

13. Jabès is quoting from 'La Chevauchée du seau' in Henri Parisot's translation.

14. Edmond Jabès, 'Quatre mystères actuels', *Eternelle Revue* 5–6 (1945), 95–7.

15. The unpublished letter is in the Bibliothèque littéraire Jacques Doucet (série ms. 41 098).

16. Parrot had spoken warmly on behalf of the war effort of French-Egyptian intellectuals in 'La France africaine', *L'Intelligence en guerre* (Paris: La Jeune Parque, 1945), 305–7. These remarks were republished in Egypt as 'La Résistance française en Egypte', *Sé* 15–16 (1946), 10.

17. Pierre Fédida's reflections on the negative presentation in the psychoanalytic 'situation' in his essay 'Le site de l'étranger' are strikingly relevant to Jabès's self-questioning in his letter to Parrot and in the passage quoted from *LQ*. See Fédida's *Le Site de l'étranger: la situation psychanalytique* (Paris: Presses Universitaires de France, 1995), 53–69.

BIBLIOGRAPHY

1. Published works written or co-written by Edmond Jabès (including books, articles, reviews, letters and poems)

(With Henri Jabès), 'Déclaration,' *Anthologie mensuelle* 1 (1929), n.p.

(With Henri Jabès), 'Alliance franco-égyptienne', *Anthologie mensuelle* 1 (1929), n.p.

(With Henri Jabès), Note to André Honnorat's speech, 'L'œuvre de la Cité universitaire: son programme, son développement, son avenir', *Alliance universelle* 6 (1930), 3.

'Tableau', *Anthologie mensuelle* 1 (1929), 12.

'Au clair de lune' and 'J'ai construit un châlet', *Anthologie mensuelle* 2 (1929), 28–9.

Review (attributed) of Jean Moscatelli's *Poèmes trouvés sur un banc*, *Alliance universelle* 4 (1930), 39.

'Epithalame', *Alliance universelle* 8 (1930), 1.

'Solitude, me voici', *Alliance universelle* 9 (1930), 5.

Review of François Moutran's *Soleil sous les palmiers*, *Alliance universelle* 9 (1930), 35–6.

Illusions sentimentales (Paris: Eugène Figuière/Les Anthologies du XXe siècle, 1930).

Je t'attends! (Paris: Eugène Figuière, 1931).

'Maman' (Cairo: La Semaine égyptienne, 1932).

'Syrinx', *Semaine égyptienne* 14–15 (1932), 13.

'Apport à la poésie: le Logisme' followed by 'Extraits', *Semaine égyptienne* 29–30 (1932), 3–4 and 5–6.

'Réalités logistes' followed by an excerpt from 'Films inflammables', *Semaine égyptienne* 35–6 (1932), 9–10.

'Dimanche (4 décembre 1932)', *Semaine égyptienne* 1–2 (1932), 22.

Les Pieds en l'air, note by Max Jacob (Cairo: La Semaine égyptienne, 1934).

Arrhes poétiques (Cairo: La Semaine égyptienne, 1935).

'L'Obscurité potable' (Paris: Guy Lévis Mano, 1936).

Review essay of Paul Eluard's *Les Yeux fertiles*, Philippe Soupault's *Poésies complètes, 1917–1937*, and Max Jacob's *Morceaux choisis*, *Semaine égyptienne* 3–4 (1938), 27.

Excerpts from 'Le Sens de l'ombre', *Le Nil* (13 Jan. 1938), 8.

Excerpts from 'Le Sens de l'ombre', *Le Nil* (25 Jan. 1938), 8.

Excerpts from *Avec l'ombre*, *Progrès égyptien* (10 Mar. 1941), 7.

Review of Ahmed Rassim's *L'Ermite de l'Attaka, poème*, *Semaine égyptienne* 11–12 (1941), 18.

'A mes amis grecs', *Semaine égyptienne* 21–2 (1941), 7.

'In Memoriam: Hector de Cattaoui', *Bourse égyptienne* (22 Feb. 1942), 2

'Hommage à Max Jacob', *Semaine égyptienne* 15–16 (1944), 5. Republished in *Saluer Jabès: les suites du livre*, ed. Didier Cahen (Bordeaux: Opales, 2000), 62–4.

Preface to Max Jacob's *Lettres à Edmond Jabès* (Alexandria: Scarabée/Valeurs, 1945).

'Quatre Mystères actuels', *Eternelle Revue* 5–6 (1945), 95–7.

(Signed 'Eddy'), 'La rue de France' (letter to the Editor), *Progrès égyptien* (25 Mar. 1945), 3.

'En l'honneur de Pierre Seghers', *Semaine égyptienne* 15–16 (1946), 11.

'Quatre chansons', *Poésie 46* 33 (1946), 58–61.

'Le Fond de l'eau' (Cairo: La Part du sable, 1947).

Chansons pour le repas de l'ogre (Paris: Pierre Seghers, 1947).

Letter to the Editor concerning the Jean Cocteau debate with René Etiemble, *Progrès égyptien* (13 Mar. 1947), 2.

'Trois Filles de mon quartier' (Paris: Guy Lévis Mano, 1948).

'Ressource du sujet', *Lettres françaises* 211 (1948), 5.

Excerpts from 'Trois Filles de mon quartier', *Loisirs* (Autumn 1948), n.p.

La Voix d'encre (Cairo: La Part du sable, 1949).

La Clef de voûte (Paris: Guy Lévis Mano, 1950).

Les Mots tracent (Paris: Librairie Les Pas perdus/L'Age d'or, 1951).

(Unsigned), Untitled poem, *Le Temps de la poésie* 6 (1952), intro. by René Char (Paris: Guy Lévis Mano, 1952), 28–30.

Paul Eluard (Cairo: La Part du sable, 1953). Republished as '"La mort d'un poète est une tache d'encre sur le poème"' in *Portrait(s) d'Edmond Jabès*, ed. Steven Jaron (Paris: Bibliothèque nationale de France, 1999), 10–15.

L'Ecorce du monde (Paris: Pierre Seghers, 1955).

'Une chance de naître', *Mercure de France* 1106 (1955), 230–6.

'La Girafe', *Calligrammes: almanach des lettres et des arts en Egypte, 1956*, ed. Raoul Parme (Cairo: Anis Abu Fadil, 1956), 103.

Je bâtis ma demeure, poèmes 1943–1957, pref. by Gabriel Bounoure (Paris: Gallimard, 1959).

'Simone Picciotto', *Sens plastique* 28 (1961), n.p.

'La Demeure de Reverdy', *Mercure de France* 1181 (1962), 148.

Le Livre des Questions (Paris: Gallimard, 1963).

Le Livre de Yukel (Paris: Gallimard, 1964).

Le Retour au Livre (Paris: Gallimard, 1965).

Yaël (Paris: Gallimard, 1967).

Elya (Paris: Gallimard, 1969).

Aely (Paris: Gallimard, 1972).

· *(El ou le dernier livre)* (Paris: Gallimard, 1973).

Je bâtis ma demeure, poèmes 1943–1957, 2nd edn., pref. by Gabriel Bounoure, afterword by Joseph Guglielmi (Paris: Gallimard, 1975).

Le Livre des Ressemblances (Paris: Gallimard, 1976).

Le Soupçon le Désert (Paris: Gallimard, 1978).

L'Ineffaçable l'Inaperçu (Paris: Gallimard, 1980).

Le Petit Livre de la subversion hors de soupçon (Paris: Gallimard, 1982).

Récit (Montpellier: Fata Morgana, 1982).

'La vraie lisibilité', *GLM* (Montpellier: Fata Morgana, 1982), 109–10.

Le Livre du dialogue (Paris: Gallimard, 1984).

Le Livre des marges (I. *Ça suit son cours*, II. *Dans la double dépendance du dit*) (Paris: Hachette/Biblio Essais (1975 and 1984), 1987).

Le Parcours (Paris: Gallimard, 1985).

Le Livre du Partage (Paris: Gallimard, 1987).

La Mémoire et la main (Montpellier: Fata Morgana, 1987).

Le Livre des Questions I (*Le Livre des Questions, Le Livre de Yukel, Le Retour au Livre*) (Paris: Gallimard/L'Imaginaire, 1988).

Un Etranger avec, sous le bras, un livre de petit format (Paris: Gallimard, 1989).

Le Livre des Questions II (*Yaël, Elya, Aely,* · *(El ou le dernier livre)*) (Paris: Gallimard/L'Imaginaire, 1989).

'Max Jacob' (new pref. to the 2nd edn. of Max Jacob's *Lettres à Edmond Jabès*) (Milan: All'insegna del Pesce d'Oro, 1989).

'Pages nouvelles II', *Instants* 1 (1989), ed. Lucie Ducel, 243–55.

'Philippe Soupault', in *Philippe Soupault, le poète*, ed. Jacqueline Chénieux-Gendron (Paris: Klincksieck, 1992), 9–11.

La Mémoire des mots: comment je lis Paul Celan (Paris: Fourbis, 1990).

Le Seuil le sable, poésies complètes 1943–1988 (Paris: Gallimard/Poésie, 1990).

Du désert au livre: entretiens avec Marcel Cohen, suivi de l'Etranger (2nd edn. Paris: Belfond, 1991).

Le Livre des Ressemblances (*Le Livre des Ressemblances, Le Soupçon le Désert, L'Ineffaçable l'Inaperçu*) (Paris: Gallimard/L'Imaginaire, 1991).

Le Livre de l'Hospitalité (Paris: Gallimard, 1991).

Désir d'un commencement Angoisse d'une seule fin (Montpellier: Fata Morgana, 1991).

Un Regard, pref. by Jean Frémon (Montpellier: Fata Morgana, 1992).

Bâtir au quotidien (*Le Livre des Marges III*), pref. by Viviane Jabès-Crasson (Montpellier: Fata Morgana, 1997).

2. Manuscript sources

Manuscripts by Edmond Jabès in the Fonds Edmond Jabès in the Département des manuscrits of the Bibliothèque nationale de France are identified by titles (e.g. 'Les Voies lactées', an unpublished tribute to Maurice Blanchard dated Jan. 1960; 'Poésie vécue', notes for a radio interview with Alain Cuny dated Feb. 1960; 'Propos d'Edmond Jabès: Paris, Tel-Aviv, Jérusalem, Sdeh Boker', David Mendelson's 1982 interview). The manuscript pages I have called 'La "matrice cachée" du *Livre des Questions*' are published in Steven Jaron (ed.), *Portrait(s) d'Edmond Jabès*, 90–101.

BOUNOURE, GABRIEL, and JABÈS, EDMOND, *Correspondance Gabriel Bounoure–Edmond Jabès, 1952–1969*. Edition in preparation, pref. by Steven Jaron, transcription and chronology by Jean-Luc Bayard. Where possible I have quoted from these letters by date.

HENEIN, GEORGES, Letter to André Breton in the Bibliothèque littéraire Jacques Doucet (BRT.C.943).

JABÈS, EDMOND, Selected correspondence in the Bibliothèque littéraire Jacques Doucet, including letters to Georges Cattaui (1993), André Frénaud (49.524–49.527), Max Jacob (8024.402), Michel Leiris (43.517; 43.518), Louis Parrot (41.098), Maurice Saillet (RDY sup. 45) and Tristan Tzara (TZR.C. 2134). Several of these letters are published in Steven Jaron, 'Repiquage poétique chez Edmond Jabès', *Pleine Marge* 24 (1996), 109–29.

SUPERVIELLE, JULES, Letter to Edmond Jabès, 31 Aug. 1959. Appendix to *Correspondance Gabriel Bounoure–Edmond Jabès, 1952–1969*.

3. Interviews and personal correspondence

AGHION, RAYMOND, Interview in Paris (25 Oct. 1994).

ARNALDEZ, ROGER, Interview in Paris (22 Apr. 1995).

BEYSSET, JEAN, Letter (24 Jan. 1995).

BOUILLIER, HENRI, Interview in Paris (10 Apr. 1995).

COHEN, HENRI, Questionnaire (by Daniel Lançon and the author) sent to Geneva (Mar. 1995).

COSSERY, ALBERT, Interview in Paris (2 June 1995).

HASSOUN, JACQUES, Interview in Paris (29 May 1996).

JABÈS-CRASSON, VIVIANE, Interview in Paris (25 Oct. 1994).

MENDELSON, DAVID, Letter (3 June 1996).

REBEYROL, PHILIPPE, Interview in Paris (31 Dec. 1994).

WISSA-WASSEF, CÉRÈS, Interviews in Paris (1 Nov. 1994) and in Cairo (with Daniel Lançon) (3 Mar. 1995).

4. Published sources

ANON.:
—— 'Assemblée générale des sionistes', *Israël* (20 Jan. 1928), 3.
—— 'Le Centre hébraïque de l'UUJJ', *Israël* (27 Jan. 1928), 3.
—— 'Organisation sioniste du Caire, appel aux anciens adhérents', *Israël* (10 Feb. 1928), 2–3.
—— 'Fête annuelle du Lycée français', *Semaine égyptienne* 17–18 (1929), 25.
—— *Israël* (13 Dec. 1929), 4.
—— Press notice for *Anthologie universelle*, *Semaine égyptienne* 5–6 (1930), 20.
—— 'L'Alliance franco-égyptienne scellée au premier banquet (9 janvier 1930) de l'*Anthologie mensuelle*', *Anthologie mensuelle* 3 (1930), 1–7.
—— *Israël* (30 May 1930), 6.
—— 'Carnet de l'UUJJ, Section du Caire: Le 4 septembre, 1 acte d'Edmond Jabès à l'UUJJ', *Israël* (28 Nov. 1930), 3.
—— *Israël* (6 Feb. 1931), 3.
—— 'M André Spire en Egypte', *Israël* (13 Jan. 1933), 1.
—— 'Un bon exemple à suivre', *Israël* (13 Jan. 1933), 4.
—— 'Le judaïsme égyptien et l'antisémitisme nazi: un meeting de protestation au Caire', *Bourse égyptienne* (30 Mar. 1933), 2.
—— 'La jeunesse juive contre l'antisémitisme allemand', *Israël* (21 Apr. 1933), 4.
—— 'Une provocation raciste au Caire: la réunion des nazis à l'hôtel Victoria', *Israël* (21 Apr. 1933), 4.
—— 'Au Caire: une réunion des jeunesses d'action juive du Caire', *Bourse égyptienne* (3 May 1933), 10.
—— 'Un roman juif sur Alexandrie: *Le Fou de Dieu* de Elian-J. Finbert', *Israël* (5 May 1933), 2.
—— 'Les juifs d'Egypte et leurs frères d'Allemagne, manifestation contre l'antisémitisme allemand à la Maccabi', *Israël* (5 May 1933), 3.
—— 'La propagande nazie en Egypte', *Israël* (16 June 1933), 3.
—— 'L'hitlérisme, dangereuse propagande du désordre social, est traîné devant les Tribunaux', *Israël* (30 June 1933), 6.
—— 'A l'étranger: en Egypte: une ligue contre l'antisémitisme, un procès retentissant en perspective', *Droit de vivre* 14 (1933), 6.
—— 'La communauté juive de Kom-Ombo possédera bientôt son temple', *Israël* (8 Sept. 1933), 4.
—— 'A la jeune WIZO, la conférence de Mlle Arlette Cohen', *Israël* (23 Mar. 1934), 5.
—— 'Protestations des organisations juives d'Egypte contre les excitations nazies au meurtre des Juifs', *Israël* (18 May 1934), 1.
—— 'Un grand mariage', *Israël* (30 May 1935), 6.
—— 'Mission laïque française', *Journal d'Egypte* (11 Feb. 1937), 55–6.
—— Review of Max Jacob's *Lettres à Edmond Jabès*, *Fontaine* 51 (1946), 676.

ANON., 'A propos de "Le Signe arabe" de Robert Blum', *Actualité* (14 Jan. 1956), 1 and 13.

—— 'Les auteurs minoritaires d'Egypte: encore une trahison des clercs', *Actualité* (14 Jan. 1956), 1.

—— 'Aux Amitiés françaises: dîner d'adieux à Fernand Leprette', *Progrès égyptien* (19 May 1956).

ADORNO, THEODOR, *Minima Moralia: Reflections from Damaged Life*, trans. E. F. N. Jephcott (London: Verso, 1974).

ALEXANDRIAN, SARANE, *Le Surréalisme et le rêve*, pref. by J.-B. Pontalis (Paris: Gallimard, 1974).

—— *Georges Henein* (Paris: Pierre Seghers, 1981).

AMER, HENRY (pseud. Henri Bouillier), review of *Je bâtis ma demeure, poèmes 1943–1957*, *Nouvelle Revue française* 81 (1959), 522–4.

ANANIAS, 'Lettre d'Egypte', *Cahiers du sud* 322 (1954), n.p.

ANTELME, ROBERT, *L'Espèce humaine* (rev. and corrected edn. Paris: Gallimard/Tel, 1978).

APOLLINAIRE, GUILLAUME, *Alcools, suivi de Le Bestiaire illustré par Raoul Dufy et de Vitiam impendere amori* (Paris: Gallimard/Poésie, 1966).

ARGUS, 'Un grand banquet démocratique et antifasciste au Caire', *La Marseillaise* (28 July 1945), 6.

ARNALDEZ, ROGER, 'La langue et l'expression', *Revue du Caire* 140 (1951), 21–34.

AUSTER, PAUL, 'Book of the Dead: An Interview with Edmond Jabès', in Gould (ed.), *The Sin of the Book: Edmond Jabès*, 3–25.

AZAR, AIMÉ, 'Jean Moscatelli, poète de l'incertitude a-t-il ému le lecteur oriental?', *Egypte nouvelle* 429 (1952), 315–17.

BANON, DAVID, 'Le livre et les livres: une écriture de l'exil', *Nouveaux Cahiers* 104 (1991), 7–8.

BARBITCH, IVO, 'Ahmed Rassim, poète d'Egypte et d'ailleurs', *Progrès égyptien* (3 Feb. 1941), 6.

—— 'Arsène Yergath ou la magie d'enfance', *Progrès égyptien* (10 Feb. 1941), 2.

—— 'Georges Henein', *Progrès égyptien* (24 Mar. 1941), 5.

—— 'Edmond Jabès ou la recherche de l'humain', *Progrès égyptien* (10 Mar. 1941), 7.

BASTIDE, FRANÇOIS-RÉGIS, 'Rendez-vous à Paris avec les Egyptiens', *Nouvelles littéraires* 1334 (1953), 5

BAUMIER, JEAN, review of *Je bâtis ma demeure, poèmes 1943–1957*, *Europe* 367–8 (1959), 291–2.

BAYARD, JEAN-LUC, 'La Demeure ou les trois temps du livre', *Quinzaine littéraire* 582 (1991), 15.

BEN-AMI, 'Les Allemands du Caire et ceux du Reich', *Israël* (11 May 1934), 1.

BENOIT, ERIC, *Ecrire le cri: 'Le Livre des Questions' d'Edmond Jabès, exégèse* (Bordeaux: Presses Universitaires de Bordeaux, 2000).

—— *De la crise du sens à la quête du sens: Mallarmé, Bernanos, Jabès* (Paris: Cerf, 2001).

BERGER, PIERRE, 'La Demeure d'Edmond Jabès ... elle donne sur le jardin de l'Espoir', *Carrefour* (30 Sept. 1959), 21.

BIDENT, CHRISTOPHE, *Maurice Blanchot: Partenaire invisible, essai biographique* (Seyssel: Champ Vallon, 1998).

BLANCHARD, MAURICE, *Les Barricades mystérieuses*, pref. by Jean-Hugues Malineau (Paris: Gallimard/Poésie, 1994).

BLANCHOT, MAURICE, 'Etre juif', *Nouvelle Revue française* 116 (1962), 279–85.

—— 'Etre juif (fin)', *Nouvelle Revue française* 117 (1962), 471–6.

—— 'La question la plus profonde', *Nouvelle Revue française* 96 (1960), 1082–6.

—— 'La question la plus profonde (II)', *Nouvelle Revue française* 97 (1961), 85–9.

—— 'La question la plus profonde (III)', *Nouvelle Revue française* 98 (1961), 282–91.

—— 'L'interruption', *Nouvelle Revue française* 137 (1964), 869–82.

—— *L'Entretien infini* (Paris: Gallimard, 1969).

—— *L'Amitié* (Paris: Gallimard, 1971).

—— Untitled, *Nouveaux Cahiers* 31 (1972–3), 51–2.

—— *Le Pas au-delà* (Paris: Gallimard, 1973).

—— 'Notre compagne clandestine', in *Textes pour Emmanuel Levinas*, ed. François Laruelle (Paris: Jean-Michel Place, 1980), 79–87.

—— *L'Ecriture du désastre* (Paris: Gallimard, 1980).

BLUM, ROBERT, *Beaux Masques: cinq actes, théâtre*, pref. by Fernand Leprette (Cairo: Lecioni, 1932).

—— *Le Signe arabe* (Cairo: L'Atelier, 1955).

BOCTOR, GABRIEL, 'Activités Essayistes', *Un Effort* 57 (1935), 23.

BOSQUET, ALAIN, 'La Poésie: recherche et ronron', *Combat* 4/692 (1959), 4.

BOUNOURE, GABRIEL, 'Prière d'insérer' (Cairo: LDF/Le Chemin des sources, 1955).

—— *Marelles sur le parvis: essais de critique poétique* (Paris: Plon, 1958).

—— 'Adresse amicale à Fernand Leprette', *Mercure de France* 1166 (1960), 367.

—— 'L. Massignon: itinéraire et courbe de vie', *L'Herne: Massignon* (Paris, 1962), 45–54.

—— 'Magicien et martyr: une complainte mystique', *Le Monde* suppl. to number 7523 (22 Mar. 1969), 4.

—— *Edmond Jabès: la demeure et le livre* (Montpellier: Fata Morgana, 1982).

E. C., 'Aux Amitiés françaises: "les jeux, miroir de l'homme et de la société"', *Bourse égyptienne* (25 Feb. 1956).

CAHEN, DIDIER, *Edmond Jabès* (Paris: Pierre Belfond, 1991).

—— 'Ecrire sa vie', in *Portrait(s) d'Edmond Jabès*, ed. Jaron, 16–67.

CASTRO, LÉON, *Le Procès de l'antisémitisme: mémoire déposé au Tribunal mixte du Caire pour Umberto Jabès et contre le Club allemand du Caire* (Cairo(?): 1934).

CATTAUI, GEORGES, *La Dévotion à l'image* (Cairo: Institut français d'archéologie orientale, 1919).

CHABANEIX, PHILIPPE, review of Jean Moscatelli's *Poètes en Egypte, anthologie*, *Mercure de France* 1112 (1956), 740–1.

CHAR, RENÉ, *Fureur et mystère*, pref. by Yves Berger (Paris: Gallimard, 1967).

—— Five letters to Edmond Jabès, *Nouveaux Cahiers* 31 (1972–3), 54–5.

CHARASSON, HENRIETTE, *Monsieur de Porto-Riche ou le 'Racine juif'* (Paris: Siècle, 1925).

COMBE, DOMINIQUE, 'Citation de Jabès', *Temps modernes* 538 (1991), 150–75.

COSSERY, ALBERT, *Les Hommes oubliés de Dieu* (Paris: Charlot, 1946).

—— *La Maison de la mort certaine* (Paris: Charlot, 1947).

DAUPHINÉ, CLAUDE, *Rachilde, femme de lettres 1900* (Périgueux: Pierre Fanlac, 1985).

—— *Rachilde* (Paris: Mercure de France, 1991).

DERRIDA, JACQUES, *L'Ecriture et la différence* (Paris: Seuil/Points, 1979).

—— 'Edmond Jabès et la question du livre' (1964), in *L'Ecriture et la différence*, 99–116.

—— 'Violence et métaphysique: essai sur la pensée d'Emmanuel Levinas' (1964), in *L'Ecriture et la différence*, 117–228.

—— 'Ellipse' (1967), in *L'Ecriture et la différence*, 429–36.

—— *De la grammatologie* (Paris: Minuit/Critique, 1967).

—— Untitled, *Nouveaux Cahiers* 31 (1972–3), 56.

DIVOIRE, FERNAND, *Stratégie littéraire* (Paris, 1928).

DIWERGE, WOLFGANG, *Als Sonderberichterstatter zum Kairoer Judenprozeß (1933). Gerichtlich erhärtetes Material zur Judenfrage* (Munich: Zentralverlag der NSDAP, Franz Eher, 1935).

DONNAY, MAURICE, *La Vie amoureuse d'Alfred de Musset* (Paris: Flammarion, 1926).

DUCEL, LUCIE (ed.), *Instants* 1 (1989).

D. E., 'Jean Cocteau sur la selette', *Progrès égyptien* (5 Mar. 1947), 2.

ELUARD, PAUL, *La Vie immédiate, suivi de La Rose publique et de Les Yeux fertiles* (Paris: Gallimard/Poésie, 1967).

—— *Le Livre ouvert, 1938–1944* (Paris: Gallimard/Poésie, 1974).

ERBERTZ, CAROLA, *Zur Poetik des Buches bei Edmond Jabès. Exiliertes Schreiben im Zeichen von Auschwitz* (Tübingen: Gunter Narr, 2000).

FARGEON, MAURICE, *L'Eternelle Tragédie ou Israël peuple immortel* (Cairo: Internationale, 1934).

FÉDIDA, PIERRE, *Le Site de l'étranger: la situation psychanalytique* (Paris: Presses Universitaires de France, 1995).

FENOGLIO, IRÈNE, 'L'activité culturelle francophone au Caire durant l'entre-deux guerres: du paradoxe à la contradiction', in *D'un Orient l'autre*, i: *Configurations* (Paris: CNRS, 1991), 457–96.

FINBERT, ELIAN-J., *Le Fou de Dieu* (Paris: Fasquelle, 1932).

FREDERICKSEN, BROOKE, 'Dwelling in Words: The Early Poetry of Edmond Jabès', *French Forum* 3 (1993), 335–54.

FREUD, SIGMUND, *Three Essays on Sexuality*, in *The Standard Edition of the Complete Psychological Works of Sigmund Freud*, vii, ed. James Strachey et al. (London: Hogarth Press, 1953).

S. G., 'Aux Amitiés françaises: hommage à Henri Michaux', *Progrès égyptien* (11 Feb. 1956).

GAGNEBIN, MURIELLE, *L'Irreprésentable ou les silences de l'œuvre* (Paris: Presses Universitaires de France/Ecriture, 1984).

GARDAZ, ELIZABETH, 'Jabès: poétique de l'exil et exil à l'œuvre', *Exil et littérature*, intro. by Jacques Mounier (Grenoble: ELLUG, 1986), 284–8.

GHARIEB, SAMIR, *Le Surréalisme en Egypte et les arts plastiques* (Giza: Prisme, 1988).

ABOU GHAZI, BADR EDDAIN, *Ramsès Younane* (Cairo: Organisation égyptienne générale du livre, 1978).

GOULD, ERIC (ed.), *The Sin of the Book: Edmond Jabès* (Lincoln, NB, and London: University of Nebraska Press, 1985).

GREEN, ANDRÉ, *Le Travail du négatif* (Paris: Minuit/Critique, 1993).

GRENIER, JEAN, *Lexique* (Paris: Gallimard, 1955).

—— *Carnets, 1944–1971*, ed. Claire Paulhan (Paris: Pierre Seghers, 1991).

GUICHARD, LÉON, *Revue du Caire* 73 (1944), 166–9.

R. H., 'Mort de la littérature: la thèse de M. Roger Caillois', *Bourse égyptienne* (14 Dec. 1948).

—— 'Les confidences d'un poète: une interview de Philippe Soupault', *Bourse égyptienne* (22 Feb. 1949).

—— 'Une introduction à la lecture de "Maldoror"', *Bourse égyptienne* (25 Feb. 1949).

—— 'Aux Amitiés françaises: émouvant hommage au Dr Taha Hussein Bey', *Bourse égyptienne* (19 May 1949).

HARLONG, R., review of *Les Pieds en l'air*, *Gringoire* 287 (1934), 4.

HASSOUN, JACQUES (ed.), *Juifs d'Egypte: Images et textes* (Paris: Scribe, 1984).

——, and NAGGAR, CAROLE, 'Le Caire quitté: conversation avec Edmond Jabès (26 juillet 1984)', *Autrement* 12 (1985), 43–7.

HEIDEGGER, MARTIN, *Poetry, Language, Thought*, trans. and intro. by Albert Hofstadter (New York: Harpers, 1971).

HENEIN, GEORGES, *Suite et fin* (Cairo: Centonze, 1934).

—— 'André de Laumois', *Un Effort* 38 (1934), 5–6.

—— (pseud. Serge Ghonine), review of *Arrhes poétiques*, *Un Effort* 55 (1935), 24.

—— review of *Les Pieds en l'air*, *Un Effort* 59 (1936), 22.

—— 'Bilan du mouvement surréaliste', *Revue des conférences françaises en Orient* 8/1 (1937), 645–54; republished in *Pleine Marge* 24 (1996), 131–44.

—— 'Note critique', *La Part du sable* 1 (1947), n.p.

HENEIN, GEORGES, 'Paul Eluard et le surréalisme', *L'Egypte nouvelle* 447 (1953), 62.

—— 'L'apport d'Albert Cossery', in Parme (ed.), *Calligrammes: almanach des lettres et des arts en Egypte, 1956*, 18.

—— *Le Seuil interdit* (Paris: Mercure de France, 1956).

HOURANI, ALBERT, *Arabic Thought in the Liberal Age, 1789–1938* (Cambridge: Cambridge University Press, 1983).

HUSSEIN, TAHA, 'France-Egypte', *Lettres françaises* 117 (1946), 5.

HYPPOLITE, JEAN, 'Commentaire parlé sur la *Verneinung* de Freud', appendix to Jacques Lacan, *Ecrits* (Paris: Seuil/Champ freudien, 1966), 879–87.

JACOB, MAX, *Lettres à Edmond Jabès*, pref. by Edmond Jabès (Alexandria: Scarabée/Valeurs, 1945).

—— *Lettres à un jeune poète, suivi de Conseils à un jeune poète*, pref. by Marcel Bealu (Paris: Gallimard, 1946).

—— *La Défense de Tartufe: extases, remords, visions, prières, poèmes et méditations d'un Juif converti*, pref. and notes by André Blanchet (Paris: Gallimard, 1964).

—— *Le Cornet à dés* (Paris: Gallimard/Poésie, 1967).

—— *Méditations*, pref. by René Plantier (Paris: Gallimard, 1972).

—— *Derniers Poèmes en vers et en prose* (Paris: Gallimard/Poésie, 1974).

—— *Advice to a Young Poet*, trans. and intro. by John Adlard, pref. by Edmond Jabès, afterword by Jacques Evrard (London: Menard, 1976).

—— *Lettres à Edmond Jabès*, 2nd edn., Milan: All'insegna del Pesce d'Oro, 1989).

—— *Lettres à Edmond Jabès*, 3rd edn., foreword by Steven Jaron, pref. by Edmond Jabès, afterword by Gabriel Bounoure (Pessac: Opales, 2003).

EL-JANABI, A. K., 'Art et liberté, points de repères', *Opus international* 123–4 (1991), 100–1.

JARON, STEVEN, 'Repiquage poétique chez Edmond Jabès', *Pleine Marge* 24 (1996), 109–29.

—— 'Une voix effacée d'une province limitrophe', *Pleine Marge* 24 (1996), 145–8.

—— 'Edmond Jabès ou le fonctionnement du palimpseste', in Kober et al. (eds.), *Entre Nil et sable: les écrivains d'Egypte d'expression française*, 191–200.

—— 'L'amitié comme "éphémères retrouvailles"', in *Portrait(s) d'Edmond Jabès*, 68–77.

—— 'La "matrice cachée" du *Livre des Questions*', in *Portrait(s) d'Edmond Jabès*, 88–101.

—— 'Jacob, mon ange qui brûle', foreword to Max Jacob, *Lettres à Edmond Jabès* (3rd edn., Pessac: Opales, 2003), 7–17.

—— (ed.), *Portrait(s) d'Edmond Jabès*, pref. by Jean-Pierre Angremy (Paris: Bibliothèque nationale de France, 1999).

KLAT, HECTOR, 'Cèdres', *Semaine égyptienne* 29–30 (1934), 2.

—— *Le Cèdre et les lys* (Beirut: Revue phénicienne, 1935).

KLOSSOWSKI, PIERRE, *Les Méditations bibliques de Hamann* (Paris: Minuit, 1948).

KOBER, MARC, FENOGLIO, IRÈNE, and LANÇON, DANIEL (eds.), *Entre Nil et sable: écrivains d'Egypte d'expression française (1920–1960)*, pref. by Robert Solé (Paris: Centre national de documentation pédagogique, 1999).

KRÄMER, GUDRUN, *The Jews in Modern Egypt, 1914–1952* (Seattle: University of Washington Press, 1989).

KRONICK, JOSEPH G., 'Edmond Jabès and the Poetry of the Jewish Unhappy Consciousness', *Modern Language Notes* 106/5 (1991), 967–96.

LACOUTURE, JEAN, and LACOUTURE, SIMONNE, *L'Egypte en mouvement* (Paris: Seuil, 1956).

LAGARDE, PIERRE, *Max Jacob, mystique et martyr* (Paris: Baudinière, 1944).

LANÇON, DANIEL, *Jabès l'Egyptien* (Paris: Jean-Michel Place, 1998).

LANDAU, JACOB M., *Jews in Nineteenth Century Egypt* (New York: New York University Press, 1969).

LANDES, DAVID S., *Bankers and Pashas: International Finance and Economic Imperialism in Egypt* (London: Heinemann, 1958).

LASKIER, MICHAEL M., *The Jews of Egypt, 1920–1970: In the Midst of Zionism, Anti-Semitism, and the Middle East Conflict* (New York: New York University Press, 1992).

LAUMOIS, ANDRÉ DE, 'Chez les Essayistes: le cénacle qui devient un club', *Bourse égyptienne* (7 Dec. 1934), 2.

LECOMTE, MARCEL, review of Georges Henein's *Seuil interdit* and Jabès's *Je bâtis ma demeure, poèmes 1943–1957*, *Journal des poètes* 3 (1960), 3.

LEIRIS, MICHEL, *Journal, 1922–1989*, ed., with intro. and notes, Jean Jamin (Paris: Gallimard, 1992).

LEPRETTE, FERNAND, *Egypte: terre du Nil* (Paris: Plon, 1939).

LEVINAS, EMMANUEL, 'Le regard du poète', *Le Monde nouveau* 98 (1956); republished in *Sur Maurice Blanchot*, 7–26.

—— 'Sans nom' (1966), in his *Noms propres* (Montpellier: Fata Morgana/ Biblio Essais, 1976), 141–6.

—— Untitled, *Nouveaux Cahiers* 3 (1972–3), 59; republished as 'Edmond Jabès' in his *Noms propres* (Montpellier: Fata Morgana/Biblio Essais, 1975), 73–5.

—— *Difficile Liberté* (3rd edn. Paris: Albin Michel/Biblio Essais, 1976).

—— *Sur Maurice Blanchot* (Montpellier: Fata Morgana, 1975).

LÉVY, S. EMILE, *Les Bourses des valeurs d'Egypte* (Cairo: Henri Schindler, 1953).

LICHTENBERGER, MARGUERITE, *Ecrivains français en Egypte contemporaine (de 1870 à nos jours)* (Paris: Ernst Leroux, 1934).

Ligue contre l'antisémitisme allemand (ed.), *L'Antisémitisme en Allemagne* (Cairo and Alexandria: 1933).

LUGOL, JEAN, *Israël et la civilisation: étude historique, philosophique et religieuse des origines et de l'évolution du peuple juif* (Alexandria: Procaccia, 1939).

LUTHI, JEAN-JACQUES, *Introduction à la littérature d'expression française en Egypte, 1798–1945*, pref. by Maurice Génévoix (Paris: L'Ecole, 1974).

—— 'Le Mouvement surréaliste en Egypte', *Mélusine* 3 (1980), 18–35.

——, VIATTE, AUGUSTE, and ZANANIRI, GASTON (eds.), *Dictionnaire général de la francophonie* (Paris: Letouzey et Ané, 1986).

MAGNY, OLIVIÉR DE, 'Le pouvoir de féerie', *Lettres nouvelles*, NS 23 (1959), 30–1.

MALLARMÉ, STÉPHANE, *Igitur, Divagations, Un coup de dés*, pref. by Yves Bonnefoy (Paris: Gallimard/Poésie, 1976).

MANDELSTAM, OSIP, *The Prose of Osip Mandelstam: The Noise of Time, Theodosia, The Egyptian Stamp*, trans. and intro. by Clarence Brown (Princeton, NJ: Princeton University Press, 1965).

Map of the Jewish quarter of Cairo surveyed in 1911 (repr. 1928), sheet 38-K.

MARTEAU, ROBERT, review of *Je bâtis ma demeure, poèmes 1943–1957*, *Esprit* (NS Dec. 1959), 792.

MARRUS, MICHAEL R., and PAXTON, ROBERT O., *Vichy France and the Jews* (New York: Basic Books, 1981).

MEGILL, ALLAN, *Prophets of Extremity: Nietzsche, Heidegger, Foucault, Derrida* (Berkeley: University of California Press, 1985).

MEITINGER, SERGE, 'Mallarmé et Jabès devant le livre: analyse d'une divergence culturelle', in Stamelman and Caws (eds.), *Ecrire le livre autour d'Edmond Jabès*, 133–45.

MERCEREAU, ALEXANDRE, 'L'Egypte nouvelle et le Droit des Peuples', *Alliance universelle* 4 (1930), 30.

—— 'Fernand Divoire', *Alliance universelle* 6 (1930).

MÉRIEL, ETIENNE, review of Max Jacob's *Lettres à Edmond Jabès*, *Progrès égyptien* (16 Sept. 1945), 5.

—— 'Lettres françaises en Egypte', *Progrès égyptien* (15 June 1955), 2.

MIATLEV, ADRIAN, comment in *Tour de feu* 60 (1958), 112.

MICHAUX, HENRI, *Plume, prédédé par Lointain intérieur* (Paris: Gallimard/Poésie, 1985).

MIZRAHI, EMMANUEL, 'La propagande nazie en Egypte', *Israël* (9 June 1933), 4.

MOLE, GARY D., 'Edmond Jabès and the Wound of Writing: The Traces of Auschwitz', *Orbis Litterarum* 49 (1994), 293–306.

—— *Levinas, Blanchot, Jabès: Figures of Estrangement* (Gainesville, FL: University Press of Florida, 1997).

Le Mondain égyptien et du Proche Orient/The Egyptian Who's Who, ed. E. J. Blattner (Cairo and Alexandria, 1935, 1939, 1945, 1954, 1957–8).

MONSIEUR L'ARCHIVISTE, 'Une lettre à propos de l'apport poétique de M Ed. Jabès', *Semaine égyptienne* 33–4 (1932), 12.

MOSCATELLI, GIOVANNI (Jean), *Poèmes trouvés sur un banc* (Cairo: Parme and Michel, 1929).

—— review of *Je t'attends!*, *Semaine égyptienne* 6–7 (1932), 13.

—— 'Pour GOHA le Simple', *Semaine égyptienne* 11–12 (1934), 31.

—— 'Pégase 6 cylindres: pages détachées d'un cahier de route', *Semaine égyptienne* 31–2 (1934), 7–8.

—— review of *Arrhes poétiques*, *Semaine égyptienne* 7–8 (1935), 15.

—— review of Georges Henein's and Jo Farna's *Rappel à l'ordre*, *Semaine égyptienne* 15–16 (1935), 18.

—— 'La Maison du Caire', *Semaine égypienne* 21–2 (1935), 2.

—— 'Notes italiennes', in Parme and Barbitch (eds.), *Calligrammes: art, science, littérature*, n.p.

—— *Roubaiyat pour l'aimée*, Arabic. trans. Habib Jamati (Cairo: Aldebarah, 1952).

—— (ed.), *Poètes en Egypte, anthologie* (Cairo: L'Atelier, 1955).

NADEAU, MAURICE, 'Pour Edmond Jabès', *Instants* 1 (1989), 9–12; republished in *Quinzaine Littéraire* 582 (1991), 13.

PARME, RAOUL (ed.), *Calligrammes: almanach des lettres et des arts en Egypte, 1956* (Cairo: Anis Abu Fadil, 1956).

—— and BARBITCH, IVO (eds.), *Calligrammes: art, science, littérature* 1/4–6 (1936).

PARROT, LOUIS, 'La France africaine', in his *L'Intelligence en guerre* (Paris: La Jeune Parque, 1945); republished as 'La Résistance française en Egypte', *Semaine égyptienne* 15–16 (1946), 10.

PARTOUCHE, MAURICE, 'Edmond Jabès, poète de l'exil et du désert', *Le Monde* suppl. to no. 11355 (2 Aug. 1981), 9–10.

PERRAULT, GILLES, *Un homme à part* (Paris: Barrault, 1984).

PEUCHMAURD, PIERRE, *Maurice Blanchard* (Paris: Pierre Seghers, 1988).

Pirkei Avot, The Complete Artscroll Siddur: Weekday, Sabbath, Festival, trans. and notes by Rabbi Nosson Scherman (Brooklyn, NY: Mesorah Publications Ltd, 1984), 544–87.

PIROUÉ, GEORGES, 'Un homme du Nord transplanté en terre d'Egypte', *Mercure de France* 1167 (1960), 551–4.

POLDÈS, LÉO, *L'Eternel Ghetto, pièce d'actualité, en trois actes sur la question juive* (Paris: Radot, 1928).

PORTO-RICHE, GEORGES DE, *Anatomie sentimentale, pages préférées* (Paris: P. Ollendorff, 1920).

PRATO, DAVID, 'Etudes sur les chants de la synagogue', *Israël* (1 Dec. 1933), 4.

RAAFAT, SAMIR W., *Maadi, 1904–1962: Society and History in a Cairo Suburb* (Cairo: Palm Press, 1994).

RACZYMOW, HENRI, 'Qui est Edmond Jabès?', *Cahiers obsidiane* 5 (1982), 158–67.

—— 'Edmond Jabès, juif contesté', *Nouveaux Cahiers* 104 (1991), 8–9.

RAPNOUIL, JEAN, *Le Temps dérobé, poèmes et commentaires* (Paris: Jouve et Compagnie, 1928).

RAPNOUIL, JEAN, 'L'influence de la culture française en Egypte', *Egypte nouvelle, livre d'or* (Cairo, 1938).

RAYMOND, MARCEL, *De Baudelaire au surréalisme* (Paris: José Corti, 1933).

RICHET, CHARLES, 'Les deux visages de l'ennui', *Revue des Deux Mondes* (15 July 1932), 313–24.

ROBERT, PAUL, *Le Grand Robert de la langue française* (2nd edn. Paris: Le Robert, 1989).

E. S., 'Aux Amitiés françaises: hommage à Arthur Rimbaud', *Progrès égyptien* (23 Feb. 1955).

SAILLET, MAURICE, 'Hommage à Gabriel Bounoure', *Lettres nouvelles* 5 (1953), 626–7.

SAINT-CHÉRON, PHILIPPE, 'Entretien avec Edmond Jabès', *Nouvelle Revue française* 464 (1991), 65–75.

SAMUEL, SYDNEY MONTAGUE, *Jewish Life in the East* (London: C. Kegan Paul and Co., 1881).

SEIFFOULA, 'L'apport poétique de M Edmond Jabès: "Le Logisme"', *Semaine égyptienne* 31–2 (1932), 12–13.

SHAW, STANFORD J., *The Jews of the Ottoman Empire* (New York: New York University Press, 1991).

SHUAL, A[DOLF], review of *Illusions sentimentales*, *Semaine égyptienne* 45–6 (1930), 20.

—— review of 'Maman', *Semaine égyptienne* 41–2 (1932), 16.

—— review of *Les Pieds en l'air*, *Israël* (29 Mar. 1934), 3.

—— review of *Arrhes poétiques*, *Israël* (4 Apr. 1935), 5.

SIMON, EMILE, 'La patrie de l'humain', *Revue du Caire* 31 (1941), 109–15.

SOULON, HENRI, 'Jules Supervielle', *Revue du Caire* 19 (1940), 128–37.

STAMELMAN, RICHARD, 'The Nomadic Writing of Exile: Edmond Jabès', in his *Lost Beyond Telling: Representations of Death and Absence in Modern French Poetry* (Ithaca, NY: Cornell University Press, 1990), 223–48.

—— and CAWS, MARY ANN (eds.), *Ecrire le livre autour d'Edmond Jabès, colloque de Cerisy* (Seyssel: Champ Vallon, 1989).

STARASELSKI, ALBERT, *Les Juifs dans les lettres françaises* (Cairo: Henri Sas [1940]).

STODDARD, ROGER E., *Edmond Jabès in Bibliography, 'Du blanc des mots et du noir des signes': A Record of the Printed Books* (2nd edn. Paris and Caen: Lettres Modernes-Minard, 2001).

SUPERVIELLE, JULES, *Le Fable du monde, suivi de Oublieuse mémoire*, pref. by Jean Gaudon (Paris: Gallimard/Poésie, 1987).

TALVA, F., review of Max Jacob's *Lettres à Edmond Jabès*, *Semaine égyptienne* 1–2 (1945), 24.

TSIRKAS, STRATIS, 'Etiemble en Alexandrie (1944–1948) ou un homme des lumières dans la ville de Cavafy', in *Le Mythe d'Etiemble: hommages, études et recherches* (Paris: Didier Erudition, 1979).

(Various participants), 'Ahmed Rassim, poète arabe de langue française', *Revue du Caire* 224–5 (1959).

VIVANTE, JEAN B., 'Ahmed Rassim ou des résonances particulières de la langue française exprimant une pensée étrangère', *Semaine égyptienne* 19–20 (1942), 20–1.

WAHBA, MAGDI, 'Cairo Memories', *Encounter* 62/5 (1984), 74–9.

—— (ed.), *Hommage à Georges Henein* (Cairo: La Part du sable, 1974).

WEISS, JASON, 'An Interview with Edmond Jabès', *Conjunctions* 9 (1986), 128–61.

WYBRANDS, FRANCIS (ed.), *Cahiers obsidiane* 5 (1982).

YAMILE, 'A la recherche d'un romantisme attardé', *Progrès égyptien* (30 Nov. 1942), 2.

ZEINAB, 'Ed. Jabès vu par Zeinab', *Semaine égyptienne* 29–30 (1934), 22.

ZUCCOTTI, SUSAN, *The Italians and the Holocaust: Persecution, Rescue, and Survival*, intro. by Furio Colombo (Lincoln, Nebraska and London: University of Nebraska Press, 1996).

INDEX

Adam, Juliette 25
Adorno, Theodor 2–3, 107, 116–17
Afifi, Anwar 70
Aghion, Raymond 76, 85 n. 78
Agnon, S. Y. 149
Ali, Mohammed 16–17
Amer, Henry 125–6; *see also* Bouillier, Henri
Amitiés françaises *see* Groupement des amitiés françaises
Antelme, Robert 139–40, 143, 146, 149
Apollinaire, Guillaume 40–1, 90, 93
aporia 157–8
Arnaldez, Roger 101
Arnaud, Noël 151 n. 26
Art et liberté 68, 70–1, 78–9, 84 n. 63
Audiberti, Jacques 104
Auschwitz 3–4, 13, 26, 41, 67, 72, 68, 139, 143, 146, 148–9, 163
Auster, Paul 88

Badawi, Abdel Hamid 100
Ball, Hugo 68
Banon, David 4
Barbitch, Ivo 71–6
Barbusse, Henri 25
Barchmann, Léon 34
Bataille, Georges 159
Baudelaire, Charles 11, 62, 99
Bayard, Jean-Luc 114
Beckett, Samuel 124
Ben Bag Bag 160
Bianchetti, Suzanne 25
Bibesco (Princess) 24–5
Blanchard, Maurice 80, 127–8, 155
Blanchot, Maurice 4, 12–13, 36, 129, 134–50, 152 n. 39, 153 n. 46, 159, 163–4

'Etre juif' 134, 137, 141–2, 145
'L'interruption' 143–6, 153 n. 46
'La question la plus profonde' 137–9
Blum, Robert 23, 83 n. 44, 108–9
Bonnefoy, Yves 80
Bordeaux, Henry 25
Bouillier, Henri 100, 125
Bounoure, Gabriel 1, 10, 12, 41, 87, 99–109, 111 n. 24, 111 n. 27, 111 n. 31, 112 n. 37, 123–8, 131–7, 147, 156, 166 n. 9
'Edmond Jabès: la demeure et le livre' 136
Marelles sur le parvis: essais de critique poétique 100
Bouvier, Emile 57
Bréchon, Robert 125
Bresle, Valentin 50
Breton, André 69–70, 79, 105, 110 nn. 6 and 8
Brulat, Paul 25
Buber, Martin 149

Cahen, Didier 33, 83 n. 36
Caillois, Roger 77
Castro, Léon 30, 32–4, 36
Cattaui, Georges 15–18, 20
Cattaui, Joseph Aslan de 30
Cattaui, Maurice 17
Cattaui, Moïse de 17, 29, 39
Cavadia, Marie 104
Cavafy, C. P. 50
Celan, Paul 149
Cervantes 117, 135
Chabaneix, Philippe 109
Champollion, J.-F. 19
Chamsi, Aly 76
Chapsal, Madeleine 2

Char, René 80, 104, 124, 126, 149,
    151 n. 24, 155
Charasson, Henriette 47 n. 81
Charpentier, Gustave 25
Chateaubriand 94
Chédid, Andrée 104
Claudel, Paul 99
Cocteau, Jean 57, 64
Cohen, Edith (*née* Cattaui) 17, 39
Cohen, Henri 33
Cohen, Marcel 18, 29, 67, 91, 155–6
Cohen, René 28
Cossery, Albert 50, 105
Couve de Murville, Maurice 100, 102
Cuny, Alain 151 n. 29
Curiel, Henri 76
Curiel, Raoul 76

David, Christian 13 n. 8
Derême, Tristan 64, 110 n. 6
Derrida, Jacques 4, 6–7, 10–11, 13, 148,
    153 nn. 44 and 50, 166 n. 9
Diehl, Charles 25
Divoire, Fernand 53, 82 n. 16, 136
Donnay, Maurice 22, 25
Drancy 98
Dreyfus affair 32
Dubois, Maurice 25
Duhamel, Georges 69
Dupin, Jacques 153 n. 46

Effendi, Haim Nahoum 28
Eluard, Paul 50, 78, 79–81, 89, 93, 106,
    136, 155, 158, 164, 166 n. 8
Essayistes 63, 69–70
Etiemble, René 76, 90
Evrard, Jacques 110 n. 11

Fargeon, Maurice 35
Fargues, Léon Paul 78
Farna, Jo 69
Faouzi, Hussein 76
Fédida, Pierre 167 n. 17
Figuière, Eugène 23, 25
Finbert, Elian-J. 35
Fink, Eugen 13 n. 8
Fondation du Judaïsme Français 161
Fouad I (King) 22, 24

Frapié, Léon 25
Frascaria (*née* Jabès), Nimet 122
Fraysse, Jean 93
Fredericksen, Brooke 114
Free Officers 99
Frénaud, André 120, 124, 155
Freud, Sigmund 51, 118, 138

Gagnebin, Murielle 5, 13 n. 8
Gaillard, Henry 22
Gaulle, Charles de 76
Gautier, Théophile 62
Genet, Jean 124
Gentilly, A.-M. 4
Geraldy, Paul 25, 49
Gide, André 50, 57
GLM *see* Lévis Mano, Guy
Goethe 50
Green, André 13 n. 8, 150 n. 8
Grenier, Jean 78, 80–1, 100, 104, 109
Groupement des amitiés françaises 76–8,
    80, 98, 100–1, 104, 107–8, 123,
    166 n. 8
Groupes d'action antifasciste et italiens
    libres 65, 83 n. 47
Guichard, Léon 76
Guilloux, Louis 104

Hahn, Reynaldo 52
Hamann, Johann Georg 10
Haraucourt, Edmond 57–8
hazard of exile 7–11, 66, 106–7, 155, 159,
    164–5
Hegel 118, 150 n. 8, 153 n. 44
Heidegger, Martin 116–17, 125
Heine 49, 141
Heinemann, Isaac 141
Henein, Georges 6, 64, 68–71, 78–81, 87,
    105, 110 n. 8, 127
Herriot, Edouard 25
Hitler, Adolf 31, 33–4, 36, 38, 64, 67, 97–8
Hölderlin 125
Holmes, Hugh 32
Holocaust *see* Auschwitz
Honnorat, André 25
Hugo, Victor 15
Hussein, Taha 77, 105
Husserl 13 n. 8

Hyppolite, Jean 150 n. 8

Ismail (Khedive) 16
Ivray, Jehan d' 24

Jabès, Arlette (*née* Cohen) 17–18, 29, 34–5,
  54, 58, 91, 101, 122
Jabès, Berthe (*née* Arditi) 1
Jabès, Edmond (uncollected verse, prose
  etc; journals and books)
  'A l'écoute des meurtres à venir' 78
  'A mes amis grecs' 108
  Alliance universelle 23–4, 49
  Anthologie mensuelle see *Alliance universelle*
  'Apport à la poésie: le Logisme' 51–3,
    58–9, 89
  Arrhes poétiques 28, 37, 49–50, 58, 61–4,
    66, 83 n. 44, 91
  Avec l'ombre 38, 71–6, 78, 89
  'Cela a eu lieu' 7
  Chansons pour le repas de l'ogre 38–40, 46,
    78, 87, 96, 99, 122, 129–31, 164
  'Le Chemin des sources' 104
  La Clef de voûte 80, 114,
  'La Demeure de Reverdy' 127–8,
    151 n. 29
  *Désir d'un commencement Angoisse d'une
    seule fin* 135, 152 n. 36
  Du blanc des mots et du noir des signes 104,
    112 n. 36, 152 n. 30
  L'Ecorce du monde 104, 112 n. 36, 121
  Elya 5, 82 n. 35
  'En l'honneur de Pierre Seghers' 50, 78,
    108
  *Un Etranger avec, sous le bras, un livre de
    petit format* 107, 110, 143, 149–50,
    152 n. 36
  'Films inflammables' 58–60
  'Le Fond de l'eau' 68, 79, 103, 134–5
  'Hommage à Max Jacob' 98, 152 n. 38
  Illusions sentimentales 23, 26, 37, 50–1,
    59, 71, 83 n. 38, 106, 119, 150 n. 4
  Je bâtis ma demeure 1, 6–7, 12, 36, 48, 80,
    87, 101, 104, 106, 114–22, 124,
    128–31, 133–7, 147, 155, 163
  Je t'attends! 23, 26, 37, 49–52, 56, 59, 71,
    106, 161
  Le Livre de l'Hospitalité 48–9, 62, 65

Le Livre des Marges 148
Le Livre des Questions (book and cycle)
  1–6, 10, 19, 30, 36, 41–2, 48, 72,
  87–8, 101–2, 118–19, 121, 128–37,
  142–8, 151 n. 29, 156–8, 163, 165,
  167 n. 17
Le Livre des Ressemblances (book and
  cycle) 21, 158, 163
'Maman' 27, 50, 60, 89, 106, 152 n. 31
Le Milieu d'ombre 101–2, 104, 112 n. 36
'La mort d'un poète est une tache
  d'encre sur le poème' 152 n. 38,
  166 n. 8
Les Mots tracent 103
'L'Obscurité potable' 37–8, 66, 71, 73–4,
  89, 93–6
Le Parcours 166 n. 12
La Part du sable 69, 78–81, 101,
  112 n. 36, 127
'Petites Incursions dans le monde des
  masques et des mots' 112 n. 39, 114
Les Pieds en l'air 35, 37, 49–50, 60–1,
  71–2, 83 n. 44, 89
'Quatre mystères actuels' 76, 164
Le 4 septembre 23
Récit 73
'Ressource du sujet' 78, 85 n. 95
Review essay of Paul Eluard, *Les Yeux
  fertiles*, Philippe Soupault, *Poésies
  complètes*, and Max Jacob, *Morceaux
  choisis* 60, 89, 152 n. 38
Reviews:
  Valentin Bresle, *Le Charme poétique* 50
  Jean Moscatelli, *Poèmes trouvés sur un
    banc* 24, 49
  François Moutran, *Soleil sous les
    palmiers* 24
  Ahmed Rassim, *L'Ermtie de l'Attaka*,
    poème 82 n. 24
'Sens de l'ombre' see *Avec l'ombre*
'Simone Picciotto' 151 n. 29
Le Soupçon Le Désert 158
'Syrinx' 50
'Les Voies lactées' 127
Jabès, Haim 2, 27
Jabès, Henri 23–6, 30, 45 n. 52
Jabès, Isaac Haim 27–8
Jabès, Joseph 27

Jabès, Joseph Elie 28, 30
Jabès, Marcelle 7, 29, 60, 95
Jabès, Solomon 27
Jabès, Umberto 28, 30–5, 63, 85 n. 78
Jabès-Crasson, Viviane 101, 122
Jacob, Max 12, 60, 64, 67, 70, 74–5, 78, 80,
    84 n. 75, 87–99, 100–2, 106, 110 nn. 6
    and 8, 110 n. 11, 111 n. 16, 123, 136,
    155, 164–5
Jewish writing 8, 40, 162
Jouve, Pierre-Jean 136
Jung, C. G. 51

Kabbalah 9–10
Kafka, Franz 46 n. 69, 129, 164
Kamil, Anwar 70
Kamil, Fouad 70, 79
Klat, Hector 62
Klossowski, Pierre 10
Krämer, Gudrun 34

Lacan, Jacques 13 n. 8
Lamartine, Alphonse de 23
Lançon, Daniel 14 n. 11, 83 n. 38
Laporte, Roger 153 n. 46
Laumois, André de 69
Lauffer, Yvonne 50
Leiris, Michel 84 n. 75, 126, 151 n. 24,
    157–8, 163, 166 n.5
Leprette, Fernand 18, 108–9
Levinas, Emmanuel 4, 138–9, 146–9,
    153 n. 50
Lévis Mano, Guy 93, 151 n. 24, 155
Ligue contre l'antisémitisme allemand 34
Ligue de la jeunesse juive contre
    l'antisémitisme allemand 34
Ligue internationale contre l'antisémitisme
    (LICA) 30–2, 34
Ligue internationale scolaire contre
    l'antisémitisme (LISCA) 34
Luca, Gherasim 79
Lundvist, Arthur 79
Lugol, Jean 32

Maccabi youth group 34
Maison des artistes 70, 92, 111 n. 13
Mandelstam, Osip 26
Maeterlinck, Maurice 25

Magny, Olivier de 125
Mahmoud Bey 25
Maimonides, Moses 27, 32
Mallarmé, Stéphane 11, 40, 53, 57–8, 93,
    121, 157–8, 163, 166 n. 5
Malraux, Clara 141
Mani, Simon 34, 36
Mansour, Joyce 105
Margueritte, Victor 25
Marinetti, F. T. 83 n. 44
Maritain, Jacques 16
Maritain, Raïssa 16
Marranos 135
Marreau, Pierre 25
Massignon, Louis 111 nn. 24 and 31
Mayo 70, 84 n. 57
Meeteren, Wilhelm van 30–2, 35
Memmi, Albert 141–3, 146, 153 n. 44
Mercereau, Alexandre 24
Mériel, Etienne 83 n. 44, 90, 109
Meschonnic, Henri 14 n. 14
Miatlev, Adrian 109
Michaux, Henri 77, 80, 99, 124, 136
Miller, Henry 105
Mizrahi, Emmanuel 31
Mole, Gary D. 10
Monsieur l'Archiviste 57, 60
Moscatelli, Jean 24, 48–51, 61–2, 64–7, 69,
    87, 92, 94, 105–6, 109
    Poètes en Egypte (ed.) 104–6, 109
Moutran, François 24
Musset, Alfred de 23, 36
Mussolini 64–5, 83 n. 44, 97

Nadeau, Maurice 114, 126, 151 n. 24
Nasser, Gamel Adbel 1–2, 105, 109; see also
    Free Officers
Neher, André 141
negative presentation 5, 36, 41–2, 118, 143,
    157, 159, 161, 163, 165, 167 n. 17
Noailles, Anna de 25
Novalis 101

Offnar, Raymond 23–4

Parme, Raoul 83 n. 44
Parrot, Louis 164–5, 166 n. 16, 167 n. 17
La Part du sable see Edmond Jabès

Partouche, Maurice 9
Pastoureau, Henri 79
Paulhan, Jean 104
Petit, René 25
Picciotto, Simone 151 n. 29
Plumont, Louis 25
Poinsot, M. C. 23
Poldès, Léo 24
Porto-Riche, Georges de 37
Prato, David 29
Prévost, Maurice 25
Proust, Marcel 16

Raczymow, Henri 14 n. 14
Rachilde 23
Rapnouil, Jean 20–1
Rassim, Ahmed 50, 56, 71, 82 n. 24
Ravel, Maurice 58
Raymond, Marcel 136, 152 n. 38
Rebeyrol, Philippe 100
récit éclaté 1, 72, 146
Reverdy, Pierre 127–8
Richet, Charles 25, 58, 82 n. 30
Rimbaud, Arthur 11, 40, 62, 99, 104
Riotor, Léon 25
Romains, Jules 50
Rommel, Erwin 76
Rothschild, Lionel de 30

Saillet, Maurice 111 n. 24
Salama, Zaki 70
Salmon, André 64, 90
Sartre, Jean-Paul 141
Scherer, Jacques 166 n. 5
Seghers, Pierre 50, 78, 108, 164
Seiffoula 55–7, 59–60, 63–4
Shaw, Stanford J. 27
Shoah see Auschwitz
Shual, Adolf 23, 51, 61, 63–4
Simon, Emile 13 n. 2
Sinai campaign 99, 107
Soupault, Philippe 77, 80, 89, 93, 98
Souza, Robert de 51, 136
Spire, André 16, 35, 46 n. 77
Stamelman, Richard 14 n. 15

Staraselski, Albert 38
Stavrinos, Stavro 50, 60
Stoddard, Roger 14 n. 11, 83 n. 44
Suez war 1–2
Sulayman, Lutfallah 70
Supervielle, Jules 72, 126, 136, 151 n. 24,
    155
Surcouf (Baron) 25

Taha-Hussein, Claude Moenis 105, 107–8
Talva, F. 90
Tardieu, André 25
el-Telmisany, Kamil 70
Terni-Cialente, Fausta 83 n. 44
Teymour Bey, Ismail 22
Touati, Charles 141
Trigano, Shmuel 14 n. 14
Trotsky, Leon 70
Tzara, Tristan 68, 77–8

Ungaretti, Giuseppe 83 n. 44
Union universelle de la jeunesse juive
    (UUJJ) 23, 45 n. 52

Vacaresco, Hélène 25, 43 n. 25
Valéry, Paul 25, 50, 69
Varlet, Théo 64
Veber, Pierre 22–3
Vichy 3, 166 n. 10
Vigny, Alfred de 23

Wahba, Magdi 12
Weissman, Jacob 36
Wolff, Pierre 25
Women's International Zionist
    Organization (WIZO) 35

Yabetz, Baruch 27
Yabetz, Ya'akov 27
Yergath, Arsène 71, 83 n. 44
Younane, Ramsès 70, 79

Zananari, Gaston 50
Zeinab 61
Zulficar, Mohamed Bey 109